AF656381

ANDHRA CULTURE

(An Obscure Phase in the Early Historical Archaeology of Andhra Pradesh)

ANDHRA CULTURE

(AN OBSCURE PHASE IN THE EARLY
HISTORICAL ARCHAEOLOGY OF ANDHRA PRADESH)

DR. S. RAMA KRISHANA PISIPATY

AGAM KALA PRAKASHAN
DELHI - 110 052

First Published 2010

© Dr. S. Rama Krishana Pisipaty

ISBN : 978 -81-7320-097-7

All rights reserved. No part of this publication may be reproduced, stored in a retrieval system or transmitted, in any form or by any means, electronic, mechanical, photocopying, recording, otherwise, without the prior permission of Author and Publisher.

Published by:
Dr. Agam Prasad, M.A., Ph.D., Diploma in Museology
For **Agam Kala Prakashan**
34, Central Market, Ashok Vihar
Delhi - 110 052
Tel.: 27212195, 47098 550, 65688806-7
Fax: 91-11-27212195
Email: agambooks@gmail.com, agambook@yahoo.com
www.agamkala.com

Composed by:
Aman Printographics
Delhi - 110 052
Mobile: 9891395309

Printed by:
Chawla Offset
Delhi-110 052

Printed in India

CONTENTS

PREFACE

Andhra Pradesh forms a distinct territorial and cultural unit on the southern side of the Vindhyan range in the Indian sub-continent. It has always appeared as a strong and independent enclave with a single linguistic unit. It covers a wide region of the Deccan plateau, which is drained by ever- flowing rivers like the Krishna and the Godavari and their tributaries. The rivers, as they come down the Western Ghats and Eastern hills, bring in through their annual cycles, plenty of alluvial soil and inundate the plains. This ensures cultivation of good quantities of food grains. Moreover, the regular flow of water makes communication stable in the plains, especially in the coastal belt. Again, the Eastern hills, the Erramalai and the Nallamala ranges are the repositories of minerals like copper, iron, zinc, lead, etc., which serve as basic raw martial for making household goods, weapons and various types of utilitarian objects for the daily life. Besides, the Srisailam range and the pebbly slopes along the river Krishna are noted for precious and semi-precious stones like diamond, carnelian, jade, etc. Thus, Andhra Pradesh has all the required geographical feature suitable for human settlements, which was utilized since the ancient times to the present day.

The purpose of this volume is to high light the hidden cultural phase of the region during Early Historical period i.m., between circa 400 BCE and CE 300. The archaeology of the region during Early Historical period is still not well known like the Gangatic region, the other part of India. For, the period between the Megalithic and the Ikshvaku i.e. circa 400 BCE to CE 300 was a time bracket during which many cultural traits such as development and mastery of art, crafts and technologies, make-up of urbanization, trade and commerce, political systems, etc., were consolidated. In spite of the extensive spade work and the large quantity of data acquired from the sites of the Early Historical Andhra Pradesh, discrepancies and vague assessments could be noticed in many of the publications. For example, quite often a group of materials i.e. from post-Megalithic to the Satavahana period is mixed together and are referred to as reminiscence of the Early Historic or the Satavahana period, giving a very broad span. One of the important reasons for such casual attitude is that the pre-Satavahana period was regarded as a 'political dark age' and the beginning of the main politico-social stream in the region was taken to be from the Satavahana period. It may be noted that though the pre-Satavahana period may not look so important for the history of political systems, culturally it was very significant. The archaeological remains unearthed from various sites of the entire region support this view. It was realized by us that the entire data in between 400 BCE and CE 300 could be classified into two distant stages. The former one, is significant and entirely independent cultural horizon, which lies between the Early Iron Age Megalithic and the late Satavahana period. The present prefers to use the term 'Andhra Culture' (c 400 BCE - CE 100) and the preceding culture as 'Satavahana Culture (c 100 – 300 CE) which was one of well known dynastic rule in the region. The present study emphasize on cultural evolution, culture process, technological developments, trade and commerce, economy, political empower, etc., traits which were not only evolved for the first time but also prevailed hundreds of years in the region. Throughout this book, developments of the region in various aspects that formulated first time in the history of Andhra will be described, analyzed, interpreted, compared and discussed.

In the preparation of this work, I have been benefitted much by many scholarly works. It would, therefore, be unfair not to record my deep sense of gratitude to the scholars whose work I have thoroughly utilized. I express my deep sense of gratitude to the Director, Department of Archaeology and Museums, Government of Andhra Pradesh, and the Director, Birla Archaeological and Cultural Research Institute, both in Hyderabad, Andhra Pradesh, for providing me with the facilities to examine the Early Historical collections of their Institutions and allow me to conduct explorations and participate in the excavations in the region. Further, they allow me to study the library collections and provide extensive facilities for the present work.

Last but not the least, I apologies to those from whom I have received help or assistance of some kind or the other in connection with this work but have not been able to acknowledge the same individually.

Salutation to the lotus feet of my respected Gurus & Parents.

Dr. S. Rama Krishna Pisipaty

SCSVMV University
Enathur, Kanchipuram-631561, India
pisipaty@indiainfo.com

Chapter 1

INTRODUCTION

In the middle of the first millennium BCE witness the beginnings of the Early Historical period in Indian subcontinent. A drastic change has been appeared in the region after a long gap for the time, which prevailed hundreds of years. In Indo-Ganga region saw the raise of large kingdoms and drastic changes in the life style of the people, from tribal nature to sophisticated way. By this time many tribal groups that are mentioned in the later Vedic literature, have carved out kingdoms for themselves. As the result sixteen monarchies and republics popularly known as *Mahagenapadas* stretches across the Indo-Gangetic plains (Afghanistan to Bangladesh in modern political division). These kingdoms comprised the existing local population as well, giving them heterogeneity, which was absent in the earlier tribal societies. It is difficult to pin-point the precise or even approximate time of this change but the middle of the first millennium BCE may be a suitable date bracket. Gradually, it spread to the Vindhyan and Deccan region also which supplanting or modifying the existing tribal cultural traits to urban or civilized and some regions braking new grounds.

This period was marked by significant changes in the socio-cultural style of the people. Besides political one, there were other unifying factor i.e. Religion. The Jaina and Buddhist thoughts, at first localized in north and northeast regions, spread far and wide from the last quarter of the first millennium BEC. These religious activities carved out for itself important centers in Deccan and Coastal region in the megalithic tribal milieu. Another important factor was evolution of Script. The Brahmi script, though it was restricted for royal edicts in the beginning, it spread all over India by the end of the second century BCE for other documental activities.

Many new other traits like introduction of coinage which facilitated trade; ports and high ways which promoted long-distance communication and commerce; extensive use of iron and other metals along alloys; large scale production which promotes merchandise; structures in permanent materials and so many were developed for the first time in the region. Even though little later, similar developments have also been noticed in the Deccan and southern part of India. It may be noted that the techno-cultural knowhow has spread in the rest of the region with in a short span due to the rapid interaction between the intra and inter regional contracts. Moreover, the Early Historic period of the south and southwest and east India seems to have had its own peculiarities. Though as in the neighboring regions, it originated in the middle of Early Iron Age Megalithic, its driving force arose not so much out of north Indian contracts but as trade with Mediterranean region and religious intrusion. As a result saw development of sea-ports and emporia and in the flow of gold coins and occasionally objects from Roman region. The epoch can therefore be regarded as the second civilization of India, which not only prevailed hundred of years but also served modern world.

Several scholars have devoted themselves to study the history, culture and the antiquarian wealth of Andhra region. Their efforts brought to light a vast collection of antiquities which date between the Early Stone Age and the Mediaeval times. In recent years, a number of systematic field investigations have been conducted in the region which has brought to light a clearer picture of the Early Historical period. For, the period between the Megalithic and the Ikshvakus, i.e., *circa* 400 BCE to CE 300 was a time bracket during which many cultural traits such as development and mastery of Art, Crafts, and Technologies, make-up of urbanization, trade and commerce, political systems, etc., were consolidated. In spite of the extensive spade work and the large quantity of data acquired from the sites of the Early Historic Andhra Pradesh, discrepancies and vague assessments could be noticed in many of the publications. For example, quite often a group of materials *i.e.*, from post-Megalithic to the Satavahana period is mixed together and are referred to as reminiscence of the Early Historic or the Satavahana period, giving a very broad span. One of the important reasons for such casual attitude, to our mind, is that the pre-Satavahana period was regarded as a 'political dark age', and the beginning of the main politico-social stream in Andhra was taken to be from the Satavahana period. It may be noted that though the pre-Satavahana period may not look important for the history of political systems, culturally it was very significant. The archaeological remains unearthed from various Early Historical sites of Andhra support this view.

It was realized by the author that the entire data (between *circa* 400 BCE and CE 300) could be classified into two stages. The former one is significant and entirely independent cultural horizon, which lies between the Early Iron Age Megalithic and the Satavahana period. The author prefers to use- the term 'Andhra Culture' (*circa* 400 BCE to CE 100) for this period and the preceding culture as 'Satavahana Culture' (*circa* 100 to 300 CE) which was one of the well known dynastic rule in the Deccan. The reasons for the use of these nomenclatures have been discussed in Chapter I.

It may also be noted that the Andhra Culture period was marked by the introduction of many new trends in the history of the Andhra for the first time. Important among them were formation of urbanization, political systems, external and internal trade network and so many cultural traits which were similar to those of the other parts of the Indian sub-continent. The previous Megalithic tribal nature of living was completely abandoned, and was altered by the extensive use of metal with advanced technologies, permanent building materials in the construction of shelters, introduction of coinage, development of trade and the organized social structures, etc., which laid the foundation for the socio-cultural trends which appears to have survived for centuries in this region.

Similarly, the following Satavahana phase is also important for the early history of the Andhradesa. From the available data gathered from different inscriptions and archaeological remains, it is clear that the late Satavahanas directly controlled the political and economic affairs of the entire region by the end of the second century CE. It further indicates that the Satavahanas were able to bring about a strong political, economic and cultural cohesion to the entire region. However, though the scholars have thrown light on the political history of the Satavahanas, the cultural pattern of the period is still in the dark.

We, therefore, feel that though the Andhra-Satavahana period is a very significant phase of the Early Historic Andhra Pradesh, a total picture of its culture has not yet been attempted seriously. The present topic, therefore, has been selected with a view to piece together the scattered evidence and reconstruct the Early Historical culture milieu, particularly of Andhra and Satavahana periods.

The present study is based on two types of data. In one category comes all the published accounts which were collected from various excavation reports and other relevant publications. The second category forms information gathered by studying the archaeological collections housed in various institutions and personal explorations in the region by this researcher. Collections from Kotilingala, Peddabankur, Kondapur, Yeleswaram, etc., stored in the Department of Archaeology and Museums, Government of Andhra Pradesh, and Veerapuram in the Birla Archaeological and Cultural Research Institute, both in Hyderabad, Andhra Pradesh, were examined. In the case of Satanikota, Salihundam and other excavated sites of the region, the published reports have been used extensively. It may be mentioned that due to the limitations and practical problems, only five excavated sites have been selected for detailed study, which represent all the three regions, viz., the Coastal Andhra, Telangana and Royalseema. These sites also belong to different types of settlements like religious, rural, urban, etc. However, other archaeological sites of the region have also been referred to in the discussion wherever it was necessary.

The artefactual remains like clay objects, metal objects, structures and other noteworthy antiquities like ornaments, coins etc., from the selected sites have been deal with in detail in four chapters, while the stratigraphy and chronology of the sites have also been dealt in a separate chapter. The cultural reconstruction of both the periods, the Andhra and the Satavahana, forms the matter of concluding chapter. A good amount of evidence is also available in the form of sculptures and religious architectures of the period under study. Though important for cultural studies, these have not been dealt with detail in the present volume because exhaustive analysis and interpretation of these have already been carried out by various scholars. Some of the important aspects have been referred to in the last chapter.

Chapter 2

ENVIRONMENT & GEOGRAPHIC SUMMERY

Of all aspects of the environment, the topography, that is, the configuration of surface and relief, changes most slowly. Nevertheless, it is important for human societies. Further, the topography can be viewed as the stage for human societies, past and present. In this part describe the environment of the region, topography, climate and characteristic assowciation of flora and fauna, soils, etc. It introduces the reader to the geography of the region, develops the environmental background for the early societies in the Andhra Pradesh.

Andhra Pradesh is situated in between the Latitudes 12° 14' and 19° 54' N and the Longitudes 76° 50' and 84° 45' E. It is bounded on three sides by the sates of Tamil Nadu, Karnataka, Maharashtra, Madhya Pradesh and Orissa, and the other side by the Bay of Bengal, in clockwise direction from south to east. The coastal line forming the eastern boundary of this area is characterized by a convex bent and is located between Gopalpur (north) and Madras (south) in a stretch of 960 Km long area. The total area administered by this state is 2, 76,754 sq km (Mangalam, S.J. 1986: 1-3).

On map, Andhra Pradesh, the region under study, is appeared on the southern side of the Vindhyan range in the triangular plateau of the Indian peninsula. The present boundaries of this state were defined in 1956. The limits of the spread of the Telugu language were determined as the area of Andhra at first by. J.M. Campbell (1874). Following Campbell, the same criterion was used by G.A. Griesen (1967: 296, 577) and the State Reorganization commission of the Government of India in 1956 (Report of the States Reorganization Commission 1955).

2.1 Topographically the region can broadly be divided into three zones, viz., Coastal Andhra, Telangana and Royalseema. The entire coastal plains and a considerable chunk of the Eastern Hills go to make the coastal Andhra. It comprises the districts of Srikakulam, Vijayanagaram, Vishakhapatnam, East Godavari, West Godavari, Krishna, Guntur, Prakasam and Nellore. The Telangana region is occupied by a part of the peneplained plateau and is situated on the north-western part of the State. It comprises the districts of Adilabad, Nizamabad, Karimnagar, Medak, Hyderabad, Rangareddi, Warangal, Khammam, Algona and Mahboobnagar. The Royalseema zone is located on the south-western region of the state, which includes four districts viz., Anantapur, Kurnool, Cuddapah and Chittoor (Jaya Rao, S.S. 1988).

2.2 Physiographically the Sate has been divided into three parts viz. the coastal plains, Eastern Hills, and western peneplains (Jaya Rao, S.S. 1988: 821-507). The coastal plains make the littoral part extend from the Bay of Bengal to the

Eastern Hills varying from 75 to 150 km. in width. It is much wider then the west coast. The Eastern Hills are a series of disjuncted hills, forming as much a crescentic border of the coastal plateau in Deccan. The western peneplains are highly eroded and isolated hillock break the monotony of the vast plains (Prasad, R.C. *et al.* 1987: 821-507).

2.3 Geologically the region constitutes a peneplained part of the ancient and stable Deccan block and is chiefly composed of the gneissic complex of pre-Cambrian origin. On the Eastern Coast, is a strip of marine sediment in more or less connected patches of Mesozic, Tertiary or Quaternary fossiliferous rock formations. These formations range from Eocene to Pliocene and the principal formation are named 'Cuddalore series' (Wadia, D.N. 1970: 313). The central Telangana region, the gneisses inter-spread with granitic intrusions, presents a surface monotony, whereas in the outskirts 'the Archaean basement is overlain by the rocks of younger series' (Singh, R.L. 1971: 824). The western and northern parts of the Telangana have got a few formations of the Deccan traps. The lower and upper Gondwanas appear in the form of a long continuous belt in the Godavari basin. In the Royalseema, the Dharwar formations which chiefly consist of schist are found to be confined to the south-west of the region. The Cuddapah system, which makes a crescentic outcrop in most of the Royalseema and part of the coastal region, again occurs in the extreme north-eastern part of the region, the Cuddapah are overlain by the rocks of ' Kurnool Series' of the lower Vindhyan System.

2.4 Rivers

Rivers with their tributary system are the main channel of the drench and drain of the land surface. The region is drained by two major river systems. The river Godavari and the Krishna cut across the entire latitude of the state. The rivers rise from the Western Ghats in Maharashtra and drain into the Bay of Bengal after crossing the Eastern Hill. There are altogether about 34 major as well as minor rivers and streams in the State (Vedantam, T. 1977: 1).

The river **Godavari,** the largest perennial river in the region, enters the State near Adilabad district in the Telangana region and fall into Polavaram in the Godavari district of the Coastal Andhra after crossing the Eastern Hills through Papi Hills. The river splits into three branches after crossing Rajahmundry in East Godavari district, *viz.* the Gautami, Vasishta and Vainalaya. These three branches join the sea near Yanam, Narasapur and Rajom, respectively in East Godavari district. The Manjira, Maner, Penganga, Wardha, Pranahita, Kadam, Indravati and Peddavagu are the other important tributaries (Rameshan, N. 1976) of the Godavari.

The river **Krishna**, another major drainage system of the sate, separates the Telangana and Royalseema region from one and the other. It enters into the Sate near Mahaboobnagar district in the Telangana region and flows through the Telangana and Royalseema region superimposing the northern end of the Cuddapah ranges. It falls into the Bay of Bengal at Divi taluka in Krishna district enclosing the island of Divi. In its strenuous passage, it receives a number of tributaries, important among which are the Tungabhadra, Dindi, Musi, etc. (Singh, R.N. 1971: 825).

The river **Penneru** originates from the Eastern Mysore plateau and flows south-easternly through the Nandyal Basin and finally joins the Bay of Bengal near Cuddalore in Nellore district of southern coastal region. The Boggeru, Cheyyaru, Chitravati, Jayamangali, Kunderu, Papagni, Punchu, Sagiteru, etc. are important tributaries of the Penneru. The river and its tributaries are not only important drainage of the Royalseema and Nellore region but these have also carved out a number of wide valleys (Raja Gopal, M.V. 1974) on their way.

The river **Tungabhadra** also originates from Mysore plateau, but Joins the river Krishna near Kudavalli Sangameshwaram in Kurnool district (Rameshan, N. 1976). The Vamsadhara and Nagawati rivers are the other notable streams in the Northern Coastal region. Besides, there are also some other important streams such as, Varahu, Eleru, Gundlakamma, Suvarnamukhi and Upputeru (Magalam, S.J. 1986: 2).

The drainage facilities which are provided by numerous flowing streams are aided by natural lakes like Kolleru and Pullikat, confined primarily to this region of the State. The Kolleru occupies the region in between the Godavari and the Krishna deltas of the middle coastal region. It is a depression cut off from the sea by the river deposits and covers 259 sq km. It is very shallow and elliptical in shape. Its islands are intensively cultivated and water of the lake is rich resource of fishes (Vedantam, T. 1977: 1). The Pullikat lake, a salt-water lagoon, is situated on the southern most part of the Nellore district in the Southern Costal region.

2.5 Climate

Climate in the region enjoys seasons with 'its characteristic rhythms' which are divided into four parts (Singh, R.L. 1971:

826), viz., (1) Hot weather seasons or summer seasons (March to May), (2) South-west Monsoons (June to September), (3) North-west Monsoon (October to December), (4) Winter seasons (December to February).

The **Hot weather season** or pre-monsoon period in the state starts from March, but during the month of April and May, it becomes the hottest period of the year throughout the region. In May 'the temperature oscillates around 38° C in most of the districts and reaches 41° C at a few places like Kurnool and Khammam. Rentachintala in Gunture district is the hottest place in the state with temperature normally touching 43.83°- 47.78° C during May and June. The scorching sun and hot winds make the season quite uncomfortable. The heat is occasionally mitigated by local thunder showers and squally weather in April and May (Raja Gopal, M.V. 1974).

The **Southwest monsoon** starts sometimes in the second or third week of June. The season reaches the peak point in the month of August in Telangana and coastal Andhra region, whereas in the Royalseema and the Eastern Hilly region, it is highest in September. In the Coastal Andhra, the rainfall decreases from the shore (140-170 cm) to the interior (70-80 cm). The Northern Andhra coast gets 78 per cent rainfall but it decrease from the shore to the interior and southwards because the region lies off the main track of the monsoon and the associated depression. The Telangana region receives 85.4 per cent of the total rainfall during the monsoon period while in Royalseema, the rainfall of the season cover 58.57 per cent (Rameshan, N. 1976) of the total.

In spatial distribution of rainfall, the North-western monsoon is just the opposite to the south-western monsoon this is due to the reversal of wind direction. The south-westerly winds coming from the Arabin sea, give way to the Northeastern monsoon coming from the Bay of Bengal. From this retreating monsoon, the coastal region receives copious rainfall, which is mainly associated with the storms originating from the depressions formed in the Bay of Bengal (Rameshan, N. 1976).

The annual rainfall in the State generally decreases from north-east to south-west and to shore to interior. The average normal rainfall of the region is about 86 cm. the coastal Andhra gets 102 cm, while Telangana 89 cm and the Royalseema only 67 cm (Mangalam, S.J. 1986: 3).

The rain shadow areas in the State are the South-western region of Karnataka plateau and the Eastern Hills. These are the 'Shadow region' for both the monsoons, where semi-arid conditions prevail (Singh, R.L 1971: 827).

The **winter season** in the entire region starts with the end of the north-eastern monsoon, sometime in the second or third week of December. In the costal region, it brings a general fall of temperature by 22° at shore and 19 to 20° C in the interior (Singh, R.L 1971: 940), Whereas in the north-western Telangana region, the temperature nowhere fall below 14° C (Singh, R.L. 1971 : 827).

2.6 The Major Soil Formations

Major soil formations of Andhra are made of two processes, viz. either from the altered residue of the underlying rocks, or the alluvial debris deposition by the rivers. These could be grouped into four main categories viz. the Black, the Red, the Laterite, the Lime and Alluvial (coastal and deltaic) soils (Vedantam, T. 1977: 1).

The **Black soils** are more fertile in comparison to the other soils and are confined especially to the low lying areas. In Andhra Pradesh this group is characterized by tropical Black clay, rich in lime, magnesium and aluminum but poor in phosphorus, nitrogen and organic matters.

Lime is another noteworthy formation that is found in the form of *kankar* nodules, often present with their concentration which increases with depth. Large stretches of it are met in the region in the part of west Godavari, Krishna, Guntur and in limited areas of Nellore district of Coastal Andhra; Adilabad and Nizamabad districts of Telangana region; Kurnool, Cuddapah and Mahboobnagar district of Royalseema region Particularly confined to the area lying between the river valleys of the Krishna and the Penneru (Singh, R.N. 1971: 827).

The **Red soil** is derived from the weathering of Archaean acid gneisses and granites. The red color is due to the presence of iron in a diffused state. These are deficient in organic matter, nitrogen, phosphorus and soluble base salts (Wadia, D.N. 1970: 516). The soil is found to be spread in a considerable part of Srikakulam, Vishakhapatnam and East Godavari districts and small areas of Krishna, Guntur and Nellore districts of the coastal Andhra zone. In Telangana, it occupies a major part whereas in Royalseem, it is one of the predominate formation (Rameshan, N. 19976).

The **Lateritic soil** is largely a deposition of the monsoon region as it is produced by the prevalence of alternate dry and most conditions (Wadia, D.N. 1970: 517). Formed primarily by the decomposition of the gneisses rocks, the important components of laterites are iron, alumina and silicic acid. Owing to its high iron contents, the soil retains a brick-red color. It is found to be poor in almost all organic matters and soluble salts and has low fertility status, thus not a suitable formation for vegetation. It occupies certain parts of the Godavari and Nellore district of the coastal region of Andhra and appears to be confined primarily to the Ananthgiri Hilly region of the western peniplain (Rameshan, N. 1976).

The **Alluvial soil** is borne depositions, soil of which are brought from the higher grounds and are deposited in the valleys and plains by water action. A series of alternate layers of sand and silt of various colors and textures characterizes this group, thickness of which increases with age (Singh, R.L. 1971: 828). In our region, the soil under consideration is generally rich in lime but poor in nitrogen and phosphoric acid. There is a wide belt of river borne alluvium at the eastern coast. Besides, in addition, the great deltaic deposits are also alluvial formation at mouths of the rivers, the Krishna and Godavari. The coastal lands are also covered often by this category of formations.

2.7 The Natural Vegetation

The natural vegetation or forests of the region cover a large zone of 64 051 sq km which account for 23.2 per cent of the total geographical area. This area has been classified into four categories (as per the chief conservator of forests) of the following types – (1) the dry, ever-green forest zone, with covers the entire coastal belt; (2) the tidal forest zone, which is confined to the heavy alluvial deposits; (3) the dry deciduous and semi-moist deciduous forest zone found in bulk, mostly in the Royalseema and Telangana region. Teak is the most important species in almost all the Telangana, Nallamali forest of Royalseema region, red sanders in Chittoor and Cuddapah hilly region of the southern region of the state;

(4) the tropical thorn forest zone, which is mainly confined to the outer edges of hill slopes (Bureau of Economics and Statistics, 1969).

2.8 Coastal Line

The long coastal line of Andhra is very important for more then one reasons. For instance, it is dotted with several ports right from the Protohistoric times. It has opened roadsteads that offer anchorages. The Vishakhapatnam, Machilipatnam, Sriharikota, etc., are some of the important port towns of today. Between the relatively negative upland and the negative coast, lies the rather limited area of the delta which is the demerit of the region. The deltas are vulnerable to floods, at times disastrous and cyclones are also a danger. However, the coast for several miles inland, is largely fringed with mangrove swamp which are valuable as a fuel reserve, and the sand dunes rising to 30-50 ft the coastal plain can be divisible into three region (Spate, O.H.K. *et al.* 1984: 421) based on physical factors and economic activities, which are – (1) North Coastal plain (2) Middle Coastal plain and (3) Southern Coastal plain.

2.8.1 *North Coastal Plain*

It covers the northern districts of the coastal range, e.g., the Srikakulam and Vishakhapatnam. Its low land narrows down to 19 km. under Mahendragiri hills, but on either side of this gate, are the embankments of the Rushikulya and Vamsadhara. High density which is found in Vamsadhara – Nagawati valley in the region, may be due to highly cultivated lands.

2.8.2 *Middle Coastal Plain*

It occupies the region between the Godavari and the Krishna deltas and can be divided into Godavari delta, Elluru region and Krishna delta. It covers east Godavari district in Godavari delta while Krishna and Guntur district are in the Krishna delta. Between these two deltas, lies the Elluru region, where the Kolleru lake is situated. The Tertiary formations of clay are deposited in Godavari district which are very suitable for ceramic production and is exploited for the purpose at Rajahmundry.

2.8.3 *Southern Coastal Plain*

It is a transitional belt between the Andhra and Tamilnadu plains. It covers both the northern and the southern region of Nellore district. The coast is fringed by a belt of alluvium upto 22.5 km wide. The region consists of Archaean gneisses and schist, lateritic and largely covered with scrub.

2.9 Ghats

The Eastern Ghats have been termed as the '**Eastern Hills**' in view of its heterogenesity (Spate, O.H.K. & A.T.A. Learmonth. 1984: 722). Less stronger in formation then the Western Ghats, the Hills of the east almost disappear between the Godavari and the Krishna rivers. They however, continue towards the south-west, and finally fuse with the Western Ghats in the Nilgiris of Tamil Nadu (Wadia, D.N. 1970: 22). In the north-east, they are marked by varied relief and rugged topography and form a highly dissected mass of older peninsular rocks. The altitude of the hills gradually increases towards the north of the rivers Godavari (Sankaram 1616 m) and south-west of the Krishna. On the other side, that is in the south-west of the Krishna. On the other side, that is in the south-west the Cuddapah range forms a different series of the hill masses of Nallamalai, Velikonda, Erramali, Seshachalam, Palakonda and Nagari (300 to 1350 m). Some of these scarps are the surviving relics of the ancient mountain-chain elevated contemporaneously with the Aravallis. The average altitude of the hill is 610 m. In normal seasons, they are only depositing agents, precipitating their silt in part of their basins, alluvial banks and estuarine flats. The hills are wooded but having very thin forest. A group of inhabitants of this region are *chenchus*, aboriginal tribe living in food collecting stage, and survive by the collection of honey, bamboos and other minor forest products (Rameshan, N. 1976).

The western peneplain is situated in the western part of the region, which is separated from the coastal region by the convex fortification of the Eastern Hills. It covers the entire Telangana and most of the Rayalseema region. The peneplained belt attains its maximum east-west width in the central Telangana and thence gradually tapers off towards the south. The altitude of the northern region varies from 530 to 660 m whereas in the southern region, it ranges from 300 m to 465m. The monotony of the common peneplain level is broken in the extreme western and northern Telangana by lava deposits rising abruptly over 600 to 800 m (above MSL). Similarly, the extensions of the Mysore plateau in the south-west Royalseema terminate without facing scarps the general slope of the region is towards the east as is evident from the alignment of the drainage. The general aspect of the peneplain consists of the undulating plain surfaces dotted with monad rocks and intersected by almost completely graded river valleys. The plateau are formed by the Archaean gneisses, a belt of Gondwanas with coal bearing formation in the north, whereas the central part is composed of the Purana series of rocks such as quartzite, dolerite, chart and chalcedony, which are abundant in this region and which attracted the lithic tool based settlements. In the southern side, the Cuddapah basin with Kunderu drained Nandyal valley (215 m) have deposits of barites, asbestos, lime stone and shale, the lime stone is one of the important building materials. The Dharwar formations with schist occupy the southern part which abounds in minerals like copper, gold etc. and are confined to the Ananthapur district (Raja Gopal, M.V. 1974).

The very structure of this natural physiographical division of the region under study seems to have determined the highways of this region. The large opening along the Krishna valley is still the main line of communication between the west and East coasts. The breaks in the Eastern Hills provide natural routes which connect the plateau and the East coast region. The East coast is dotted with several convenient anchorages and had developed several ports and port towns which open roadsteads as a consequence of brisk trade and religious propagation from the Protohistoric period. Another important pass in the Nalamalai range leads to the extreme west and south. These natural passes seem to have provided highways to the region in the prehistoric to Historic periods. Now, these natural routes have been developed into regular modern highways.

Another interesting feature of this region is the river valleys which provide agricultural lands. This is the most important determinant factor for the agricultural nucleus around which again settlements for cluster. The fertile Godavari and Krishna valleys and the open coast line were two prominent geographical units attracting major settlements in this region. These units rich in natural resources seem to have been fostered so as to attract population for centuries with the result that the area had continuous and undisrupted history and could develop into a common linguistic-cum-socio-religious unit. It also evolved a high culture recognizable within the periphery of Indian civilization (Yazdani, G. 1960).

REFERENCES

Griesen, G.A. 1967. (reprint). *Linguistic Survey of India*. Delhi.

Jaya Rao, S.S. (ed) 1988. *Census of India*. Andhra Pradesh Serious No 2. Hyderabad. IA and XII.

Magalam, S.J. 1986. *Historical Geography & Toponomy of Andhra Pradesh*. New Delhi.

Prasad, R.C. and O. Singh. 1987. *India-A Regional Geography*. Varanasi.

Raja Gopal, M.V. (ed).1974. *Andhra Pradesh District Gazetteers*. Hyderabad.

Rameshan, N. (ed). 1976. *Gazette of India*, Andhra Pradesh. Hyderabad.

Sigh, R.L. (ed) 1971. *India: A Regional Geography*. National Geophysical Society of India. Varanasi.

Spate, O.H.K. & A.T.A. Learmonth. 1984 (3rd edition). *Indian and Pakistan*: A general and Regional Geography. New Delhi.

Vedantam, T. (ed). 1977. Administrative Atlas. *Census of India 1971*. Andhra Pradesh Series No 2. Hyderabad. IX-A.

Wadia, D.N. 1970 (reprint). *Geology of India*. London.

Yazdani, G. 1960. *The Early History of the Deccan*. London.

Chapter 3

HISTORY OF ARCHAEOLOGICAL RESEARCHES

The first discovery of the existence of man in Andhra Pradesh was made as early as in 1844 when captain new bold reported some animal bones and a human tooth of the upper Paleolithic period from the famous Billasurgam caves in Kurnool district of the Royalseema region (Newbold, T.J. 1844). The archaeological remains of the region attracted the attention of many geologists and amateur archaeologists since the middle of the eighteenth century. A. Rea, R.B. foot and L.A. Cammiade were the pioneers of the south Indian Archaeology, who explored various regions with a view to finding out remains of ancient man. Their efforts brought to light a vast collection of antiquities which date between the early Stone Age and the mediaeval times. As a result of these discoveries, archaeological investigations were subsequently carried out in a number of regions of Andhra Pradesh, which gradually started filling up gaps of Andhra history. The painstaking efforts made by pre-historians brought to light remains of all the three phases of the Paleolithic period e.g., the Lower , the Middle and the Upper in varies region such as Krishna and Godavari valleys and Kurnool, Nellore, Guntur district , etc. (Jayaswal, V. 1978). Some of the finds such as the Acheulian occupation site of Hunsgi (Paddaya, K. 1985), Kurnool cave (Murthy, M.L.K. 1985: 106-128) deposits of the Upper Paleolithic phase have added new date to the Indian Prehistory. The Department of Archaeology and Museums, Government of Andhra Pradesh from its inception has successfully conducted many explorations which finally resulted in excavations. In the process, sites pertaining to Prehistoric period have been noticed by the Department at Naderipally, Amarabad, Yeleswaram, Gundala, Peddamarur, Ketavaram, Gollavaram, Gavigudem, Kazipalley, Narasapally, Wankhedi, Belum, Billagudem, and Kudelocherolopalli. At Amarabad a Lower Paleolithic site in Mahaboobnagar district excavation laid bare a large number of hand axes to cleavers. Near Godavari Khani, Lower Paleolithic tools, lithic blades and bone tools along with fossilized faunal remains of oxen, buffalo, deer, sheep are also collected.

But, true Mesolithic deposits could not be ascertained so far in the region under study. Through significant for the early history of man, these remains fall much beyond the spent of time which is the subject matter of this volume.

R.B. Foote (1987) discovered the first Neolithic site Vadamanu in Guntur district of Andhra Pradesh. Succeeding him other scholars like K.V. Soundara Rajan (1952: 64-92), V.R. Reddy (1976) and others explored and discovered many Neolithic sites in the entire region, which are situated in the districts of Vishakhapatnam, Krishna, Guntur Nellore, Hyderabad, Karimnagar, Kurnool, Cuddapah , Anantapur, etc. Some of these were also excavated. Among them, Ramapuram,

Togarrai, Polakonda, Budigapalli, etc. are noteworthy excavations. Neolithic period of Andhra is the first stage from which the entire history is found in uninterrupted way. Neolithic habitation sites are excavated by the Department of Archaeology and Museums, Government of Andhra Pradesh at Utnoor, Chinnamarur, Polakonda and Hulikallu. The department also undertook excavations at Neolithic-Chalcolithic sites at Guttikonda (Guntur district), Belum (Kurnool district), Chinnamarur and Karapakala in Mahaboobnagar district.

The second categories of sites belong to the megalithic tradition of the Early Iron Age. E. H. Hunt (1924: 14), V.D. Krishmaswami (1949) K.R. Srinivasan and N.R. Banerjee (1953: 103-118), M.A. W. Khan (1963), H. Sarkar (1969: 12-26), K.P. Rao (1988: 19-32) and many others have discovered and excavated many megalithic sites in Andhra Pradesh. Different types of burial monuments were discovered. Besides, a few habitational sites were also excavated (Rao, K.P.1988). During the last three decades, the Department of Archaeology and Museums, Government of Andhra Pradesh, have conducted excavations at various Megalithic sites. Among them, Yeleswaram, Pochampad, Kadambapur, Agiripalli, Peddamarur, Chinnamarur, Tenneru, Jonnawada, Uppalapadu, Chagatur, etc., are some of the noteworthy sites. At Chinnamarur a Neolithic cemetery was noticed in Megalithic habitation while Megalithic cemetery was noticed at Neolithic habitation which represents the transitional phase.

In the earlier phase of archaeological investigations in Andhra region, there existed, in fact, two trends. In one case, Stone Age remains were the basic period, which received attention of the field investigation. All the discoveries of Paleolithic,

Neolithic and Megalithic (an Early Iron Age trait) mentioned above are the result of such efforts. In the other, remains of religions establishments were being looked for. The stupa architecture and sculptural wealth of the ancient Andhradesa were the main groups witch was under study. for example, the famous sits of Amaravati was excavated a number of times e.g., in 1845 by W. Elliot (1845), subsequently by R. Sewell (1877), J. Burgers (1887), A. Rea (1909), etc. The sculptural yield and the architecture of the famous stupa at Amaravati were highlighted at this time. However, in later years, a series of archaeological investigations were again conducted with a view to bring forth the entire nature of this Buddhist establishment (*IAR 1973-74*: 4). Similarly, more then six dozens Buddhist sites were studies in Nineteen Sixties and Eighties. Noteworthy among them are Salihundam, Samkaram, Bhavikonda, Thotlakonda, Guntupalle, Kesarapalli, Gantasala, Jaggayapeta, Bhattiprolu and Chandravaram.

As a result of the above investigations, the picture of two phases of Andhra History, the very early period, the stone and Early Iron age and the Historical period were becoming clearer day by day. But the intermediary stage, the Early Historical period was still shrouded in mystery. In Nineteen forties, there were isolated attempts made to unveil the evidence for the Early Historical settlements like Kondapur in Medak district which was excavated by the Nizam's state Department of Archaeology (*ARN 1940-41*). An early town of Andhra period which was a noteworthy centre of craft and Buddhist monument was exposed. But systematic investigations for accumulating evidence for the early Historical period were conducted during the last three decades. Many Early Iron age settlements with remains of antiquities were discovered and some were also excavated. The Department of Archaeology and Museums, Government of Andhra Pradesh, under the supervision of V.V.K. Sastry, discovered hundreds of Early Historic sites in the region. The main area under investigation by this team was Telangana region. Important Early Historical sites were Peddabankur, Dhulikatta, Chinnabankur, Vamanur, Kapparaopeta, Kotilingala, Kachapur, Bodagutta, Karnamamidi, Polakonda and Bomany. Some of these sites were also excavated such as Yeleswaram, Peddabankur, Dhulikatta, Kotilingala, Chandavaram, Thotlakonda, Bhavikonda, Gopalapatnam, Pavurallakonda, Dantapuram, Nelakondapalle and Keesaragutta. Besides, many rock paintings have been noticed, for instance, Budigapalli, Regonda, etc. (Sastry, V.V.K. 1983: 239).

The Birla Archaeological and Cultural Research Institute, Hyderabad, under the leadership of T.V.G. Sastry, located a number of sites. Three of which, viz., Veerapuram (Sastry, T.V.G. *et al.* 1984), Vaddamanu (*IAR 1981-82*: 1) and Hasmathpet (Sastry, T.V.G. *et al.* 1984) are noteworthy. Vaddamanu (*AAR 1981-82*: 1) and Hasmathpet (Sastry, T.V.G. 1981) were also excavated. In Nineties the same institute also conducted excavation at Garapadu (*IAR* 1992-93: 1), Puduru (*IAR* 1994-95: 2), etc. I. K. Sarma, southern circle of the Archaeological Survey of India, explored the lower Krishna Valley and the coastal region. Many Buddhist establishments (Sarma, I.K. 1987: 17-22), ports and port towns (Sarma, I.K. 1990: 19-23) of the Early Historic period were recognized by him. He excavated religious sites like Amaravati (Buddhist), Guddimallam (Saiva), etc., culture have come to light as a result of these investigations. Besides, some Universities like Telugu University, Srisailam and Nagarjuna University, Guntur have also conducted explorations in the region and traced many sites. Among them, at Elchuru (*IAR* 1988-89: 3-5) and Srisailam (*IAR* 1989-90: 2-4) of Telugu University and Gandluru (*IAR* 1982-83: 1-2; 1983-84: 1-2) of Nagarjuna University excavated reports are also important.

The salvaging operations, which were carried out in the valley of Nagarjunakonda in early fifties, need special mention. This was not only the first protective efforts to save the monuments from submergence at the time of the construction of the Nagarjuna sagar Dem but the archeological operations carried out at this time by the Archaeological survey of India, brought to light a full cultural sequence from the Early Stone Age to the Mediaeval period (*IAR* 1955-56: 23- 26; Subrahmanyam, R. *et al.* 1975).

3.1 GENERAL CULTURAL SEQUENCE OF ANDHRA PRADESH

The archaeological discoveries made so far in the region under study, have revealed at least five cultural stages in the Prehistoric and the Early Historical periods. In the following table these stage have been mentioned along with their date brackets and typical features.

This sequence has been more or less corroborated by the archaeological sites of the Deccan, such as Maski (Thapar, B.K. 1957: 4-142), Piklihal (Alchin, P.R. 1961), T-Narsipur (Seshadri, M.1971), Brahmagiri (Wheeler, R.E.M. 1947-48:181-310), Nagarjunakonda (Subrahmanyam, R. *et al.* 1975), Veerapuram (Sastry, T.V.G. *et al.* 1984), etc.

Table 1

3.1 General Cultural Sequence of Early Andhradesha

Phase		Culture	Date Bracket	Typical Artifacts
I		**Paleolithic**	70,000 BP	Hand as us, Cleavers, Scrapurs, Borers, Worked Flakes, etc.
II	A	Early Neolithic	2500-1800 BCE	Coarse Grey Ware, Red Ware, Polished Stone Axes
	B	Late Neolithic (mixed with Metal Age)	1800-100 BCE	Painted Pottery, Black-and-Red Ware, Spouted Vessels, Ground Stone Axes, Metal Objects
III	A	Early Iron Age Megalithic	800-400 BCE	Black-and-Red Ware, Black Ware, Metal Objects, Funerary Monuments
	B	Late Megalithic	400 BCE onwards	
IV		Andhra	400 BCE – CE 100	Russet Coated Painted Ware, Imported & Imitation Wares, Fortified planned Urban settlements, Religious establishments, etc.
V		Satavahana	100 - 300 CE	Red Polished Ware, Grey Ware, Satavahana coins, Metropolis cities

The archaeological date in this region, seem to indicate that the Neolithic sites were mostly concentrated around the river Krishna and its tributaries. Main subsistence and economy of these communities were incipient agriculture and tending of cattle and other domestic animals like goats, etc. Finds of accumulated debris of ashes, presumably of burnt out cow-dung, seem to indicate that these were seasonal camp sites, which were associated with such religious festivals as the modern *pongal* (Allchin, F.R. 1963). An analysis of the components of an ash mound seems to indicate wet climate. The area was perhaps better wooded and covered largely with grass land (Majumdar, G.G. *et al.* 1966: 54). This Neolithic cultural complex appears to have continued upto the beginning of the first millennium BCE. During the entire time span of this phase, there was a gradual increase of food production by means of agriculture (Subrahmanyam, R. *et al.* 1975:77-80).

The Neolithic settlements of Nagarjunakonda (Subrahmanyam, R.*et al.*1975), Veerapuram (Sastry, T.V.G. *et al.* 1984), Ramapuram (*IAR 1981-82*:3-8), etc., are characterized by pit-dwellings which were of circular, oval, oblong and irregular in shapes. Others types of dwellings, such as circulars, square or rectangular huts have also been unearthed. The walls seem to have been matted with clay and supported by earth-fast posts'. Evidence for inter-regional contacts of the Neolithic folks of the Andhra region has also been reported. For it is apparent that the painted pottery and blade tradition (Reddy, R.V. 1985 a) were not local industries. Besides, petrological analysis of the granite axes also supports the above presumption (Allchin, B. and F.R. Allchin. 1968: 268). Such inter-regional contact seems to have helped developing the growth of trade routes, which is supported by the location of the small settlements on the trade routes. Discovery of Neolithic sites indicates that the significance of the region with rich natural resources was realized even before the early Historic period (Sankalia, H.D. 1963: 198). The openings of Andhra ware the main avenues and eastern regions of the Andhra Pradesh, as well as, other intra-regions.

Artifacts belonging to pecked and ground stone industry and bland industry were collected from the region along with several pot shreds. The tool types consist of axes, chisels, adzes, chopper-chopping tools, picks, core scrappers flake tools, by product flakes, rubbing stones, hammer stones, mace-heads, saddles querns, etc. (Reddy , R.V. 1976). The ceramic industry includes blotchy Grey and dull Red wares (Reddy, R.V. 1985). It is entirely handmade. The common shapes are globular vessels of various sizes with constricted and concave necks and flared rim. The other shapes include spouted pots, rimless bowls, lipped, legged pots etc. The common decorations are red ochre painted, incised, impressed designs, etc. Certain culture elements of the Chalcolithic period such as painted pottery and or Early Iron Age appear during the later phase of Neolithic culture complex. There is, however, no evidence for the existence of independent culture horizon of Copper / Bronze Age in Andhra.

In the beginning of the first millennium BCE, iron technology was introduced, which changed the earlier façade of the lithic, based culture. Since the advent of iron, there has been great change in the socio-economic conditions of the entire region. But the earliest stage of Iron Age is marked by tribalism. The chief characteristic of this stage was a new mode of burying the dead, which involved constriction of imposing funerary monuments. The most common types of monuments were cists, passage graves, dolmens which involved construction of imposing funerary monuments. (Dikshit, K.N. 1992: 31). A great number of cairn burials are noticed in the megalithic Andhra. Only a few habitation deposits of these people have been noticed in close proximity to the megaliths (Rao,

K.P. 1988: 19-32), *viz.*, Veerapuram (Sastry, T.V.G. *et al.* 1984), Kesarapalli (Sarkar, H. 1966), Mudigal (Reddy, R.V. 1985), Dendulure (*IAR 1958-59*: 68), etc. At Kesarapalli, the habitational deposits were located close to a cluster of rectangular cist burials. It was found inter-locked with the late Neolithic levels and a still later culture complex with the Rouletted ware. Occurrence of the Rouletted ware was perhaps due to the contact with interaction of western inhabitants. It appears that small settlements with entirely temporary rural base were in existence during this period. These communities were surviving primarily on incipient farming and were utilizing iron objects, a tradition still common in some of the tribal communities of India.

The use of iron, including evolved types of tools and weapons certainly indicate a period of developed food producing economy in which agriculture might have played an important role. Compared to the dwellings of this phase, the burial architecture of the people was impressive and also varied in types. The ceramic types are Black and Red ware, Black ware, Red were, coarse Grey ware, etc. Majority of them are wheel made. The common shapes are shallow dishes, rimless bowls, and globular pots with concave or constricted necks and beaded out clubbed or beveled rim. Sometimes carinated pots and ring stands also occur.

The stage of urbanism in Andhra begins in the middle of the first millennium BCE or around fourth century BCE when permanent settlements with on exceptionally rich array of defensive devices appear along with developed iron technology. It was also a time of surplus food production and long distance trade. The characteristic ceramic type, the Black and Red ware, of the earlier period had stabilized as a standard ceramic with certain technological and morphological modifications. Similarly, the impressive Megalithic burial practices also continued. But, in spite of the continuation of some of the earlier cultural elements, Andhra Pradesh can march a step forward from the tribal tradition to the stage of civilization. It may be worth while to mention to this connection that the extensive use of iron tools and implements and decorative objects in gold, silver and brass, which have come to the light from the Megaliths at Nagarjunakonda (Subrahmanyam, R. *et al.* 1975) and Yeleswaram (Khan, M.A.W. 1963), suggest that mastery of a number of metal technology was a local feature of the Neolithic times, which gave impetus to the development of crafts and technological skills of the Early Historical period.

In the last quarter of the first millennium BCE *i.e.*, Andhra phase, the region was marked by significant changes in the cultural pattern. By this time, some of the tribes had carved out kingdoms *(Ganarajyas)* for themselves and dominated over the other groups. As a result, many political localities developed, which had clusters of small settlements. With the exploitation of natural resources, not only agriculture but many crafts were also developed. This promoted in the region, many new small and large settlements around the natural resources. From the hinterland, several crops and goods could be brought to the large settlements along the river. Sometimes the small settlements served as satellite centers of the nearby towns. This enabled the people to exchange food grains and other commercial products resulting in extensive trade activities. At the same time, coinage was introduced in the region, which further facilitated trade activities in the region. Iron was used extensively. Structures of kiln-burnt brick were made which provided durability to the settlements. A strong defensive mechanism was developed as result settlements were fortified. These activities had hastened the process of urbanization. Another advantage enjoyed by this region was the hinterland of the rivers and a long coastal line. It had brought the maritime people closer inviting foreign merchants for exchange of market produce from different lands. The merchandise made the people rich. With the development of trade and cultural activities, attention had to be paid to framing of moral codes, law and order, conservancy facilities, education and many other institutions, which acted as the motivating factors in urbanization.

The Satavahanas were gradually extending their regime in Andhra through Telangana region in around first century CE. By the end of second century CE, it had witnessed the consolidation of the entire region for a politically unified leadership for the first time in the history of Andhra Pradesh. The evidence for Satavahana hegemony in the region appears as in the form of a good number of coins and relics of plastic art, besides a few inscriptions and literary sources. It may also be noted that the economic conditions of the region has been increased during this period. It shows in the form of art activity, Jaggayapet, Bhattiprolu, etc., sculptural embellishments on stupa were enlarged during this period. In the case of urban characters, trade and commerce and other cultural activities were also developed under the atmosphere of political stability.

Since the periods mark the beginning of the historical period of Andhra Pradesh, a few numismatic and epigraphical evidence also are available, which provide additional information about this period.

Table 2

3.2 Numismatic and Epigraphic Evidences

Name	Date bracket	From of evidence	Reported	Reference
raja Kuberaka	3rd cent BCE	inscriptions	Bhattiprolu	Buhler, G. 1894: 328-9
raja Somaka	2nd cent BCE	inscriptions	Vadamanu	Sastry, T.V.G. 1983
raja Ashoka	Ist cent BCE	inscription	Salihundam	*EI*. XXXI: 87, 88
Ayira Manasada	Ist cent BCE	inscription	Velpuru	*EI*. XXXII: 86
rajakumari Sammali	Ist cent BCE	inscription	Amaravati	Sarma, I.K. 1988
raja Bala	Ist cent BCE	inscription	Amaravati	Sarma, I.K. 1988
Ayira Siri Saka Sada	Ist cent BCE	coins	Amaravati	Sarma, I.K. 1980
Gobhadra	2nd –Ist cent BCE	coins	Kotilingala	Sastry, P.V.P. 1979:17-28
Sama Gopa	2nd –Ist cent BCE	coins	Kotilingala	Sastry, P.V.P. 1979:17-28
Kamvaya	2nd –Ist cent BCE	Coins	Kotilingala	Sastry, P.V.P. 1979:17-28
Narana	2nd –Ist cent BCE	coins	Kotilingala	Sastry, P.V.P. 1979:17-28

The inscription form the coastal Andhra region (between 300 BCE and CE 100) speak of *raja* or *rajkumari* which suggest that the king was more a leader of the community in the earlier phase. It can be said that they were the rulers whose authority was recognized in a localized area. The inscribed coins, providing the names of their issuers, reveal the political profile of emergent localities for the first time across the Andhra region. From all such evidence, it can be inferred that the region consisted of only a number of *Ganarajyas*, each with a chief under the name Andhra *jatiya*. So there were several chief of Andhra origin calling themselves as *raja*, who used to exercise some authority in their traditional way of administration during the last quarter of the first millennium BCE and the first one and a half century of the beginning of CE. The *Puranas* do not mention their names because they were petty chiefs without imperial status.

A little later, Satavahanas, perhaps a clan of the Andhras, rose to power in the north-western region. The Satavahana dynasty *(kula)* appears to be identical with the Andhras in the puranic texts such as Maitreya, Vayu, Brahmanda, Vishnu and Bhagavata Puranas. They were called Andhras because they were of Andhra origin (*jati*). On the basis of the finds of the Kondapur coin (Rao, R.M.1961), Telangana region could be ascertained as the original home of the Satavahana ruler. K. Satyanarayana (1975:110) is of the opinion that the Satavahanas established their hegemony first in the Telangana and then spread their empire west wards, north wards and south wards. The archaeological evidence, viz., coins from the stratified layers of Satavahanas suggest that only after the first century of the CE in the north-western region was under the rule of Satavahanas. For the occurrence of coins of Gautamiputra Satakarni (*c* 75-102 CE) suggest that the Andhra region was their domain onwards (Datta, M.1990: 5).

Wheeler (1947-48: 180-310) for the first time used the term 'Andhra Culture'. A specific ware of this group was also termed as 'Andhra ware' (Russet Coated Painted ware) by him as per the remains of the Brahmagiri site. But, Wheeler used the term 'Andhra' for the group of Satavahana antiquities, including the coins. He might also have had the same opinion regarding the Satavahana origin like Satyanarayana and others, which has been quoted above. But the present author applied the term 'Andhra Culture' for pre-Satavahana cultural context of the Andhra Pradesh. This was the crucial period in the history of the early Andhradesa, where the major cultural formulation took place. We therefore, feel that the term 'Andhra Culture' is more appropriate to this period as in the case of the Andhra Pradesh.

In spite of the extensive spade work which has been briefed above, and good accumulation of archaeological data, the earliest phase of the Early Historical period of Andhra Pradesh is not very well reconstructed. There are detailed reports on individual excavated sites, and isolated attempts to study one or two aspects of the history and culture of the period. But, a total picture of the culture has not been attempted seriously. It is true particularly for the period, which lies between the Megalithic period (*circa* 800 to 400 BCE) and the Satavahana period (100 to 300 CE). It may be noted that this time-span viz., *circa* 400 BCE to CE 100 is very significant for the entire Indian sub-continent. As this was the period which marked by the introduction of many new trends in India History for the first time. Important among these were the formulation of second urbanization, political systems, trade and commerce and a number of culture traits related to complex but systematic living. The Gangetic plains had emerged as a nucleus region where these developments have been studies in detail. Glimpse of somewhat similar situation can be envisaged in Andhra Pradesh also, which need to be examined carefully.

In Andhra the time-bracket under consideration can be termed as 'pre-Satavahana' or 'Andhra Culture' (these terminologies have been discussed in detail a little later in this chapter). It was this period when basic culture traits had formulated, which later on continued for number of centuries. A major charge in the living pattern is also evident. There was in fact a transition from pre-literate and tribal societies to the literate and more organized mode of living. For the Megalithism of the preceding period, gradually evolved into a culture system, which though adopted some of the earlier traits such as ceramics and the disposal of dead, was heading towards urbanization and socio-economically complex societies. This culture progress culminated into the imperial power beside society of the Satavahana period. From Satavahana period, a continues dynastic history is available in the region. But, it is also apparent that the remains of the material culture used by the common people have not been fully utilized for the reconstruction of the history of peoples of the Satavahana times. It was, therefore, though useful to put together all the archaeological evidence in view to reconstructing the cultural history of the Early Historical period of Andhra, particularly of the 'per-Satavahana/Andhra Culture' and 'Satavahana Culture'. Because, in the remains of this period evidence for the foundations of a number of culture traits such as the urbanization and rise of political organization, etc., are embodied. Scrutiny with the help of historical accounts has been attempted in the present volume.

Before discussing the potentiality of the material culture of the region, it would be logical to admit the limitations of our research work. Almost the entire data, which has been studied, is based on the reports and observations of the respective excavators. For, it was not possible for the author to actually excavate any relevant site in the region independently. It was however, tried to examine the excavated remains in person wherever possible along with excavators either in the site or stored collection. But quiet a few discrepancies come of in this study, which were due to the imperfect nature of the collections. For example, the earlier archaeologists were interested in unique and beautiful things of aesthetic value and structural remains of religious nature. As a result of this, may other antiquities were discarded during excavations. The majority of the reports mention only the important objects and then speck of large number of minor antiquities, which are not described in detail. It is know that the minor antiquities are also of much significance and for complete understanding of any archaeological horizon all categories of antiquities must be analyzed properly. The biased and partial collections which are large in number thus minimize the liability of many of our conclusions. The other problem that was faced by this researcher was of dating the collections. In majority of the cases, all the antiquities of third century BCE to second/third century CE have been grouped together by the field investigators. The separation of the group particularly within per-Satavahana /Andhra Culture and Satavahana Culture was very difficult. But there are few recently excavated sites where demarcations of these two culture periods have been mentioned, which provided reliable base to our study. With the above mentioned in mind, the present study has been conducted as far as possible on the usable available data. Further, in ancient times, the Andhradesa had its boundaries much beyond the present administrative state unit of the same name. But, for the sake of convenience, the modern administrative land coverage of the Andhra state has been accepted as the select area of the present dissertation. It may be mentioned that this region includes more or less the nucleus of the linguistic as well as the culturally homogeneous unit of Telugu population.

On the basis of the material remains such as clay objects, metal objects, structure remains and other noteworthy antiquities recovered from the various sites like Salihundam, Peddabankur, Kotilingala, Satanikota, Veerapuram and other excavated sites (*cf* Table 4) within the State along with a comparative analysis with the other excavated sites of the rest of India for the potentiality of the region during the Early Historical period has been attempted in the present volume.

3.3 TERMINOLOGY

The term 'Andhra' is used in more then one ways, particularly for a region and also for a group of people from the ancient times. In ancient texts, the region under study has been variously referred to as 'Antaka' or 'Andhaka' (Cowell, E.B.1990: 135) and 'Andhra' (Majumdar, R.C.1980: 193-195). The Kumbha and Samkicca Jatakas (Cowell, E.B. 1990: 10, 134) refer to the 'Andhras' as well as Andhra country and Andhra city. All these terms have been taken to be derived from a single linguistic unit.

The use of the term 'Andhra' for a particular group of people is also found side by side to the name of the region in ancient literature. The earliest reference to the Andhras is found in the Aitareya Brahmana (Agoshe, K.S. 1986), which speaks of the Andhras as non-Aryan exiled sons of Vishwamitra. They are said to occupy the bordering region of the Aryan settlements. The Andhras are also referred to in the Sankhyayana Srautasutra, the Mahabharata (Edgerlon, F. 1944) and the Ramayana (4: 41) along with the Cholas, Ceras and Pandyas. All these references suggest that a particular section of the population of the ancient India were known as Andhras. Further, these were perhaps the native people different from the Vedic groups of northwestern region. That the Andhras continued to be recognized as a separate group of people during the Early Historical period is also attested by the inscriptions of Mauryan king, Asoka. One of his Rock Edicts (Hultzsch, E. 1969: 83) refers to the Andhras along with the Pulindas as the inhabitants of the border lands. The Anguttara and the Vinaya, the Buddhist texts also mention the Andhras in their list of *Janapada* (Rhys, T.W.1903: 23 - 287). Roy Chodhuri observed that the Andhras occupied the lower valley of the Godavari and the Krishna. But a small section of them have lived near the Vidarbha, as the people called 'Andhs' and are still found in the district of Buldana in Maharashtra (Yazdani , G .1960 : 15). K.P Jayaswal (1916: 82) refers to the Andhra as one of the enclaves of the powerful and independent State between the Godavari and the Krishna rivers, in the vast empire of Bindusara (*c* 300-273 BCE). The historical evidence, thus, refers to a group of people, perhaps of non-sindh vedic stock as Andhras.

Wheeler, for the first time used the term 'Andhra culture' while describing the excavated remains of Brahmagiri (Wheeler, R.E.M. 1947-48:180-310). But he used the term Andhra for a particular ware e.g. Russet Coated Painted Ware or the 'Andhra Ware'. Which he had found to associated with typical Satavahana antiquities such as coins, etc. But in recent years, the archaeological evidence collected, suggest that Russet Coated Painted ware was the characteristic ceramic type of the pre-Satavahana levels though it associates also at times the Satavahana culture horizons.

It may be mentioned that there are enough evidence unearthed during the last three decades in the Andhra Pradesh, an account of which has already been briefed above, which reveals two distinct culture levels during the Early Historical period. The present researcher prefers the term 'Andhra Culture' to the 'pre-Satavahana Culture' for the first period of the Early Historical Andhradesha. This is, because it was realized by him during the course of examination of the archaeological collections that between the two well established cultures e.g., the megalithic and the Satavahana, there existed an entirely independent culture complex. This intermediatery stage needed to be emphasized and given a name. There were two alternatives, e.g., to prefix it with the know levels such as post-Megalithic or pre-Satavahana, or use a new term. The term 'post-Megalithic' was not found appropriate, as the complex under consideration had undergone so much change that the basic nature of tribal and rural culture of megalithic tradition had almost lost its identity. Similarly, the 'pre-Satavahana' nomenclature also does not appear to reveal the true significance of this culture horizon. 'Andhra Culture' therefore, was found suitable label for more then one reasons.

As was discussed above, the historical accounts suggest that there was a separate recognized group of people in the region under study, which was identified as Andhras. There appear under to be a group of indigenous people, who were the inhabitants of the border land of Mauryan empire. The list of *Janapadas* also includes Andhras. It may be argued that these references could not have been for the Megalithic population, which could not rise from the tribal way of life. Nor could this be for the Satavahana, who post date *Janapada* time and the Mauryas. Under these circumstances, the Andhras of the Early Historical times could only identified with the archaeological remains of the post-Megalithic and the pre-Satavahana times, which can be referred to as 'Andhra Culture'. Andhra culture of *circa* 400 BCE to CE 100 was widespread in most parts of Andhra Pradesh. It appears to have evolved from certain basic traits of Megalithic system of local chiefdom. Introduction of coinage, use of permanent material for buildings, development of trade and organization of social structures were such aspects of the time which laid the foundation for the socio-cultural trends which prevailed for centuries in Andhra Pradesh. It is, therefore, that the use of this term was thought to be very logical for the pre-Satavahana archaeological horizon, of the region under study.

The subsequent culture stage of the Early Historical period of Andhra Pradesh derives it name from the famous dynasty of Satavahanas, who rose to power between 100 and 250 CE in the region. Since this dynastic label is freely in use for culture traits also, such a Satavahana art, etc., it was found logical to use it for denoting such a culture level which was almost contemporary to the said dynasty. Besides, the growth of imperial power also is well reflected in the culture contents, particularly in the case of settlements and building activities. But, it may be mentioned that the time-bracket of Satavahana culture extends beyond the period of the hold of the imperial power. For example, an account of the radiocarbon dates the Satavahana horizons could be dated to *circa* 150 to 300 CE, while the extent of Satavahana's rule was between 100 and 250 CE. Further, it may be added that though there appears to be drastic change in the politico-administrative setups from the *Janapada* system of the Andhra period to the monarchical system of the Satavahana times, the cultural transition from the first to the second stage was smooth and in the form of acultural process of development.

The other terms which denote individual artifact categories like, pottery, beads, etc., are used as per the convention in the archaeological studies, Terms denoting specific types such as Russet Coated Painted ware, Rouletted ware, etc., have been discussed in the respective sections which deals with the details of various artifact types.

REFERENCES

Allchin, B. and F.R. Allchin. 1968. *The Birth of Indian Civilization*. Harmondsworth.

Allchin, F.R. 1960. *Piklihal Excavations*. Andhra Pradesh Government Archaeological Series. No 1. Hyderabad.

Allchin, F.R. 1961. *Utmur Excavations*. Andhra Pradesh Government Archaeological Series No 5. Govt. of Andhra Pradesh. Hyderabad.

Allchin, F.R. 1963. *Neolithic Cattle Keepers of South India. A Study of Deccan ash mounds*. Cambridge.

Allchin, R. & B. Allchin. 1983. *The Rise of Civilization in India and Pakistan*. New Delhi.

Annual Report of Archaeological Department of His Exalted Highness of the Nizam's Dominions. 1940-41 (abbreviated as *ARN*) Department of Archaeology. Hyderabad.

Basak, R.D. (ed). 1971. *Gatha Saptasati of Hala*. Calcutta.

Burgers, J. 1987. *Buddhist Stupas of Amaravati and Jaggayyapeta*. Archaeological Survey of South India. London.

Cammiade, L.A. and M.C. Burkitt. 1930. Fresh Light on the Stone Age of South East Asia, India. *Antiquity*. IV: 3227-39.

Cowell, E.B. (ed). 1990 (3rd edn.) *The Jatakas or Stories of the Buddha's Former Births*. Translated by H.D. Francis. New Delhi. 530:138. 135: 512-10.

Dikshit, K.N. 1992. Iron Age and Peninsular India. *Puratattva*. Bulletin of Indian Archaeological Society. No 22 (1991-92). (ed) Dikshit, K.N. New Delhi: 31-34.

Dutta, M. 1990. *A Study of the Satavahana Coinage*. New Delhi.

Edgarton, F.E.D. 1944. The Sabhaparvan. *The Mahabharata* (19 Vols). (eds) V.S. Sukhtankar and S.K. Belvalkar. Poona. II.

Eggeling, J. (Translated). 1990 (reprint). *Sacred Books of the East*, The Satapatha Brahmana. (ed) F. Maxmuller. New Delhi.

Foote, R.B. 1887. Notes on some Recent Neolithic and Paleolithic antiquities in South Indian. *Journal of the Asiatic Society of Bengal.* LVI, 3: 259-82.

Foote, R.B. 1916. *The Foote Collection of Indian Perhistoric and Proto-historic Antiquities*: Notes on their Ages and Distribution. Madras.

Hultzsch, E. 1969. *Corpus Inscriptionum Indicarum.* Vol I. Inscription of Ashoka, (new edition). Varanasi.

Hunt, E.H. 1924. Hyderabad crain burials and their significance. *Journal of Royal Anthropological Institute of Great Britain and Ireland:* 14.

Indian Archaeology 1955-56, 58-59, 73-74, 74-75 81-82, and 82 -83 *A Review* (abbreviated as *IAR*). (ed) Director General. Archaeological Survey of India. New Delhi.

Jayaswal, K.P. 1916. The Empire of Bindusara. *The Journal of the Bihar and Orissa Research Society.* IT, 1: 82

Jayaswal, V. 1978. *Palaeo History of India* (A Study of the Prepared core Technique). Delhi.

Khan, M.A.W. 1963. *A Monograph on Yeleswaram Excavation.* Andhra Pradesh Archaeological Series XIV. Government of Andhra Pradesh. Hyderabad.

Krishna, M.S 1982. *Geology of India and Burma.* New Delhi.

Krishnaswami, V.D. 1949. Megalithic Types of south Indian. *Ancient India*, Bulletin of Archaeological Survey of India. No 5. New Delhi.

Kumari, M.A. & B.R. Subramaniyam 1991. The Paleolithic Archaeology of Gundlakamma Basin. *Indian Archaeological Heritage* (SH. K.V. Soundara Rajan Felicitation volume). (eds) C. Margabandhu, K.S. Ramachandran, A.P.Sagar & D.K. Singhal. Agam Indological series. No 11. New Delhi.

Majumdar, G.G. & S.N Rajaguru. 1966. *Ashmonud Excavations at Kupgal.* Poona.

Majumdar, R.C. (ed). 1980. (5th edn). *The Age of Imperial Unity the History and culture of the Indian People.* first edition 1951. Bombay.

Mangalam, S.J. 1986. *Historical Geography and Toponomy of Andhra Pradesh.* New Delhi.

Murthy, M.L.K. 1985. Blade-and Burin and Late stone Age Industries around Renigunta, Chitoor district. *Studies in Indian Archaeology.*

Professor H.D. Sankalia Felicitation Volume. (eds) Deo, S.B. & M.K. Dhavalikar. Bombay: 106-128.

Newbold, T.J. 1844. Notes on the Osseous breccia and deposit in the caves of Billa Soorgum Lat 15° 28' Long 78° 15', S. India. *Journal of the Asiatic Society of Bengal.* 13, 2: 610-615.

Paddayya, K. 1985. The Blade-Tool Industry of Shorapur Doab. *Studies in India Archaeology.* Professor H.D. Sankalia Felicitation Volume. (eds) Deo, S.B. & M.K. Dhavalikar. Bomay: 165-190.

Prasad, R.C. and O. Singh. 1987. *India-A Regional Geography.* Varanasi.

Rameshan, N. (ed). 1976. *Gazette of India,* Andhra Pradesh. Hyderabad.

Rao, K.P. 1988. *Deccan Megaliths.* Delhi.

Rao, N.S. 1980. Unexcavated Megalithic Sites in Karimnagar district of A.P. *Ithihas.* VII 2: 155-158.

Rao, R.M. 1961. *Satavahana coins in the Andhra Pradesh Government Museum.* Andhra Pradesh Government Archaeological Series. No 2. Govt. of Andhra Pradesh. Hyderabad.

Rays, D.T.W. 1903. *Buddhist India.* London.

Rea, A. 1990 (reprint). Excavations at Amaravati. *Archaeological Survey of the India Annual Report 1908 -09.* New Delhi: 88-91.

Reddy, R.V. 1976. *The Prehistoric and Protohistoric Cultures of Palauoy, South India: with a Special reference to Ashmound problem.* Andhra Pradesh Govt. Archaeological Series. No 43. Hyderabad.

Reddy, R.V. 1978. *A study of the Neolithic culture of South India: with a special reference to Ashmound problem.* Andhra Pradesh. Archaeological Series. No 43. Hyderabad.

Reddy, R.V. 1978. *A study of the Neolithic Culture of South-Western Andhra Pradesh.* Archaeological series. No 51. Govt. of Andhra Pradesh. Hyderabad.

Reddy, R.V. 1985. Mudical: A Megalithic site in Anantapur district, Andhra Pradesh. *Culture of the Past, Current Anthropological and Archaeological perspective.* Volume 3. (ed) Bhowmik, K.L. New Delhi. 3: 133-142.

Reddy, R.V. 1985a. First forming communities in Anantapur district Andhra Pradesh. *Culture of the Past, Current Anthropological and Archaeological perspective.* Volume 3. (ed) Bhowmik, K.L. New Delhi: 142-154.

Reddy, V.V. 1991. *Neolithic and post- Neolithic Cultures.* New Delhi.

Sankalia, H.D. 1963. *Pre- history and Proto-history in India and Pakistan.* Bombay.

Sankar, H. 1973 (reprint). Kesarapalli-1962. *Ancient India*. Bulletin of Archaeological Survey of India. No 22. New Delhi: 37-274.

Sarma, I.K. 1987. Buddhist sites in Andhra Pradesh. *Archaeology of Andhra Pradesh, A Souvenir.* (ed) Sastry, V.V. K. Hyderabad.

Sarma, I.K. 1990. Ancient Andhra ports, Religion centers and sea faring. *Journal of Marine Archaeology.* I: 19 -23.

Sastri, T.V.G. (ed). 1983. Vaddamanu Excavations and Explorations in Krishna Valley. *Bulletion of Birla Archaeological and Cultural Institute.* Hyderabad.

Sastri, T.V.G., Bai, M. K. & J.V. Rao. 1984. *Veerapuram*, A type site for culture study in the Krishna Valley. Hyderabad.

Sastry, V.V.K. 1983. *The Proto and Early History of Andhra Pradesh.* Govt. of Andhra Pradesh. Hyderabad.

Sastry, P.V.P. 1978. Unknown coins of Satavahana and their Predecessors. *Numismatic Digest.* 2, 1: 10-21.

Sastry, P.V.P.1979. Some more coins from Kotilingala. *Numismatic Digest.* 3, 2: 17-28.

Sasrty, P.V.P. 1989. Political system in Early coastal Andhra. *Ajaya Sri, Recent studies in Indology.* Prof. Ajaya Mitra Sastri Felicitation Volume. (ed) Hande, D. New Delhi.

Satyanarayana, K. 1975. *A study of the history and culture of the Andhra* (from Stone Age to Feudalism). New Delhi.

Schoff, H.W.1974 (reprint). *The Periplus of the Erythraean Sea* (Travel and Trade in the Indian Ocean by a Merchant of the First Century A.D.). first published in 1912. New Delhi.

Seshadri, M. 1971. *Report on the Excavations at T. Narsipur.* Bangalore.

Sewell, R. 1972. (reprint). *Lists the Antiquarian Remains in the Presidency of Madras. Archaeological Survey of India* (New Imperial Series Volume VII). Delhi.

I Sewell, R. 1973. (reprint). *Report of the Amaravati tope and Excavations on its sites 1877.* Varanasi.

Soundara Rajan, K.V. 1952. Stone Age Industries near Giddalur, district Kurnool.

Ancient India. Bulletin of Archeological Survey of India. No 8. New Delhi: 64-92.

Srinivasan, K.R. & N.R. Banerjee. 1953. Survey of South Indian Megaliths. *Ancient India.* Bulletin of Archaeological Survey of India. No 9. New Delhi: 103-118.

Subrahmaniyan, R. (ed). 1975. *Nagarjunakonda* (1954-60). Memories of the Archaeological Survey of India. No 75. New Delhi: I

Sukhtankar, V.S. 1955. *Cambridge History of India.* (ed) F.J. Rapson. Delhi. I.

Thapar, B.K. 1957. Maski, 1954: A Chalcolithic site of the Southern Deccan. *Ancient India.* Bulletin of the Archaeological Survey of India. No 13. New Delhi: 4-142.

Wheeler, R.E.M. 1947-48. Brahmagiri and Chandravalli, 1974: Megalithic and other Culture in the Chittaldurg district, Mysore state. *Ancient India.* Bulletin of the Archaeological Survey of India. No 4. New Delhi: 181-310.

Yazdani, G. (ed). 1960. *The Early History of the Deccan*. London.

Chapter 4

DISPERSAL OF SETTLEMENTS

Settlement patterns and localities of the Early Historic people in the region under study have been attempted in this part, basic data for which is derived from various publications and explorations. Map (No 1) showing the location of the sites yielding Early Historic antiquities reveals number and spread of Early Historical settlements in the region. It may be mentioned that the total count of Early Historical sites in the state which are reported so far comes to around four hundred [AAR; IAR Sastry, V.V.K. 1983.

Map (No 1) showing sites of the Early Historical period, reveals that the distribution pattern of the sites of this category is very wide and extends almost all over the state. Within this wide dispersal of settlements, there are a few noteworthy patterns. A dense clustering of sites, particularly of small dimensions, is formed in the central portion of the coastal Andhra region of the state. These small settlements are closely located and are found along the rivers Godavari, Krishna and Gundlakamma and their delta regions. Similar type of settlement pattern can be seen in the south-western region of Telangana in the delta areas of the river Krishna and its tributaries. In the other part, i.e., in the northern region of the Telangana, pockets of Early Historical sites occur particularly along the river Godavari and its tributaries. The region the marked by a number of Early Historical sites which are located at almost in every alternate village of the region (Sastry, V.V.K. 1983: 123). In the Royalseema region, these settlements are scattered and located mainly around rivulets or small streams. There are however, a few pockets of sites on the confluence of the large rivers like Krishna and Tungabhadra. These may be taken to be exception to the general distribution of sites.

The central Telangana region was not suitable habitat during the Early Historical period. Similarly, the southern most part of the sate was also a neglected area as it was not inhabited by these settlers. Except for these few significant variations the region under study has come from one physiographic unit. Further, the size and the nature of sites suggest that these settlements show very close affinities with one and the other. It seems that at first, there were a number of small settlements which had agricultural base. A little later, some of these emerged as important settlements where along with agrarian base, gradual concentration of power and population started accumulating. Such centers were also surrounded by a cluster of small dependent settlements some of which were new establishments.

The data, which is available from the field survey though represents that the area was under occupation during the Early Historical times, yet it is difficult to ascertain the nature of the settlement pattern. Because, in most of the cases, antiquities are collected from the surface and their original cultural contents could not be known. The sites with potentialities for presenting precise stratigraphical contents were not many and some of these were subjected to small scale diggings. These probings, however, were not taken up as regular horizontal excavations, and hence, the data available lacks details and are scanty in nature. Due to this situation, only those sites have been selected as representative settlements which have been extensively excavated and provide factual details.

All the reported sites have been divided within three topographical region of the state, viz., the Coastal Andhra, Telangana and Royalseema.

The Survey data indicates that the river valley sites are numerous in the entire three regions. The Krishna and Godavari valleys and their delta areas were the nucleus zone of habitation during the Early Historical times. Most importantly in most of the cases, a large portion of the catchment areas, especially of small river plains were selected. The fertile plains lying in the vicinity of the small and large rivers appear to be the preferred habitat as 155 sites of this category have been reported so far, which forms nearly half of the total number of know ancient settlement of our area study (Sastry, V.V.K. 1983; Pisipaty, S.R.K.1983.

The alluvial plains another important role in the formulation of the Early Historic settlements in the Coastal Andhra, from where a total of fifty sites have been brought to light. Due to the fertile nature of this deposit, the concentration of settlements shifted from the previously unoccupied areas to these plains by the end the last millennium BCE because agriculture based economy had reached its zenith.

The coastal plains and on-shore sites are obviously important localities in the coastal region. The main concentration in these areas may be due to the ports and anchorages. It seems that these places were suitable for the prophets also. Nearly a quarter of the total sites of the region (90 in all) are recognized as the coastal plain localities. Among these, a good number are religious (Buddhist) settlements by nature (Map V; Pisipaty; S.R.K. 1983).

The hillocks or foot hills were also important areas in the arid and semi- arid regions, such as in Telangana and Royalseema region, from where 20 sites are reported. The reason for selecting this region was their rich forest products as well as mineral resources.

4.1 STATIGRAPHY & CULTURAL SEQUENCE

The chrono-cultural sequence of the Early Historical period of the region under study, has been discussed in this part with the help of excavated sites. The stratigraphy of the excavated sites and the available Radiocarbon dates obtained from the various unearthed horizons, have been evaluated for the purpose of dating.

Representative Sites

Representative Sites: from the group of over three dozen excavated sites (Map V), the following sites (Table 3) have been selected for detailed analysis.

It may be note that these sites have not only yielded good amount of excavated material, but also represent all the three geo-physical units of Andhra Pradesh.

Table 3

Sl. No.	Site	Region	Nature	Significance
1.	Salihundam	Costal Andhra	Coastal Plain & Hill top	Religious Centre
2.	Peddabankur	Telangana	River Valley	Urban Centre
3.	Kotilingala	Telangana	River Valley	Political Centre
4.	Satanikota	Royalseema	River Valley	Fortified Town
5.	Veerapuram	Royalseema	River Valley	Rural Centre

Salithundam

Salihundam (18° 13'N Lat 84° 15'E Long), the ancient Buddhist site, is situated on the fringes of the Eastern Hills in Srikakulam district in the northern Costal Andhra region. It lies on the right bank of the river Vamsadhara. The famous ancient sea port, Calingapatnam (now a defunct sea port), is dotted on the By of Bengal and located within an earshot distance (8 km) from Salihundam towards the east. The excavation at Salihundam was initially carried out by the directorship of A.L Longhurst (1919-20: 30). It was subsequently re-excavated by R. Subrahmanyam due to which details sequence of archaeological debris and a monastic establishment was brought to light (Subrahmanyam, R. 1964).

The excavation brought to light three periods of occupation with a clear-cut break in between each of these. Besides three distinct occupation levels, a group of well documented religion structures, particularly Buddhist, was unearthed which date from the Andhra period upto the Historical period (Subrahmanyam, R. 1964; *IAR* 1953-54: 11). Table 4 presents the stratification and important antiquities from Salihundam. All the unearthed evidence from Salihundam proves that the first settlers at this sits were the Andhra Culture people. It also appears from the archaeological remains that this settlement flourished primarily under the influence of Buddhism. On the basis of the Punch Marked coins and other datable remains (inscriptions), this period can be assigned a date bracket of late third century BCE or the beginning of the second century BCE to first century CE. The structures of period II at this site could be dated between second and third century CE and were built perhaps by the Satavahanas and their immediate successor (*IAR 1953-54*:11). But on account of the inscribed ceramics, seals and coins, a more precise time bracket for this period e.g. the 1st to 3rd or 4th century CE can be ascertained. The uppermost period, which has yielded modern looking pottery and other artifacts of the later period, has been dated to *circa* 4th or 5th century CE to 7th or 8th century CE.

Peddabankur

Peddabankur (18° 30' N Lat 79°30' E Long) is an ostentatious modern village in the Peddapalli taluk of Karimnagar district in the northern Telangana region. This Early Historical sits, covering approximately an area of 30 hectares, is situated adjacent to the Karimnagar-Peddapalli road. The site is located on the bank of a *nallah*, known as Hussainvagu.

The excavation at Peddabankur was carried out by the Department of Archaeology and Museums, Government of Andhra Pradesh. These field investigations were conducted by Khan, M.A.W. (*IAR* 1967-68: 2; 1968-69: 1-2), and V.V.K.

Sastry (*IAR* 1970-71: 2; 1971-72: 2-3; 1972-73: 3; 1974-75: 5; 1977-78: 12-13).

The sits and its surrounding are covered by alluvial black soil which is spread on a disintegrated granite *morrum*. The secondary minerals such as carnelian, jasper, chalcedony, crystal and quartz are available in good quantities in this region which was useful media for tools and ornaments (Sastry, V.V.K. 1983: 124). The archaeological debris of 11 m was divided into four layers are suggestive of two periods (*cf* Table 4). The earliest habitation in the mound was confined to layer 4. It is a thin gravel layer. Layer 3 overlying layer 4 and evidence a change in the cultural composition. It is 56-70 cm in thickness. The culture change is marked by the increase of pottery wares both in quantity and types. Layer 2 is characterized by the loose grayish and types. Layer 2 is characterized by the loose grayish earth mixed with fine sand which bears traces of continuous cultivation. The archaeological remains of this layer correspond with layer 3. But it can be differentiated from the earlier layer due to the increase of structural activities and the occurrence of Satavahana and Roman coins. Layer 1 is composed of loose earth characterized by surface humus (*AAR* 1970-71: 1-2; 1971-72: 1-3; 1972-73; 1974-75: 1-3).

The cultural sequence of the sits begins with the late Megalithic period and continued upto the post-Andhra or Satavahana period with a time bracket of fourth century BCE to second century CE (*IAR* 1978-79: 103). It has been reported that the sits was suddenly deserted in the post-Satavahana period due to perhaps some natural calamities. Table 4 presents the stratigraphy and cultural sequence of the material remains at this site.

Kotilingala

Kotilingala (18° 30'N Lat 79° 30'E Long) is situated in Peddapalli taluk of Karimnagar in the northern Telangana region. It is located on the southern bank of the river Godavari. It was excavated by the Department of Archaeology and Museums, Government of Andhra Pradesh, by a team of archaeologists (*IAR* 1980-81: 2; *AAR* 1981-82; 1983-84: 37).

The Early Historical mound with a height of nearly 6 m above the plain, is roughly 50 hectares in extant. The entire mound yielded the Early Historical pottery and other antiquities. The mound retained a cultural deposit as thick as 2 to 2.5 m and was marked by several habitational floors. The three areas which were excavated in the central and northern parts of the mound, revealed evidence for two cultural phases of a homogeneous culture of the Early Historical period. In all six layers were exposed which rested one above the other over the natural soil. Table 4 show the archaeological remains of the site.

The evidence unearthed here, suggests that the Early Historical settlers occupied this in two stages. The earliest phase is characterized by the mud rampart along with the bastions on four corners, advanced ceramic remains, terracotta figurines, metal objects and other antiquities. The occurrence of the coins of the Andhra kings, who were purely non-Satavahanas, such as Gobadha, Samagopa, Satasa, etc, are the other important finds of this phase. On the basis of palaeographic characters (on coins), the date bracket suggested for this phase is third to first century BCE. The archaeological contents in the second phase were very similar to phase Ia. The noteworthy differences were the increase of structural activities. Use of bricks in the construction of fortification wall is the significant evidence. Besides, brick was also used in bastion and gateways. The city also evidence planning in the form of well arranged dwelling. The urban stage of this phase is also reflected in certain categories of antiquities, such as molded figurines. In this case, special mention may be made to the double molded terracotta female figurines, which are very typical of this period. On the basis of the Satavahana coins and style of terracotta figurines, this phase has been dated between circa last quarter of first century BCE and second century CE.

Satanikota

Satanikota (15° 55‘N Lat 78° 14‘E Long), the ancient fort site, was discovered near a small hamlet in Kurnool district of the northern Royalseema region. Satanikota (*kota* means a fort, in regional language) lies on the right bank of the river Tungabhadra, near the Kudavalli Sangamesvaram, where it meets the river Krishna.

In order to find out the archaeological potentiality of the site, the Department of Archaeology and Museum, Government of Andhra Pradesh, carried out small scale excavation (*IAR 1967-68*: 2). Later, the Excavation Branch of the Archaeological Survey of India , conducted scale excavation at the site under the supervision of N.C. Ghosh (1986; *IAR 1974-7* : 5; 1976-77: 7; 1977-78: 3-11; 1979-80: 2-6).

The major portion of the village mound which yielded the Early Historical antiquities is now under occupation. However, the habitation on the western and eastern ends of the Village are still mentioned by their traditional names as *Enugula kota* (elephant stable) and *Gurrmula kota* (horse), which is away from the bank of the river Tungabhadra,

Megalithic burials were brought to light during the course of documentation of the archaeological remains in the region. Digging of about 1.5 m thick habitational deposit at this site has been divided into 3 cultural periods. Period II has further been separated into three different phases (Ghosh, N.C. 1986). Table 4 briefs the stratification as well as the major finds from Satanikota.

In the absence of absolute dates, the archaeological remains of Satanikota have been dated relative dating. For instance, on the basis of lithic tools, the lowest implementiferous horizon has been dated to the Mesolithic period. The second period is characterized by the Rouletted ware, Russet Coated Painted ware, circular and barrel shaped beads, coins inscribed in *Brahmi* etc. which are datable between *circa* first century BCE to the third century CE. The uppermost level of period III, which has yielded Mediaeval pottery and other contemporary antiquities, has been dated to *circa* 14th or 15th century CE.

Veerapuram

Veerapuram (16° Lat 78° 95' E Long) is situated in Nandikotkur taluk of Kurnool district in the northern Royalseema region. The Early Historical site at Veerapuram is located at a distance of 2 km north-west of the present Village of the same name. It is situated on the right bank of the legendary Krishna, near Chakrateertha sangam, where the river Bhavanasi joins it.

The excavation at Veerapuram was carried out by the Birla Archaeological and Cultural Research Institute, Hyderabad, by T.V.G. Sastri and his team between 1978 and 1980 (Sastri, T.V.G. *et al.* 1984; Sastri, T.V.G. 1981).

The archaeological at the site was found scattered in an approximate area of 9.5 acres. The stratification of the site is discussed with the help of cutting on the central and western mounds, one of which is 23 m in length and the other 11 m. It presented a continuous cultural sequence right from the Neolithic upto the Early Historical Period. It also revealed evidence for three successive cultures with a break between the first two. The first period, belong to the Neolithic period and could be divided into three phases, e.g., Neolithic extending between phase I and II, and Chalcolithic. The entire relics existed in fifteen layers (Table 4).

Neolithic assemblage includes stone blade industry, hand made pottery remains, circular dwellings (with post holes), etc. Overlying Neolithic deposits is the settlement remains of the Chalcolithic people. The general culture trait during this period remained unaltered except for the use of copper technology. A thick sterile layer seals the Chalcolithic deposit. The sterile deposit shows desertion of the site and accumulation of thick silt due to the closeness of the river. The same site was reoccupied by the Megalithic people in about 500 BCE. The evidence for the construction of circular and rectangular houses wit hearths and some with garbage pits, demonstrate that Megalithic characteristic way of living was established here. The successive order of the next occupancy was of Andhra culture, with in fact appears to be an extension of the Megalithic period. For it is characterized by the dominance of Megalithic Cultural components alone with some new features. The final stage, of occupancy is marked by the post-Andhra or Maharathi period, which is characterized by the mature stage of structural activities (Sastri, T.V.G. *et al.* 1984: 20).

Table 4

4.2 CULTURAL SEQUENCE & ANTIQUITIES

Name of the site	Period	Culture/date brackets	Antiquities			Datable materials	Reference
			Pottery	Structures	Other objects		
Peddabankur	II	Satavahana Ist century CE – 250 CE	B & RW, RW, RCPW, RuW, BPW, RPW. GW.CW	Civilized structures	DM TC & kaolin fig., beads, metal objects	C_{14} 1975 ±110 (25 BCE) C_{14} 1960 ± 105 (10BCE), Satavahana & Roman coins	*IAR* 1967-68:2; 1968-69:1-2; 1970-71:2; 1971-72:2-3; 1977-78:12-13; *AAR* 1970 to 75; Sastry, V.V.K.1983.
		Andhra c. 200BCE – Ist century CE	B & RW, BPW, RW, GW, CW, RCPW, RuW	Brick structures, town planning wells & cisterns	TC & kaolin fig, seal, metal objects	inscriptions	
	I	Megalithic C. 4BCE	B & RW, BPW, RW	Baked brick structures, mud & rubble foundations	Polished stone implements, metal objects	Megaliths, ceramic types	

Contd...

Kotilingala	I	Ib	Satavahana Ist BCE – Ist/ 2nd CE	RuW, GW, along with phase Ia	Brick fortification with bastions, well planned houses, advanced stage	Similar to phase Ia	Satavahana coins	*IAR* 1980-81:2; *AAR* 1981 to 1984.
		Ia	Andhra c. 3rd – Ist BCE	B & RW, RW, CW, RPW, BPW, RCPW	Mud rampart with bastions, brick houses, stupa	S&DM TC fig., metal objects, beads, coins, etc.	Andhra coins	
Satanikota	III 1 & 2		Mediaeval					Ghosh, N.C.19 IAR-1974 to 80
	II	b 3	Post-Andhra/ Satavahana	Continuation of phase a	Continuation of phase a	Continuation of phase a	Satavahana coins	
		a 4 & 5	Andhra	B & RW, BW, RPW, RPW, RCPW, KW, RuW	Rock cut moat, fortified wall, gateways, well planned brick constructions	TC fig., beads tiles, metal objects	Ceramic tradition	
	Sterile layer of redeposit morrum							
	I layer 6		Mesolithic			Scrapers, blades, burins	Microlithic tools	

Contd...

Name of the site	Period		Culture/date brackets	Antiquities			Datable materials	Reference
				Pottery	Structures	Other objects		
Veerapuram (16°N Lat. 78°95" E)	III	c	Late Maharathi (300-400 CE)	GW	Brick temple		Late Maharathi, Ikshvaku coins	Sastry, T.V.G. et al 1984; Sastry, T.V.G. 1981
		b	Marathi/ Satavahana (50 BCE-CE 300)	B & RW, BW, BPW, RPW, RCPW, RuW	Mature stage	DM TC fig., beads, metal objects	Satavahana coins	
		a	Andhra (300-50 BCE)	B & RW, BW, RCPW, RuW	Stone structures, town planning	S & DM T C figs., beads, metal objects, PM coins	Ceramic tradition	
	II		Mesolithic (500-300BCE)	B & RW, RW, BW	Circular, rectangular houses with post hole	Beads of TC, metal objects	C^{14}	
	Sterile deposit							
	S layers 15-12		Neolithic	GW, RW	Circular house plan	Ground stone industry	C^{14} dates	

Contd...

Salihundam ($18^0$13'N Lat $84^0$15'E Long)	III	Historical (4th-7/8th CE)	RW,BW, CW	Similar to period II	Similar to period II	Ceramic tradition	Subrah-manyam, R. 1964; *IAR* 1953:11
	II	Satavahana (Ist-3rd/4th CE)	B & RW, RW, RPW, RuW, GW	Well planned houses, stone built path ways, etc	Inscribed conch shell, bricks, TC fig., beads, etc.	Satavahana & Kushana coins, inscribed shreds	
	I	Andhra (Ist BCE-Ist CE)	B & RW, RW,GW, RuW	Brick platforms, monastic establishments, houses, etc.	Iron objects, beads, TC seal	Inscription on ceramics, seals, PM coins	

B & RW – Black-and-Red Ware, BW – Black Ware, BPW – Black Polished Ware, CW – Chocklet Ware, GW – Grey Ware, KW – Kaieolin Ware, RW – Read Ware, RPW – Red Polished Ware, RCPW – Russet Coated Painted Ware, RuW – Rouletted Ware, DM – Double Molded, SM – Single Molded, TC – Terra Cotta.

4.3 OTHER IMPORTANT EXCAVATED SITES

4.3.1 Coastal Region

The coastal Andhra region, which is nearly 600 km long coastal line, have been dotted with several major and minor ports right from the very early period of its history. The long coastline has several convenient anchorages. Some of the important ancient ports are Calingapatnam, Baliapatnam (Bhimilipatanam at present), Vishakhapatnam, Vengipura (Peddavegi), which are not far from Salihundam in the Northern Coastal Andhra region. In the central and southern Coastal Andhra region, Maisolia (Machilipatanam), Dhanyakataka (Amaravati), etc., and Maipadu, Krishnapattanam, Kothapattanam, Durarajupattanam and Baripeta (presently Sriharikota is the Rocket launching station) are the noteworthy settlements (Sarma, I.K. 1990: 19 -23). Though a few of them are now defunct ports, most of them are active ports even today. The reasons for the development of several port towns were brisk trade and religious establishment. Machipatnam (Machilipatanam) was one such great market port town of the Andhras (Schoff, W.H. 1912: 62; Sastry, M.S.N. 1927). Evidence for sea route and inland trade comes from inscriptions found at Mahanagaparvata (Guntupalli) and Kantakossala (Gantasala), which mention sea route navigators, port and also the land routes connecting ports (Sarma, I.K. 1988: 2). It may be noted that the find spots of these inscriptions is close to Salihundam. The region also became prominent due to religious activities. The Buddhist monks and missionaries perhaps moved through these coasts to south-east Asia and Ceylon (Sarma, I.K.1990: 19-23). The lower Krishna which hand the double advantage of abundant supply of marble and of easy accessibility to sea through the river, become the favorite venue for the location of Buddhist establishments like Goli (Ramachandra, T.N. 1929), Garikapadu, Jaggayapeta (Sarma, I.K. 1988: 11), Gudivada (Ray, A. 1983: 168), Kesarapalli (Khan, M.A.W. 1969); Gantasala (*IAR* 1984-85: 5-6) and so many.

The following sites need mention as the archaeological remains unearthed and supplement the evidence obtained from the above mentioned representative sites.

Amaravati

In 1797, the potentiality of this religious establishment was recognized by the then Surveyor General of India, Col. Mackenzie's (quoted Fergusson, J. 1968) discovery of sculptured stones. A series of archaeological investigations were conducted subsequently (Burgers, J 1887; Ghosh A. and H. Sarkar, 1967: 168-77), which revealed quite a large number of NBP ware shreds from the pre and contemporary layers coeval with the foundation of the main stupa, suggesting that this Buddhist establishment was important settlement of the Early Historical period.

Stupa at Amaravati (*IAR* 1953-54: 5; 1973-74: 4-5; 1974-75: 2) and the fortification at Dharanikota (*IAR* 1961-62: 1; 1962-63: 1-2; 1963-64: 2-5; 1964-65: 2-3) in Guntur district have yielded burnt brick structures and Black and Red ware along with NBP ware and iron objects. The lowest level at these sites (period I) is datable to *circa* fourth century BCE. The Radiocarbon dates from Dharanikota are 2425 ± 100 (475 BCE) (*IAR* 1965-66: 86), and Amaravati 145 + 199 BCE (250 + 100 BCE) (Sarma , I.K. 1988: 6), which more or less confirms the above time brackets for the lowest habitation levels at these sites. The period of Amaravati, which was unearthed at the Mahachetya locality, is characterized by the earliest occupation. The habitational levels here have yielded 190 NBP ware shreds, two inscribed pot shreds in early *Brahmi* Characters, iron objects, and remains of huts made of thatched roofs, etc. the stupa at this time appears to be a low mound of mud. In period IB, which is dated to *circa* third century BCE has revealed an equal number of NBP ware shreds and a granite railing found *in situ* near the stupa. Period II roughly coincides with the second or first century BCE and coeval with phase I of Barhut and Sanchi (in North India). It has yielded only 39 fragments of NBP ware shreds and number of Punch Marked coins. At this stage, evidence for intensive structural activities was brought to light in the form of a gateway, inscribed and finely caved cross bars (Ghosh, A. 1969), etc., pottery and antiquities, also inscription (Luder's List No. 1248; Sarkar, H and S.P Nainer. 1972: 15; Sarkar, H. 1970-71: 7-8, III, IV, V) and the early issue coins in copper, lead, potin (*IAR 1973-74*: 4).

Bhattiprolu

Bhattiprolu in Guntur district though is an insignificant place today, was once a thriving Buddhist establishment. The excavation at the Bhattiprolu has revealed that the ruined stupa inside of the dome, had a casket which contained a crystal phial along with a pearl, a few bits of gold leaf and some ashes. Besides, three caskets with Brahmi inscriptions of second century BCE were discovered. The finds in the caskets included copper and gold rings, pearls, coral gold beads, gold flowers, *trisulas*, gold leaf, etc. (Sewell, R. 1972: 20-21; Sarma, I.K. 1988: 30; *IAR* 1969-70: 1). No habitational debris was obtained for this site. But the evidence indicates strong Buddhist hold in the region during Early Historical period.

Ghantasala

Ghantasala, a market town, lies nearly 25 km far from Machilipatnam port and not very far from the bank of the river Krishna. The spade of archaeologist brought out a good number of Roman coins and hundreds of Satavahana coins including one with typical ship motif. Besides, other antiquities and inscriptions were also discovered which indicate the prosperity of this settlement at the end of the second century CE. It appears to be an important centre of the Indo-Roman trade (*IAR* 1984-85: 5).

Nagarjunakonda

Nagarjunakonda in Guntur district had reached its position of prosperity and importance at the beginning of first century CE. The Indo-Roman trade was known here which is evident not only from the finds of Red Glazed Roman Pottery together with Roman lamp, glass wares, sprinklers, Roman coins, but also from the structures which has been identified as an amphitheatre (Sarkar, H. & B.N. Misra. 1987; Subrahmanyam, R. 1975; *IAR* 1955-56:23-26; 1956-57: 35-38; 1957-58: 5-9; 1958-59: 5-10; 59-60: 5-10)

Pavurallakonda

Pavurallakonda or Pavurallabodu near Bhimili about 30 Km from Visakhapatnam, nearly 14-16 rock-cut troughs or cisterns were found into the bed rock with two Brahmi label inscriptions (3rd BCE and 2nd CE). Excavations in the habitation area have revealed the foundations of viharas with cells and common verandah, circular chaityagrihas, votive stupas, halls etc. Associated with the structures were found two Satavahana coins, a Roman coin, inscribed pot shreds, besides Black and Red ware, Black Polished ware and beads (*IAR* 1991-92: 3).

Bavikonda

Bavikonda lies at a distance of 16 km from the town of Visakhapatnam, along the beach road, leading to Bheemunipatnam. Excavations (*AAR* 1982-87) on the hilltop brought to light an extensive Buddhist establishment consisting of a Mahachaitya, embedded with relic caskets, large vihara complex, a number of votive stupas, a stone pillared congregation hall, rectangular halls, a refectory etc. In association with these structures were recovered, a Satavahana lead coin, three Roman silver coins, fragments of inscriptions (in *Brahmi*), *Buddhapada* slabs decorated with *asthamangala* symbols and other Early Historic cultural antiquities (3rd BCE to CE 3rd). While attending to the conservation work of the Mahachaitya, five receptacles containing silver and gold caskets were recovered.

Chandavaram

At ***Chandavaram*** exposed Mahastupa built on terraced platform, apsidal chaityagriha, votive stupas, drum slabs, Satavahana coins, *Brahmi* inscriptions (between *circa* second BCE and second CE) were recorded.

Dantapuram

Dantapuram excavations revealed four brick votive stupas associated with structures, good number of antiquities such as beads of Terracotta, semi precious stone beads, ornaments, stone objects, etc.

On the fringes of the Eastern hills, in the northern Coastal Andhra region, it seems that Buddhist activities had a strong hold in the region from the very beginning. Among the above sites, Sankaram (Rea, A. 1907-08:149-180), Ramatirtham (Rea, A. 1907-08: 1908-09:10-11), Thotlakonda (Sastry, V.V.K. 1991: 13-15), etc., are other noteworthy Buddhist establishments in the region. It seems that the Buddhists were occupied and established settlements here at the end of first millennium BCE.

4.3.2 Telangana Region

Phanigiri (Snake-hood hill) village lies on the left bank of the rivulet Aleru, a tributary of the river Musi. The Buddhist site is located on hill-top about 150 feet high and 110 km from Hyderabad in Nalgonda District. At present, the rivulet Aleru flows 2 km away from the habitation in north-south direction.

The Buddhist site at Phanigiri was selected for preliminary excavations in the year 1941 by Sri Khaja Mahamad Ahmad, the then Director (1941-1944). Fresh excavations were conducted by the State Archaeology during 2001-2002, 2002-2003, 2004-2005 and 2006-2007 (*AAR*) field seasons and brought to light a Mahastupa (18 m diameter), apsidal Chaityagrihas, Votive stupas, pillared congregation halls, *viharas,* four *ayaka platforms* (4 × 1.25 m) on cardinal directions, staircases at various levels, sculptural panels with Brahmi label inscriptions of the Satavahana and Ikshvaku times, apart from the Early Historic culture milieu datable to the period between the first century BCE and CE third century. On the south-western corner of the platform are found 42 lead coins of Mahatalavarasa. The bricks used in construction measure 50 × 25 × 7 cm. It may be noted that Phanigiri may be one of the important Buddhist monasteries strategically located on the hill top, on ancient trade route connecting the west and the east Coast of the Deccan. It may also be found that the monastic establishment at Phanigiri standing for a longer duration. A cluster of Early Historic sites (Vardhamanukota, Gajulabanda, Tirumalagiri, Nagaram, Singaram, Arvapalli, Iyyavaripalli, Arlagaddagudem and Yeleswaram) cropped up in close proximity is attesting the above argument.

Gajulabanda, another Buddhist site situated on the left bank of the river Aleru near Etoor village, is 3 km away from Phanigiri on north-west. Minor excavations were conducted by the State Archaeology (AAR 1978-79) and traced a monastery comprised of a Mahastupa, Vihara, votive stupas platforms and early historic materials. The Mahastupa (9.60 m in diameter) is located on the north-western part of the hillock with *ayaka* platforms (1.10 x 1.75 m) on four cardinal directions. A broken pillar-base and a square brick platform (1.65 × 1.40 m) were also brought to light on north-west corner of the stupa. A broken pillar (1.00 m height) with half lotus medallion intercepted by octagonal shaft is an interesting architectural member found on south-western side of the stupa. A *vihara* (14.30 × 7.85 m) with a common verandah was exposed on the south-eastern side of the monastic complex. A broken stone plaque depicted with srivasta, sankha and stupa, a fine sharp copper hook, stucco pieces of lotus flowers of different shapes and sizes, decorative potsherds of various designs such as stamped, linear and etched types, along with Satavahana coins were also reported.

Vardhamanukota, an Early Historic Buddhist site is located on the left bank of the rivulet Bikkeru or Aleru, on Phanigiri-Suryapet road. It appears that the present village itself lies on high ancient mound encompassed by a brick fortification wall which locally known as *Kotadibba* (fort mound). Buddha (standing) statue and inscribed slab with *Brahmi* characters (first century CE), coins and broken sculptural panels were reported from the site. The trial digs here brought to light alignments of limestone columns in a row, broken panels, beads, terracotta figures, Satavahana and Mahatalavara coins, pottery etc., besides brick structures such as a chaitya, vihara, a brick platform, etc. The size of the brick used in the construction measures 58 × 26 × 7 cm (AAR 1984-85).

Tirumalagiri, another Buddhist site lies on Suryapet-Jangoam road. It appears that the present habitation is cropped up over an ancient mound. Broken limestone sculptured panels namely, a circular lotus medallion, a decorated pedestal with a central socket, a balustrade with lotus medallion were recovered earlier from the site. Even today also brick alignments can be seen at certain places in the village. Similar Buddhist remains are also reported from Nagaram and Singaram villages in Nalgonda District.

Arlagaddagudem near Chinnasuraram is an Early Historic site located 15 km from Nalgonda town. Roman Gold Coins of Augustus, Tiberius and Nero were reported.

4.3.3 Royalseema Region

In the Royalseema region, the Mauryan contact over the region is more authenticated by the Ashoka edicts. These edicts are situated in such places as Rajulamandagiri and Jonnagiri of this region. According to R.E.M. Wheeler (Wheeler, R.E.M. 1947), during the period of Aryaputra (Ashoka), the territories of the Deccan were constituted as separate provinces with his capital at Isila or Suvarnagiri, modern Brahmagiri in Karnataka State. Some scholars are of the opinion that the present Jonnagiri near Pattikonda in Kurnool district is the ancient Suvarnagiri which is mentioned in the Ashokan inscriptions (Pandey, R. 1964: 119-122). If we accept this suggestion, it can be held that these regions were included in the Mauryan empire during the regime of Ashoka. Unfortunately, no site has revealed traces of material culture of the Mauryans, which could compare with the nucleus region of this empire. However, a good number of Punch Marked coins were reported from the north-western region of Andhra Pradesh (Gupta, P.L. 1963), suggesting Mauryan contact with the region. The riverine tract of the Krishna and Tungabhadra doab had enough potentialities to play a vital part in the history of the trade and commerce of this region. The rule of powerful dynasties like Mauryans and Nandas in Andhras was perhaps more in term of control of trade and commerce and did not change the general/culture milieu of daily life of the people directly.

A comparative study of the stratigraphy of the archaeological sites of the region under study, roughly speaking, would show that there was a somewhat common pattern in the Early Historical evolution of human civilization. The foregoing account indicates that the foundations of urbanism in

Andhra region were laid over the Megalithic culture horizon. The traits of Megalithic culture which basically belonged to non-urban or rural category, appears to have developed in urbanism during Andhra Culture period on account of political, religious and commercial factors. The material remains unearthed at various sites evidence the existence of long distance trades both inland and foreign, infusion of Buddhism in this region from the north and also domain of Nanda and Mauryan dynasties. It may be noted that these aspects were also responsible for the growth of urbanism in the Gangetic valley around fourth/third century BCE. The second cultural period of Andhra Pradesh, the Satavahana period, was the continuation of the Andhra culture, but there was decline in the trade activities and certain crafts like pottery, etc. In spite of these, the entire region had a strong political organization of its own, which is reflected through wide use of coinage, stylistical production of sculptures, both of stone and clay, and regular planned townships. Further, majority of the Buddhist sites are located on trade route from Kalinga to Sri Lanka and another Kalinga to Karnataka via Rayalseema area. The excavations conducted at the Buddhist sites in North Coastal Andhra, Telangana, Rayalseema areas proved to be centers of Theravada School of Buddhism that flourished almost contemporaries on the hill tops.

REFERENCES

Ahmad, K.M. 1950. *Inscribed and Riveted Pottery from Kondapur.* Kondapur Series No1. Hyderabad.

Annual Administrative 1970-71, 71-72, 72-73, 73-74, 74-75, 81-82 and 82-83 Reports (abbreviated as *AAR*). Government of Andhra Pradesh. Hyderabad.

Annual Report of Archaeological Department of His Exalted Highness of the Nizam's Dominion. 1940-41. (abbreviated as *ARN*). Department of Archaeology. Hyderabad: 16-18.

Basham, A.L. 1990. Geographical Factors in South Indian History. *South Indian Studies*. (eds) Nayak, H.M. & B.R. Gopal. Mysore.

Beck, H.C. 1941.The Beads from Taxila. *Memoirs of Archaeological Survey of India*. No 65. New Delhi.

Burgers J.1887. *The Buddhist Stupas of Amaravathi and Jaggayyapeta*. Archaeological Survey of South India. London.

Campbell, J.H. 1874. *Specimens of Languages of India including those of Aboriginal Tribes of Bengal, the central Provinces and the Eastern Frontier*. Calcutta.

Champion, H.G. & S.K. Seth (eds) .1968. *A Revised Survey of the Forest Types of India*. New Delhi.

Dikshit, M.G. 1952. *Some Beads from Kondapur*. Hyderabad Archaeological Series No 16. Hyderabad

Dutta, M. 1990. *A study of the Satavahana coins*. New Delhi.

Dutta, N.V. B.S. 1981. *Geology and Mineral Resources of Andhra Pradesh*. Hyderabad.

Ghosh, A & H. Sarkar. 1967. Beginnings of Sculptural Art in south-east Asia: A Stele from Amaravati. *Ancient India*, Bulletin of the Archaeological Survey of India. No 20 and 21 (1964 and 1965). New Delhi:168-177.

Ghosh, N.C. 1986. *Excavations at Satanikota (1977-80)*. Memoirs of the Archaeological Survey of India. No 82. New Delhi.

Grierson, G.A. 1967 (reprint). *Linguistic Survey of India*. Delhi.

Imperial Gazetteer of India (IP). 1908. Published under the Authority of His Majesty's Secretary of State for India in Council. Oxford.

Imperial Gazetteer of India. 1909. Provincial Series. Hyderabad State. Calcutta.

Indian Archaeology A Review (IAR). (ed). Director General of Archaeology in India. Archaeological Survey of India. New Delhi.

Khan, M.A.W. 1969. *A Monograph on Early Buddhist Stupa at Kesarapalli*. Archaeological Series. No 27. Government of Andhra Pradesh. Hyderabad.

Mangalam, S.J. 1986. *Historical Geography and Toponomy of Andhra Pradesh*. New Delhi.

Pisipaty, S.R.K. 1993. *Early Historical Archaeology of Andhra Pradesh. A Study of Andhra and Satavanana Cultures.* Unpublished Thesis. Banaras Hindu University. Varanasi.

Ray, A. 1983. *Life and Art of Early Andhradesa.* Delhi.

Rea, A. 1990 (reprint). *Excavations at Amaravati.* Archaeological Survey of India Annual Report 1908-09. New Delhi.

Sankalia, H.D. Deo, S.B. Ansari, Z.D. & S. Ehrardt. 1960. *From History to Prehistory at Nevasa (1954-56).* Poona.

Sastri, T.V.G., Bai, M.K. & J.V. Rao 1984. *Veerapuram* . A Type site for cultural study in the Krishna Valley. Hyderabad.

Sastry, V.V. K.1983. *The Proto and Early History of Andhra Pradesh.* Government of Andhra Pradesh. Hyderabad.

Sastry, V.V. K., Subramanyam, B. & N.R.K. Rao. 1992. *Totlakonda* (A Buddhist Site in Andhra Pradesh). Andhra Pradesh Government of Archaeological Series. No 68. Hyderabad.

Sewell, R. 1972 (reprint). *Lists-The Antiquarian Remains in the Presidency of Madres.* first published in 1982. Archaeological Survey of India. New Imperial Series No VII. Varanasi.

Sigh, R.L. (ed) 1971. *India: A Regional Geography.* National Geophysical Society of India. Varanasi

Spate, O.H.K. & A.T.A. Learmonth. 1984 (third edition). *India and Pakistan*, A General and Regional Geography. New Delhi.

Subrahamanyam, R. 1964. *Salihundam* - A Buddhist site in Andhra Pradesh. Andhra Pradesh Government Archaeological Series. No 17. Hyderabad.

Subrahamanyam, R. Banerjee, K.D., Khare, M.D., Rao, B.V., Sarkar, H., Singh, R. Joshi, R.V. Lal, S.B.., Rao, V.V. Srinivasan, K.R. & K. Totadri. 1975. *Nagarjunakonda* (1954-60). Memories of the Archaeological Survey of India. No 75. New Delhi. I.

Wadia, D.N. 1970 (reprint). *Geology of India.* London.

Wheeler, R.E.M. 1984 (reprint). Brahmagiri and Chandravalli, 1947: Megalithic and other Cultures in the Chitaldurg district, Mysore. *Ancient India.* Bulletin of the Archaeological Survey of India. No 4 (1947-48). New Delhi: 181-310.

Yazdani, G. 1941. *Excavation at Kondapur*: An Andhra town (200 B.C.-200 A.D.). Annals of the Bhandarkar Oriental Research Institute. XXII: 171-185.

Chapter 5

CLAY OBJECTS

Modeling of clay is one of the most common practices of ancient India. Free accessibility of the raw material, in desirable quantities, to all the craftsmen throughout the human habitat and the inexpensive nature were such basic qualities which promoted adoption of this medium for a very long time in human history. The plasticity and the softness are other added advantage of this medium. Besides, the only disadvantage of brittleness could easily be overcome by firing the products of clay, which after barking, acquires imperishability. As a result of all these qualities, clay objects are found in abundance from almost all Cultural Ages. In vogue, the making of the pots and pans or the utility items related primarily with food consumption and other items can be seen in the from of modeling of figurative forms which cater to the decorative, amusement and religious needs of man. Due to the diversity of the utility as well as their techno-typological features, both of these categories have been dealt separately in the present chapter under the heading – Pottery and Terracotta.

5.1 POTTERY

History Of Ceramics – The history of potting crafts in Andhra Pradesh also commences with the emergence of the food producing economy, e.g., the Neolithic period in around third millennium BCE. The ceramic remains of the Neolithic stage of our region are characterized by very coarse fabric and crude forms which were attained primarily by hand modeling. Noteworthy types of this earliest group of pots were Grey, Buff and Red wares (Table 5). Evidence of pre-firing painting are found, at time, on the exterior face of some of the vases of Red and Buff wares, which are reported from Veerapuram (Sastri, T.V.G. *et al.* 1984: 44), Nagarjunakonda (Subrahmanyam, R. 1975), Palaver (Reddy, R.V. 1968), Ramapuram (*IAR 1980-81*: 3-7), etc.

The morphology as the quantity of the remains of pottery not only suggest imperfect stage of clay modeling technology but limited number of unearthed post – shreds also indicates restricted use of post during the early food producing stage of this region. However, pot making of this stage, through crude, is important as it laid the foundation for the production and use of the earthen vessels.

No definitive evidence for the existence of Copper-Bronze Age has so far come to light from Andhra (Dikshit, K.N. 1992: 31).

The early Iron Age communities, who were building of Megalithic monuments, were also using earthen post. The potting craft during this culture period seem to emerge in fully developed form. The extensive use of wheel in the modeling of utensils, various methods of baking and variety of decorative methods were the new dimensions added to the ceramics, which were almost negligible in the earlier stage. For, except for decoration of archaic type, none of the technological advancement in the pot-making was noticeable during Neolithic period of this region.

Table 5

5.1.1 Chronology of Ceramic Traditions

S. No.	Typical Pottery	Date Brackets	Cultural stage
1	Dull Red ware	2500-1800 BCE	Neolithic
2	Grey Ware	1800-800 BCE	Neolithic
3	Buff Ware	1800-800 BCE	Neolithic
4	Black & Red Ware	800 BCE-CE 400	Megalithic, Andhra & Satavahana
5	Black Ware / Black Polished Ware	500 BCE-CE 400	Megalithic, Andhra & Satavahana
6	Russet Coated Painted ware	200 BCE-CE 300	Andhra & Satavahana
7	Rouletted and other imported & Imitation wares	100 BCE-CE 200	Andhra & Satavahana
8	Red Polished ware	100-800 CE	Andhra, Satavahana & post-Satavahana
9	Chocolate Ware	100-800 CE	Andhra, Satavahana & post-Satavahana

The characteristic industry of this region during megalithic culture stage is Black and Red ware. Other noteworthy wares which are found in association are Red ware, Black ware and Black Polished ware (*cf* Table 5). The major shapes which are found in the Black and Red Black wares are bowls and dishes, while common forms of Red ware are vases, lids and miniature post. There are, the hourglass type of stand of Black ware as well as in Red ware. These new shapes appear to suggest that the potters of this period were influenced by some other distant ceramic traditions. The shapes of pots in the habitational layers and the burial areas of Megalithic sites, in general, correspond with each other. For instance, bowls, dishes, miniature pots, etc., are found from both of the contexts (Khan, M.A.W. 1963: 25-31). However, there are a few exceptions to this pattern. The unique shapes of Black ware and Red ware, referred to earlier, are associated only with the burials. The group retaining the features of non-Andhra ceramic character appears to be confined to the ritualistic and funerary customs of the period.

The ceramic remains of the Megalithic period evidence not only a sudden advent of advanced potting technology, but it served as a firm ground for the continuation and prevalence of the major pottery tradition of the ancient Andhradesa. For, all the three ceramic types, e.g., the Black and Red ware, the Black wares and the Red wares continued in the later period that is Andhra and Satavahana cultures with or without modification.

In Andhra cultural period, the major ceramic tradition continues both in their forms and with modification. For instance, a bulk of Black and Red ware, Black ware and Red ware of Megalithic period also are found in this period without marked techno typological change. However, a section of the post Black and Red wares were modified by the application of a new technique to the surface treatment. This modification is known as 'Russet Coating' (the technique has been enumerated in this very chapter, a little later). The

Russet Coated Painted ware appears to be the diagnostic ceramic trait of the Andhra culture, and was perhaps a local innovation. Besides these indigenous varieties, there was a strong tendency to imitate non-Indian pots, both their technologies and forms during the period under examination. This observation is supported by the recovery of Rouletted ware, Aretino ware, Amphorae and Red Polished ware, etc. Some pots of these categories could even have been imported from their respective regions of the west. Besides, some of the archaeological horizons of the Andhra culture, particularly the ones exposed in the coastal region also have yielded Indian but non-Andhra tradition of pottery. The Northern Black Polished ware remains are the illustrative example. Similarly, the epicentre of the Red Polished ware has recently been determined in the western part of the Indian sub-continent (Rao, S.R. 1966: 51-59). Adoption of the Red polished ware from the west and Northern Black Polished ware from the Gang plains in Andhra is, thus, a plausible situation.

Along with a large range of indigenous and foreign pottery tradition, Andhra culture period also has a wealth of numerous forms and sizes of clay pot. This includes, table wares like dishes, bowls, cooking vessels such as globular pots, storage jars of various kinds like Amphorae, etc., and some decorative or other utility forms like sprinklers, etc. On account of this, it may be held that earthen pots in the Andhra region had acquired the status of one of the most important group of antiquities of the Early Historical Period.

In Satavahana period, the ceramic industry has stagnated. There was not neither imitation or invention or new potting technologies, nor were efforts made to model new forms. The earlier ceramic traditions, more or less continued in this period also. However, their variation in the frequencies of the ceramic traditions is noteworthy. For instance, the Black and Red ware tradition had lost its significance during this period and was just surviving in low proportion here and there. In contrast to this, the Red Polished ware, Chocolate ware and Grey ware become more popular then these wares in the earlier period. Beside, by the end of the Satavahana period, the utility of the Rouletted ware and other imported wares also appear to have lost grounds. Similar was case with the Russet Coated Painted ware, which also has lower frequency in Satavahana culture phase. Therefore, a general degeneration and dis-use of deluxe and decorative, pots can be seen during Satavahana in the Andhra Pradesh. In sprit of this tendency, utility of clay vessels remained unchanged in this period also. Plain simple variety of Red pottery with usual utilization forms was being produced to cater to the need of pots pans.

5.1.2 Major Ceramic Traditions

It is evident from the historical description of the pottery that there were a number of ceramic traditions prevalent during the Early Historic times in Andhra Pradesh (*cf* Table 5). Brief account of each of the important pottery category is, therefore, given in Table 6.

Black And Red Ware

Black and Red ware have the longest history of survival in Andhra Pradesh (Table 6). For its' appearance in the Megalithic culture context is datable to *circa* 800 BCE, as has been reported from sites like – Vaddamanu, Mallipadu, Nagarjunakonda, Peddabankur, Yeleswaram, Veerapuram, Satanikota, etc. Contrary to this, the later dates, which are assigned to the post – Satavahana period, determine the closing bracket in around 400 CE. Evidence for such determination has been unearthed at sites like Salihundam, Amaravati, Dharanikota, Vaddamanu, Mallipadu, Gantasala, Chandravaram, Nagarjunakonda, Peddabankur, Kotilingala, Dhulikatta, Yeleswaram, Satanikota, Veerapuram, etc. During the entire period, almost more than a decade centuries, Black and Red ware is found to be traversing at least three different culture stages, e.g., the Megalithic or the proto-Andhra Phase, the mature Andhra phase and the post-Andhra are marked change in the techno-typology of this ceramic tradition could be noticed during the entire history of its survival in Andhradesa.

Table 4

Period Wise Distribution of Important Ceramic Types

S.No.	Site	Megalithic	Andhra	Satavahana
1	Salihundam	-	B & RW, GW	B & RW, RW, GE, RPW, RuW
2	Amaravati	-	B & RW, BPW, RW NBP, RuW	B & RW, RW, RPW, KW
3	Dharanikota	-	B & RW, BPW, RW GR, RuW	B & RW, RW, BPW, RW, GR, RuW
4	Vaddamanu	B & RW, RW	B & RW, NBP	B & RW, BPW, RW, GR
5	Mallipadu	B & RW, BW, RW	B & RW, BW, RW, RuW	B & RW, RW, BW, RW

Contd...

S.No.	Site	Megalithic	Andhra	Satavahana
6	Gantasala	-	B & RW, RW, RuW	B&RW, RW, RPW,
7	Chandravaram	B & RW, RW	B & RW, RW, RuW	B & RW, RW,
8	Nagarjunakonda	B & RW, BPW, RW	B & RW, BPW, RW RPW, RuW	B & RW, BPW, RW, RPW, RuW, GW
9	Peddabankur	B & RW, BPW, RW	B & RW, BPW, RW RCPW, RuW, GW, CW	B & RW, BPW, RW RCPW, RuW, RMW, GW, CW
10	Kotilingala	-	B & RW, RSW, CW RPW, BPW	B & RW, RSW, CW RPW, RuW, GW
11	Dhulikatta	-	B & RW, RW	BRW, RW, RPW
12	Kondapur	-	B & RW, BPW, RW RuW, RCPW,	B & RW, BPW, RW RuW, RCPW, MW
13	Yeleswaram	B & RW, BPW, RW, IW	B & RW, BPW, RW, RPW	R & RW, BPW, RW
14	Satanikota	B & RW, BW, RW	B & RW, BW, RW RCPW, RuW	B & RW, BW, RW, RPW,
15	Veerapuram	B & RW, BW, RW	B & RW, BW, RW RCPW, RuW	B & RW, BW, RW,RPW,

B & RW - Black-and-Red Ware BW - Black Ware, BPW - Black Polished Ware, CW - Chocolate Ware, GW - Grey Ware, IW - Imitation Ware, KW - Kaicolin

Ware, RW - Red Ware, RPW - Red Polished Ware, RCPW - Russet Coated Painted Ware, RuW - Rouletted Ware

Besides its longevity, Black and Red ware also had a very wide area of occupation in the region under consideration. Because pot shreds of this tradition have been reported from almost all the important excavated sites (Map II). Noteworthy among these are – Salihundam, Amaravati, Dharanikota, Amllipadu, Chandravaram, Gantasala, Nagarjunakonda, Peddabankur, Kotilingala, Dhulikatta, Yeleswaram, Satanikota, Veerapuram, Kakanur, Annangi, Polakonda, Yapaladevipadu, Gudimallam, Calingapatnam, Kandi, Kesanapalle, Vaddamanu, Thotlakonda, Bhavikonda, Vaikuntapuram, Chebrolu, Mukhalingam, etc. Black and Red were as not only introduced in this region during Megalithic period, but it acquired the status of the chief ceramic industry of the time. It may be noted that the evidence collected so far suggests that this pottery tradition was not a local innovation but was an intrusion to the area of our study. Because, no pottery of the earlier phase, e.g., the Neolithic period has correspondence with Black and Red ware, as to suggest an indigenous development of this tradition from proto-types. In fact, developed technological skills such as wheel modeling, surface treatment and special firing technique are apparent from the collections of all the cultural stages with which this ceramic is associated. Another fact also is noteworthy. That is the early dates of Megalithic remains and the associated Black and Red ware from the neighboring regions of Maharastra (Deo, S.B. 1969: 27-37) and Tamilnadu (Gurumurthy, S. 1981). Under these circumstances, the making and the use of Black and Red were appears to be one such culture trait, which was an intrusion to the Andhradesa from north-west and / or south. But this trait got soon well adopted within the culture environment since the Megalithism also came in this region and had acquired a firm footing during *circa* 800 BCE to CE 400. Black and Red ware continued as a popular ceramic tradition during Andhra culture and Satavahana culture periods. However, its frequencies appear to have gradually decreasing during the later periods, e.g., the Satavahana and post-Satavahana. It may be noted that in general, the post-Satavahana or Ikshvaku level yielded very limited number of Black and Red ware shreds (Sastry, V.V. K. 1983: 189). Examination of the Black and Red ware collection revealed that the pots were made of fine levigated clay in which sand, quartz particles, and husk, etc., occasionally mixed. Due to this, the fabric of Black and Red ware ranges from fine to medium qualities.

The pots were made on fast rotating wheels. After modeling the shape, the surface of these utensils was carefully treated. A slip has applied first to both the exterior and the interior surfaces of the pots. Thereafter glazing was done by constantly rubbing the surface. It has been suggested that salt glazing (Ghosh, N.C. 1986: 115) was applied to the pots in which minute cracks emerge but if the same portion is rubbed continuously for a long duration, the cracks are overpowered by their luster. For, burnished pots are many in the Black and Red ware remains of the Andhra Pradesh. Painting of the surface by kaolin, incised and impressed designs are often found on this category of shreds, which is not a very common feature of the Black and Red ware of the Indian sub-continent (Sastri, T.V.G. *et al.* 1984: 60; Subrahmanyam, R. 1964: 47). Decorating the pots appears to be a noteworthy feature, particularly of the Andhra culture stage.

Firing technique is one of the most important technological stages of the Black and Red ware. The inverted firing process, described above, it the only way to obtain half black and half red surface of a pot. Pots in this method were placed in an inverted position (one the other). The interior and a portion of the top turn black due to firing under reduction temperature, while most of lower outer portion is fired under oxidizing condition i.e., having access to the oxygen, and as a result turn red brown in color.

Black and Red ware was the ceramic of bowls and dishes. Because not only these two categories are numerous but varieties in each group can be encountered. For example, in bowls, important forms are straight sided, globular or spherical and concave sided, etc. Besides, on account of the types of the rims too, quite a few variations can be noticed (Fig 1). In the group of dishes, deep and shallow varieties are prominent.

A rare type of this ceramic, the dish-on-stand, which has black dish and red stand, has been reported from Polakonda (*IRA 1976-77*: 10). Besides, the other uncommon forms of Black and Red ware of Andhra Pradesh are globular pots with short neck or bottle neck, carinated vases and deep basins (Fig 1). On account of their forms, Black and Red ware appears to be a table ware, as dishes and bowls can logically be also associated with food consumption habit of man. Occurrence of globular pots and large bowls or basin may also indicate the utility of short duration or restricted amount of storing food and drink items.

Russet Coated Painted Ware

The Russet Coated Painted ware is a distinctly characteristic pottery of the Early Historical period (*c* second century BCE to third century CE) of the lower Deccan and South India. The earliest discovery of this pottery probably goes back to 1880 (Foote, R.B. 1916). The later discoveries of this ware by wheeler were designated to 'Andhra Ware' (Wheeler, R.E.M.1947-48: 280). On account of its technical characteristics, the group was named by B. K. Thaper (1957: 17) as 'Russet Coated Pained ware', a ware appropriate term.

Made on fast wheel, the Russet Coated Painted ware can be divisible within two types, e.g., the Black and Red ware based variety and the Red ware based variety. Specimens of both the fine and coarse fabrics are encountered in these, but the most distinct and common feature to the entire group of pottery is the special decorative surface treatment. Chemical examination of the shreds revealed that a thin slappy paste of Kaolin or lime was applied to the areas of elaborate decoration. With the use of brush, this paste was applied in various patterns to the surface of the pot. The wealth of designs which were executed include - linear patterns, essentially rectilinear, criss-cross, radiating lines, rows of dote, frond like strokes, and combinations of one or two patterns. Thereafter, the same surface was coated with a russet colored wash prepared out of red ocher. The vessel thus prepared was fired in the kiln even or constant temperature so as to acquire a high glass like polish. When examined under the microscope, the red pigment surface shows a network of cracks. These cracks indicate that the vessels were probably salt-glazed. With the exception iron content in the clay, no other coloring material could be identified in the make up this pottery.

The main shapes of Russet Coated Painted were are the deep bowl with indistinct disc or round bottom and vertical side, shallow bowl with sagger base, vase without carves ring convex body and round bottom (Fig 2).

The ceramic under scrutiny appears to be a specialized but characteristic industry of the Early Historical period of Andhra Pradesh. It has been reported from more then a dozen excavated sites (Map III) and that too in good proportion. Noteworthy sites are – Satanikota (IAR *1977-78*: 3-11), Veerapuram (Sastri, T.V.G. *et al.* 1984: 59), Kotilingala, Kakanur (*IAR 1959-60*: 12), Kondapur, Gujulabanda, Nelakondapalli, Phanigiri, Tolkatta, Gurjala, (Wheeler, R.E.M. 1947-48: 308-309), Manjra, Jangoam (Ghosh, A. 1989 : 258), Rekulapadu (*AAR 1983-84* : 3), Gudimallam (*IAR 1973-74*: 2), etc.

As was stated above, Russet Coated Painted ware has wide distribution in south India and, Andhra Pradesh forms an integral part of this ceramic spread. But, the chronology and culture context of this ceramic tradition reveal regional variation. For example, in Karnataka, the area lying west and north-west of the region under study, Russet Coated Painted ware is found in association with the Rouletted ware and Arretine ware of the early CE (*c* 100 CE) (Wheeler, R.E. M. 1947-48 : 280). In the extreme south, the date for this ware was pushed back to *circa* 300 BCE (Mahalingam, T.V. 1970: 15; Rao, B.K.G. 1972; Rajan, K. 1991: 241-245). But in Andhra, this ware appears to have an earlier beginnings, as it first emerge in Black and Red ware horizons of *circa* 200 BCE, and thereafter continued with Rouletted and Red Polished wares in Andhra Culture phase of *circa* 50 BCE and CE 200. Its undisrupted prevalence in Satavahana times stretches its date bracket to *circa* 300 CE. In post-Satavahana Period, the utility of Russet Coated Painted ware ceases to exist or faded out.

It may be noted that the association of Russet Coated Painted ware with independent Black and Red ware, and also inclusion of this type as the basic ceramic of the Russet Coated Painted ware, may suggest that the ceramic tradition under discussion was a special treatment of the surface of the russet coating to a group of Black and Red ware and Rea ware was given to those pots which, perhaps had very pronounced in this ceramic tradition, and also dishes and bowls are the main shapes, it may be suggested that Russet Coated Painted ware was a *deluxe* variety of table-ware, which was in use by a particular section of the population. Its popularity with the development of the stage of urbanism in Andhra Pradesh might further indicate the urban utilization tendency of this decorative.

Red Ware

The group of Red wares in fact includes more then one pottery tradition which is marked by general characteristics of being of red color. As in the case with Early Historic and Protohistoric remains of India, this group of ceramic is a common variety in Andhra Pradesh also. Their existence in each of the culture periods, from Megalithic to the Satavahana and Ikshvaku periods is in high proportion. But due to their unspecific characteristic and ageless features, the group can best be termed as 'associated ware' even through their quantity is pronounced and types varied. One notices more then one modeling techniques, ingredients, mixture in clay surface treatment and multiple forms. For instance, both wheel-made and hand-modeled pots were made in this case. Also, the tempering materials such as grit, husk, mica, etc., have been freely mixed in various proportions so as to give a range of medium to coarse fabric to the shreds that have been unearthed from the various sites of Andhra Pradesh. The shreds of these collections were also found to be slipped or washed or were left with untreated original modeled surface as a result of which different shades of dull Red ware, pale Red ware, etc. formed. When decorated, the pots were painted with simple lines or by appliqué motives or by finger nail or tip patterns. In the wide range of shapes, important ones are – conical dish with flat vase, carinated vases, lid-cum-bowl, pots with spherical or oval bodies, high necked vessel, sprinkler, spouted vessel, storage jars, etc. Multifarious utility of Red wares is apparent, as storage jars of various kinds and cooking vessels of daily utility appear along with table-ware types and also special forms such as sprinklers. It may noted that in general, there is a dearth of cooking vessels and storage pots in other wares like Black and Red ware, Russet Coated Painted ware, Black wares, etc.

Chocolate / Brown Slipped Ware

The group under discussion is in fact a variation of Red ware industry. For, the Chocolate or Brown slipped pots was also made in fine to coarse fabrics. Bur, this group is modeled primarily on fast wheel and bear thick slip. Noteworthy forms of this ceramic group are dish and bowl, on account of which it can be classified as Table 7 were as it has typological closeness with Black and Red and Black wares. This group is found to be associating Andhra and Satavahana cultures.

Red Polished Ware

Through a variety of Red ware, this category is distinct from the above mentioned two groups, the Red ware and the Chocolate/ Brown ware, for a very specific treatment of the surface and a few typical shapes. This ceramic category is made of very well levigated clay, giving fine texture to its fabric. The thick slip over the surface was well polished and the vessels were fired at a high temperature, as a result of which, metallic sound and sturdy red to pink color fabric could be acquired. The fine finishing of this group is associated with the "Roman Samian ware" (Rao, S.B. 1958: 46:71). The local adoption of this pottery is testified by the occurrence of sprinkler type, a feature of the early present era of the northern region, and the production of various other forms in good quantity (Rao, S.R. 1966: 51- 59). In Andhra Pradesh too, local production of this ware is seen. Through the sprinkler seen to continue to the coastal region, other common types such as jar with grooved rims, flaring necked and bulbous bodied pots, vessels with footed base and bowls with incurved beaded rim and carinated shoulder, etc., were widely utilized. Through the remains of Red Polished ware have been found from the early centuries of CE, in most of the parts of North India as well as the Andhra Pradesh, this ceramic gained momentum in post-Satavahana times. The noteworthy sites of its occurrence are Veerapuram, Satanikota, Salihundam, Peddabankur, Kotilingala, Peddamarur, Calingapatnam, Amaravati, etc., while important post-Satavahana remains were uncovers from Yeleswaram and Nagarjunakonda.

Black Ware

Mode of fine levigated clay and modeled on fast wheel, the fabric of the Black ware is generally of medium quality. After the surface was treated by thick slip containing iron oxide and manganese, the pots in this slip containing iron oxide and manganese, the pots in this tradition were fired under reduced condition. Prior to firing, a colorless varnish used to be applied which was a mixture of salt petrel and soda (Marshall, J. 1951: 432-33; Misra, A.K. 1989). The common shapes of this variety are deep bowls, dishes and miniature pots.

It was also noticed that in Andhra Pradesh, this ceramic not only has sporadic distribution at a few select sites, but it also forms low proportion of the pottery collection. The noteworthy sites where remains of Black ware were unearthed, are - Salihundam and Thotlakonda, where the horizon is date between second century BCE to first century CE (Sastry V.V. K. *et al.* 1991 : 58-59), Kesarapalli (*IAR* 1961-62: 1), Peddabankur (*AAR 1976-77*: 13-17), Yapalaḍivipadu (*AAR 1975-76*: 13-21); Kotilingala and Bhavikonda (*IAR 1985-86*: 15), etc. It may be recalled that J. Marshall (1951: 432-43) has named this ware as Greek Black ware that imply foreign production of the ceramic. The limited proportion and restricted disposal of this ware during Andhra culture may indicate the import of this class of pottery through long distance trade.

Northern Balck Polished Ware

The famous NBP ware, which is known for thin and fine quality of fabric and the black highly polished surface, has limited occurrence in Andhra Pradesh. So far only four sites have been reported to have considerable proportion of NBP shreds. These are Amaravati, Vaddamanu, Chebrolu and Kesarapalli. All of these are located on the coasted region of Guntur and Krishna districts.

The Spread of NBP ware in Andhra Pradesh was much later in comparison to the north, e.g., Gangetic plains, which was the nucleus region of this ceramic based culture (Roy, T.N, 1986). Because, except for Amaravati, were an early date bracket of 475 BCE, has been determined, in the rest of the region, its spread is assigned to *circa* 300 BCE. Occurrence of NBP ware in this region is associated with the spread of Buddhism. It may by mentioned that both in the technology and the typology, the NBP ware remains of Andhra correspond well with that of Gangetic plaint. It is difficult to determine in the present state of our knowledge, whether the Andhra group was an import or a local production. The distribution of sites, their limited number, etc. does promote one to believe that NBP ware too, was brought in this region as part of the interval trade items.

Rouletted Ware

Recognized first at Arikamedu in Tamil Nadu as foreign pottery (Wheeler, R.E.M. 1947-48: 45), Rouletted ware is known to be Mediterranean origin. The pot of this tradition is made of fine well levigated clay and is a model of fast rotating wheel. The wet surface of the pot was first subjected to pricked decoration by revolving a toothed nail. The flat inner surface of dish, a common form, was thus grooved in concentric circles or rouletted pattern providing a contrast to the otherwise very smooth surface of the rest of the pot (Fig 3). The Rouletted design forms are concentric circles, miniature triangles, dots, vertical lines and ovoid patterns.

Before firing, the entire pot was also treated with slip. Due to the application of inverted firing, the inner side of the pot to turn black, while the exterior retained various shades of gray and brown. Various types of combination of black and red colors can be encountered on the Rouletted ware. It has appeared at least four distinct types e.g., Red surface with Black exterior base; Red top with both surfaces having black color; Red exterior and black interior; and black external sides and red inner body. This pattern is indicative of various types of arrangement of pots during the firing. Rouletted ware in Andhra Pradesh has been reported from a number of sites (Map IV). Noteworthy among these are – Mukhalingam (*IAR 1961-62*: 3), Calingapatnam (*IAR 1977-78*: 14), Bhavikonda (*IAR 1985-86*: 15), Gantasala (*IAR 1977-78*: 15), Annangi (*IAR 1977-78*: 1), Kesa:rapalli (*IAR* 1961-62: 2), Amaravati (*IAR 1973-74*: 4), Dharanikota, Mallipadu (*IAR 1987-88* : 20), Vaikuntapuram (*IAR 1974-75*: 2), Chebrolu (*IAR 1959-60*: 1), Satanikota, Salihapura, Veerapuram, Kondapur (Dikshit, M.G.1952 : V), Simhapura (*IAR 1961-62* : 92), Pithapuram (*IAR 1961-62*: 96), Chintamandi Dibha (*IAR 19771-72* : 4), Nerada Bandagudu (*IAR 1971-72*: 44), Nagarlapet (*IAR 1976-77*: 10), and Paritala (*IAR 1961-62*: 1).

On shred from Kesarapalli is important as this was riveted with an iron pin (Sarkar, H. 1973: 37-74). This evidence may suggest the value of the Rouletted ware. The high price attached to this category may indicate specific and restricted local production or be and article of import from a long distance like Mediterranean region. The possibility for the import of Rouletted ware in the area our study appears to be greater, as majority of the sites yielding the remains of this ceramic tradition are located in the Coastal Andhra region *i.m.*, on the trade route.

Amphorae

The category under discussion is not a ceramic tradition in which a number of shapes were produced. But it is represented by a class of specifically made form. Amphorae has usually a long cylindrical body with a painted base, a long narrow neck and two straight handles. Pike fabric with yellow slip is the other characteristic features. On account of the chemical examination of the inner coat of these pots, a resinous asphalt like material was identified (Margabandhu, C. 1985: 133). The coat was meant to reduce the porosity of these vessels as these are believed to be jar for storing wine and oil. Their Greco-Roman Mesopotamian origin has been ascertained at Taxila (Marshall, J. 1951: 407-8, 415-416). But in Andhra Pradesh, one finds both, the imported variety comparable to the Taxila example and a local produce. The later are jug shaped vessel with two handles, which were local imitation for the storage of other articles then wine and oil. However, their occurrence in Andhra culture level at only a few sites like Salihundam, Kondapur (Sankalia, H.D. 1957: 207-208) etc., may suggest very specific and restricted use this earthen form.

Arretine Ware

This ware deriver its name from the place manufacture Arretine (Arezzo) in Italy. Arretine ware is in fact a glazed Red ware with stamped designs 'terrasigillata' (Comfort, H. 1992: 134-150). This ware was first unearthed at Arikamedu in Tamilnadu (Wheeler, T.E.M. 1947-48). In Andhra, remains of this ware are restricted. The noteworthy remains have been reported from Dharanikota and Salihundam, where dish and cups with stamped designs were found. The restricted occurrence and very limited number of Arretine ware shreds can also be taken to represent import of this ceramic to Andhra region by long distance trade. The occurrence of Arretine ware in Andhra culture is in correspondence with the common practice of import of earthen vessels from far and near in the area of our study.

Mould Made Ware

Mould made ware has also been recovered from Kondapur excavation (Yazdani, G. 1941: 171-185). It was another new technical adoption by the regional potters, who were inspired by the Romans. It is made of will levigated clay and turn of wheel. The decorations were produced out of moulds in which the pot was pressed while it was in leather hard condition (Deshpande, M.N. 1961: 70-72). The designs include lotus leaves and buds followed by a band of long petals, a band of creeper and half rosettes thick cable border, etc. Majority of the shapes are bowls and cups. Among them, a few shreds prove to be imported wares. The bulk of them were regional products. The method employed in the texture, slip, variations in shape and size, decoration motifs, etc., are strongly indicative of their indigenous nature (Begly, V. 1992: 157-176). These are similar to some of the finds at Ter (Deshpande, M.N. 1965: 607-609), Nevasa (Sankalia, H.D. *et al.* 1955, Figs 142, 143, 151), etc.

5.1.3 Important Pottery Forms

The ceramic remains of the Early Historical period of Andhra Pradesh reveal that almost all the vessel utility forms were produced in clay during this period. The typical forms, the general utility shapes and the rare types have been shown in

Table 13 which also mentions the occurrence of pot shapes under the particular ceramic frame. All the important pottery shapes of the pots are described in the following:

Bowls

This is one of the most common groups of pot. Moreover it is not only has good representation in each of the stage of the Early Historical Andhra but also have a number of varieties. Except for two ceramic industries, *viz.*, Rouletted ware and Amphorae, bowls are the most typical shape of all the important pottery traditions (*cf* Table 7). It may further be noted that in most of the cases, this form was used undecorated be noted that in most of the cases, this from was used undecorated as there is in general, lack of painting or any other type of decoration on this variety. But, in case of Russet Coated Painted ware, there was a definite attempt to decorate the surface.

Table 7

5.1.3.1 Typical Pot Shapes of Important Ceramics

S.No.	Ceramic Type	NOTEWORTHY SHAPES		
		Typical	Casual	Rare
1	Black & Red ware	Bowls, Dishes	Globular pots	-
2	Black wares	Bowls, Dishes	Globular pots, Vases	Tulip shaped vases, Hour glass stands, sprinklers
3	Northern Black polished ware	Bowls, Dishes	-	-

Contd...

S.No.	Ceramic Type	NOTEWORTHY SHAPES		
		Typical	**Casual**	**Rare**
4	Red ware	Bowls, Dishes	Globular pots, Vases, vases jugs, lids, basins, *lotas*, miniature pots, troughs	Hour glass stands, lamps, spouts, pedestal cups
5	Russet Coated Painted ware	Bowls, Dishes	Globular pots	-
6	Red Polished ware	Bowls	-	Sprinklers
7	Rouletted ware	Dishes	-	-
8	Mould made ware	Bowls	-	-
9	Arretine ware	Dishes	-	-
10	Amphorae	-	Jars	-
11	Chocolate ware	Bowls	Basins, troughs	Sprinklers
12	Grey wares	Bowls	-	-

The other noteworthy feature of this pot type was that there is no marked change in their varieties during the course of three to four centuries (the period under present study). For instance, the general shapes of bowls, such as spherical bowl with convex sides, straight and concave sides, which have featureless rim, curved rim, flaring or flanged rim occur in the entire period in more or less equal proportions. Carinated bowls appear to be a special from which had limited proportion then the other general forms mentioned above. Deep bowl were very common ceramic collections of the early Andhra Pradesh. The bowls of our region in technology and typology have closeness with the earlier stages of the neighboring areas. For instance, the remains of Navdatoli, Chalcolithic site of Maharashtra (Sankalia, H.D. *et al.* 1958: 191, Fig 38, Type 28-2c, Pl 16: 114), have correspondence with our plain convex sided bowls (Fig 6, 10). The variety of shapes encountered in bowls, appear to suggest that this category belonged to multifarious variety of kitchen ware and was perhaps also used as table ware. The preponderating proportion of bowls in all the ceramic industries, and the low to very low proportion of storage and cooking vessels such as *handi,* jar, etc., would further support this presumption. It can be argued that for a specific group of people common storage and cooking vessels are used, while for the food consumption, each of the individual need separate utensil/ utensils. On account of their sizes, these bowls could be divided into three groups, viz., 8 to 15 cm - small; 15 to 20 cm - medium and 20 cm and above as large (in diameter). These groups may denote different types of utility of the bowls.

Dishes

Dishes form another major production of ceramic industries of the area of our study. This again is in accordance with the frequency of the shape of pottery of the early Indian archaeological remains. Most of the dishes of our region are made in Black and Red ware fabric but this shape is also common to other ceramic traditions (*cf* Table 7). It was noted that the dishes of Andhra level generally bear high polish. More variations in the form of dishes with reference to their sides, depth and from of rim could be noticed. The noteworthy features are shallow depth, carinated waist and flat or convex base, sloping sides and sager base, prominently in curved sides with featureless nail head rounded rim, etc. A size range of 15 to 35 cm (in diameter) was noted in the region. The decorated dishes of Rouletted ware and Russet Coated Painted ware appear to be *deluxe* category of table ware. The type appears to have been used primarily as plate or *thali* for food consumption but it could also have served as kitchen ware for instance, tasks like kneading of flour, covering of cooking vessels, etc., could easily be performed by this shape of pottery. This category also, like bowls, did not undergo major typological changes during the entire span under consideration.

Storage Jars

These are common in general to the Red and the Tan or Chocolate ware. But, Amphorae could also be classed into this group. These were generally used for storing grains, water and for other kitchen need. They are naturally thick sided globular in shape, thick rimmed with flat and round base. Some of them are decorated with designs. It is also found at Peddabankur storage jai that there is a lot of lime coating as a preservation of food grains. In contrast, a squattish jar from Yeleswaram, 56 cm in diameter at the mouth and 65 cm high inside (Noorjahan, B. 1979: 115-117) is noteworthy. It is decorated with an incised fish pattern at the top of the flat rim and gadroomed knobs at the edges. The tree symbols were stamped over the shoulder. Below the shoulder, is another band of circular cusps bearing the figures of bull, horse, lion and *Gajalakshmi*. At the middle is appliqué band of oblique strokes (now it is in Yeleswaram Pavilion Museum, Director of Archaeology & Museums, Government of Andhra Pradesh, Hyderabad). In Kondapur, the storage jars were inscribed with Brahmi letters on the outside (Fig 7). Some of them were joined with rivets (Ahmad, K.M. 1950, Pl VIII, IX, X). Many water vessels are also noticed. It consists of pots of gourd or globular in shape and were convenient for carrying water. The rims are sometimes beaded, flanged and grooved or simply flanged or externally thickened. Majority of them are devoid of any decoration and slip. If slipped, it is abased due to constant use and the moisture content suggesting further storage of water or some such liquid.

Lotas

These are small to miniature vessels with globular body and round base. A common variety of this vessel is narrow neck and out turned rim. Besides some other sub-types such as elongated neck and an out turned splayed out rim with a flange, ellipsoidal body with convex base or tapper to flat base, out turned rim with corrugated body and convex box are also noteworthy in this category. In general, these are plain but sometimes embossed band at the neck and incised circle at the shoulder may be noticed. Its size and shape suggest that it was used for consuming liquids or could be measuring vessel or even storing vessel for small amount of liquids. In general, the size of this type is about 15 cm high with a capacity of 250 ml. The type was very well represented at Peddabankur, Kotilingala, Salihundam, etc., and associate with Red, Black and Red and Chocolate wares of Andhra and post-Andhra culture periods. Similar *lotas* are also found at Nagarjunakonda sculptures (Murthy, K.K. 1977: 146, Fig. 10).

5.1.3.2 Rare Pot Forms

(a) Brazier or hot case

A unique specimen like brazier or hot case has been found from Yeleswaram excavations (Fig 5, No 1). It is in Black ware. The stand had a perforated wall with triangular and rectangular designs and projection at the periphery of the rim. The projections may be for carrying large size dishes. It has also sockets (3.55 cm in diameter) and straight sided wall. The lid has a loop at the top and grooves and graffiti marks over the body (now it is in Yeleswaram Pavilion Museum, Director of Archaeology and Museums, Hyderabad).

(b) Hour glass stands

It has been found in Red ware as well as Black ware in different sizes. For example, at Nagarjunakonda, Yeleswaram, etc., similar objects are noticed from Megaliths. From Yeleswaram, a small Black ware stand with Black Polished ware vessel has been noticed (Fig 5, No 4). The vessel has a globular body and neck with flared rim and is covered with a knobbed.

(c) Tulip Shaped Vases

Tulip shaped vases (Fig 5, No 2) with funnel shaped lid is another interesting shape. It is in Black ware. Majority of them occur in the Megalithic context, e.g., Yeleswaram, Nagarjunakonda, etc.

(d) Sprinklers

It is a popular type in Red Polished ware during the post-Andhra periods. Occasionally, these are found in Chocolate ware and Black ware. Several Red Polished sprinklers have been found during the study period (Fig 4). Some of them are finer specimens which were imported from of Samarian ware from the Mediterranean regions, e.g., Yeleswaram, Kondapur, etc. From Yeleswaram, variety of Red Polished sprinkler with a high burnished surface has been noticed (Fig 4). It has straightened narrow neck and splayed out flange and printed knob. It has a perforation at the top running through the neck. The shoulder is provided with a spout. Majority of them are imitations and local production. According to M.G. Dikshit (1955: 79), the sprinklers and spouts are special water vessels used by the Buddhists.

5.1.4 Detailed Analysis of Ceramic Industries

The details of pottery found in Andhra culture and the Satavahana culture, which forms the subject of this section, is based on the excavated remains of five select sites. Two of these, Kotilingala, Peddabankur are such sites, reports of which are not yet published. The observations made here, thus, are based on the examination of the excavated collection by the present author. These represent the Andhra and Satavahana culture of the Telangana region. Besides, the two other represented sites which fall within the boundaries of Royalseema region are Satanikota and Veerapuram. The Ceramic collections of both the sites are reported in detail e.g. Veerapuram (Sastri, T.V.G. *et al.* 1984: 57-72) and Satanikota (Ghosh, N.C. 1986). Besides using the published details, the present research also could lay hand on the collection of Veerapuram. The following account also embodies our own observations.

PHASE I: The Andhra Culture Period

Black and Red ware is one of the characteristic ceramic types of the period, which forms 18% of the collections. It is well levigated clay with ingredients like sand, quartz and husk being sparingly used. The section ranges from medium to thick. The ware is coated with slip at the surfaces. There are also some burnished pots. Occasionally salt glazing is also noticed. The general types occurring in this ware are the bowls and dishes.

Black Wares constitute about 22% of the ceramic collection of which, Black polished variety forms 80%. The polished variety of pottery is made of fine clay and is of fine to medium fabric and free from degradients. A few of them are treated with slip uniformly on both sides. In certain shreds, only external surface retains slip and burnishing. Important shapes, which were noticed in this ware, are – dishes. Besides, dish stands, finials, carinated vases, lid-cum-bowls, *lotas, etc.,* also occur as less frequent types.

Red ware, another predominant ceramic of this period, forms 32% of the total collection. A small proportion of these are slipped and the remaining is of dull Red unslipped variety. The color of the slip ranges from dark brownish red to dull red. The fabric in both the cases is medium to coarse and degradients like sand, grit, husk, etc., were generally mixed in the clay. The Majority of them are wheel made with a few exceptions like storage jars, troughs, etc. Almost all of them are well fired with a few exceptions having unoxidized smoky core. In some cases, these are decorated with a wavy and finger-tipped designs at the flange, a hand pinched triangles below concentric grooves near the neck, etc. Majority of the decorated shreds are storage jars.

In **Chocolate ware,** a good number of shreds (12%) are noticed. This group has a distinct slip which has closeness to Red were in nature but varies in color from deep brown to Yellowish brown, sometimes turning towards blackish red or black. However, it is distinct from both Red and Black wares. The fabric of the pots are medium quality bearing traces of tempering materials like sand, frit, husk, etc. the typical forms of this ware bowls, large size basins, troughs, etc.

Russet Coated Painted ware in this phase is represented in very low quantity (1.5%). It is made of well levigated clay and is fine to medium in fabric. It is found in Black and Red ware (1.1%) and Red slipped ware (0.4%). The paintings are rectilinear in pattern. The designs are composed of vertical or oblique lines to from *zig-zag,* criss-cross or latticed patterns. The paintings are made on the external surface of sides. The main types of this ware are dishes and bowls.

Rouletted ware is found in very meager quantity in this site. Some of the pieces are of fine fabric with thin section made of well levigated clay and exhibit superior workmanship, while a few of the shreds of medium fabric indicate their local character. The ware occurs in Black and Red and in Red. Majority of them are Black and red ware. The lower bottoms of these are dishes depict a series of designs in rouletting pattern. These are incised and include concentric bands of dots, dashes, etc. Dish is the main type of this ware.

Red Polished ware occurs in very meager quantity (5%) in this phase. The ware is of extremely fine levigated clay and very thin in section. It is uniformly burnt in brick-red color. The outer surface gets a very fine smooth polish from orange pink to dull red. It may be due to the ferrous slip. The types available in this are the sprinklers, bowls and miniature bowls or cups.

Kaolin ware is noticed in this site represented by only a few shreds (0.02%). The only from available in this is sprinkler.

There are a few other types of wares like Grey ware, ill-fired ware, different shades in ranges between red to black, etc. All these are in coarse to medium fabric. Majority of them are vases and bowls, and appear to from the miscellaneous bulk of the ceramic group of phase I.

PHASE – II: The Satavahana Period

The ceramic tradition of the second phase, i.e., the Satavahana Period, show similar tendency at site, which were noticed in the earlier period. However, there is a little variation in the proportion of the ceramic types. For example, the Black and Red ware during this phase lost its significance and gradually decreased (18 t0 11 %). The type also is devoid of burnished variety and appears to have mediocre look. Generally it is in medium fabric. In contrast to this, there is an increase of Red ware (from 30% to 36%) and Red polished ware (5% to 12.3%). But Russet coated painted ware and Roulette ware are also noticed in less Proportion. Besides, the Chocolate ware also shows a tendency of losing popularity in this phase. Though a little variation in the Proportion of some of the ceramic types is noticeable in this phase, yet there is no change in the general techno-typology of the pottery in this period and the Andhra culture phase at this site.

Table 8 represents the frequency of ceramic traditions in the Telangana and Royalseema region representative sites such as Peddabankur, Kotilingala and Veerapuram. It is apparent from the frequency figures that at both of these sites of different regions, there are only minor variations in the prevalence of important industries of earthen pots between the Andhra and Satavahana cultural phases. Andhra culture appears to be richer then the other in terms of foreign or imitation wares like Russet Coated and Rouletted ware as well as some other special varieties such as Chocolate ware and Black ware. Only Red Polished ware is a noteworthy industry that appears to get a boost in the later culture period. Moreover Grey ware is not prominent ware at Veerapuram. Further, some of the vases are appended with graffiti marks on the external surface. A few bowls are represented with incised *Nandipada*, Brahmi '*ma*', etc. symbols. These symbols and the inscribed labels indicate the labeling of earthen ware for socio-religious reasons.

Table 8

Frequency of Ceramic Types

Ceramic types	Peddabankur		Kotilingala		Veerapuram	
	*I	II	I	II	I	
Black and Red ware	18%	11%	16%	9%	**14%**	9%
Black ware	22%	23%	21.5%	24%	21%	24%
Red ware	32%	36%	35%	37%	36%	38%
Russet coated Painted ware	1.5%	0.5%	1%	0.2%	2.1%	4%
Rouletted ware	1%	0.2%	0.5%	0.2%	1.78%	3.5%
Red polished ware	5%	12.3%	7%	11.5%	3%	7%
Chocolate ware	12%	5.1%	8%	6.5%	3.5%	4%
Grey ware	4%	7%	2%	5%	-	-
Others	4.5%	4.9%	9.5%	6.6%	19.2%	10.5%

* Note: I – Andhra Culture II – Satavahana Culture

The foregoing account of the clay pots of the Early Historical period of Andhra reveals some important ceramic trait, which are as follows.

The Black and Red were is the tradition, which evidences continuity of the Megalithic cultural element in the Andhra culture. However, the techno-typological adoption of this ceramic tradition in this period was in two ways. One, the exact reproduction of the Megalithic trait e.g., fine texture, burnishing and slipping; and the other, the mediocre reproduction in the form of coarse variety of Black and Red ware. The second type would indicate the establishment of popularity which was acquired by the Black Red ware during the Early Historical period.

The Red wares, through from the major bulk of pottery in all the levels of the period under study, there appear to be non-classical and featureless types. But most of the utility pots of all the categories were produced in this tradition. Even the hand-modeling, a rare practice of the Early Historical period, was in vogue only in this ware. It may be interesting to note that the proportion of Red wares increases at all the sites of Satavahana habitation by five to ten per cent. It may be worthwhile to enquire the reasons for the popularity of non-specific ceramic category with the rise of the popularity of non-specific ceramic category with the rise of the Satavahana political establishment, reasons for which are not very clear at the present state.

Another noteworthy feature was that the coastal region has concentration of imported pots. This is demonstrated by distribution and frequency of such ceramics like Rouletted ware, Russet coated painted ware, Red Polished ware and

Northern Black Polished wares. The later three ware perhaps indigenous pottery traits while the former one had their root in far distant region. The import of technology and/or articles during the Andhra Culture period appears to be primarily by trade route.

It was further observed that the urban stage, during Andhra Culture period appears to provide impetus for the use and production or acquisition of various types of ceramic industries with an emphasis on quality and variety of decor and colors. This tendency, perhaps, became less pronounced during Satavahana times, when through general type continue, yet the finer varieties such as Rouletted ware, Russet Coated Painted ware, etc., appear to have lost grounds. It may be noted that the general pottery yield of the consumers do not appear to care much for *deluxe* varieties.

In correspondence with the general tendency of the Proto and the Early Historical periods of the Indian sub-continent, in Andhra region also, the most common earthen from is bowls. This is not a type but appears to be a verity, as the variation of their body form, rim and size may suggest more then one type of utility, e.g., table ware, kitchen ware and perhaps small storage ware. Similarly, dishes too, are a common variety. But most of these appear to be table ware. In comparison to these two, the vases and the jars or large pots are very limited in all the periods *viz.* Megalithic, Andhra and Satavahana. The later group of storage and cooking utility utensils are restricted because in such task, one pot appears to cater to the need of the unit of a family or community, while in case of table ware each of the individual needs one or two more vessels to himself. It, therefore, appears to us that the inflated proportion of the bowl-dish category was the table ware while the lower ratio of the jar/vase category was of storage and cooking vessels, which were used perhaps by the group of people.

5.2 TERRACOTTA

Terracotta art tradition had also started in Andhra along with the potting craft. The early farmers and the pastoral communities of the region had initiated the production of clay figurines probably for ritualistic purposes. Crude and archaic forms of bulls were the main category in use during the Neolithic times. Such terracotta figurines have been reported from Veerapuram, Ramapuram, Nagarjunakonda, etc. These clay forms were hand-modeled and undecorated.

The utility of terracotta figures appear to have increased considerably during the Early Iron Age. The Megalithic builders of this region were producing and utilizing objects of daily utility. Lagged Sarcophagus in different forms and sizes were in use for disposal of dead body. This category is a unique example of artistic amplitude of clay modeling (Raghavan, M.O. *et al.* 1974: 29-31). Besides, other noteworthy products in Terracotta are gamesman, ornaments, spherical balls, animals and mother goddess type ritualistic figurines, etc. However, there is no change in the modeling technique. Noteworthy sites are Nagarjunakonda, Ramapuram, Peddabankur, Yapaladevipadu, etc.

During the Andhra Culture, the terracotta craft developed in accordance with the aesthetic value of the society. Introduction of mould was an innovation, which could produce large number of artistic compositions in very short duration. In this technique, use of double mould is particularly significant the domestic utility of the terracotta also increased. For example, terracotta ring wells, pipes, tiles, crucibles, dabbers, gamesman, etc., are such multifarious production as to suggest the typo-technological development in this craft. Yeleswaram (Khan. A.M.W. 1963: 45), Kondapur (Yazdani, G. 1960: 775-76), have yielded noteworthy finds of the terracotta art in the region.

During the Satavahana period, the terracotta flourished in the form of a style and school in this region. The double molded sumptuous and hollow figurines are attested examples of the Satavahana art in this region. Besides the ornamented clay composition mirror the affluent society of the period. Noteworthy examples have been reported from Nagarjunakonda (Murthy, K.K. 1977: 61).

During the Early Historical period (400 BCE to CE 300), there were two broad categories of terracotta, viz., 1. Figurines and 2. Other products. Among this elaborate typology, the most important and significant feature of the region was figurines (secular and religious in both human and animal forms). It may also be noticed that the kaolin is more suitable clay for the figurines, with was also used for making figurative forms in this region, particularly Telangana.

The terracotta art dose not seems to have flourished in the Deccan before the Christian era, and that too, was confined to only a certain region. The main difficulty that artisan faced was the lack of rich fine clay. So he had to work with Kaolin, a kind of clay which is the product of the Deccanese trap (Wadia, D.N. 1975: 420-421). Its plasticity and durability are far superior to clay. Kaolin or china clay is also known as *Hyderabad aluminium silicate* (Al_2O_3 SiO_2) (Whitten, D.G. A. *et al.* 1972: 231). The name Kaolin is a corruption of the Chinese *kauding*, which means 'high ridge' and also the name of a hill east of king-te-chen. The composition of the clay is SiO_2 - 48. 3%; $A1_2O_3$ - 37.6%; Fe_2 O_3 – 0. 5%; CaO – 1 %; H_2O

–12.5%. The absence of iron is particularly important for the color point of view (Fenwick, I.M. *et al.* 1982).

Process in the preparation of clay for figurine is similar to that of ceramics, of which has been described previously in this chapter. Further, the clay was mixed with powdered lac and decoction prepared from the barks of fine milky trees like Banyan, Pipal, Khadira, etc., for pottery figurines. The mixture is then pressed and kneaded and again allowed to dry. Sometimes the clay was mixed with barley, *mash* (black gram), *guggula* (incense), etc. Oil ash, cotton and mica were also mixed to prevent the clay from cracking.

Table 9

5.2.1 Modelling Technique and Forms

Modeling type	Time brackets	Culture	Forms
Hand modeling	*c* 1500-800 BCE	Neolithic	Bull type figures
Hand modeling	*c* 600-100 BCE	Megalithic & Andhra	Archaic human and animal figurines
Single Mould	*c* 200 BCE-CE 100	Andhra	Plaque
Double Mould	*c* 50 BCE-CE 400	Andhra, Satavahana & Ikshvaku	Human and Animal figurines

The production of terracotta in the region of our study demonstrates that the terracotta figures were produced in four stages. These are marked by distinct chronological periods with an emphasis on technical and stylistically peculiarities. However, regional variations are found in the proportions of the modeled forms and objects. In the first stage, purely hand made modeling was in vogue. In this case the figures were reduced to the simple forms. Mostly female figures of religious nature were modeled in this stage, which has a span from Neolithic to the last quarter of the first millennium BCE. In the next stage *i.e.*, Andhra culture period (during second and first century BCE) use of single mould was initiated and used extensively. Use of mould not only helped increasing the production but it also improved the execution quality of the objects. Hand modeling and archaic form continued to prevail side by side. In the third stage, e.g., during late Andhra times, use of double mould was introduced to the terracotta modeling. The terracotta art reached the stage of high specialization at the time of Satavahana when the artisans were successful in producing hollow terracotta figurines like stone sculptures. In the fourth stage, the earlier modeling traditions continued but show deterioration during the Ikshvaku period (Sankalia, H.D. & H.K. Dhavalikar. 1969: 44). Details of three modeling techniques have been enumerated below.

5.2.1.1 Hand Modeling

Hand made terracotta have a wide distribution in the entire Andhra Pradesh both in terms of time bracket and the spatial occurrence. The clay modeling in this case is performed by pressing and pinching the clay lump which is extracted from the lump of prepared clay. In this technique, usually archaic models of animals and human forms are found, which are termed as 'Ageless' or non-stylistically figurines. A good quality of hand made figurines have been found in our region from all the three cultural periods, e.g., Megalithic to Satavahana times. In human forms, female figurines are dominated. These figurines are characterized by featureless face and halo like dressing of hair locks. However, in some figures the hair is shown with incised lines. The hands are pinched and are in the form of pointed masses or horizontal tapering projection without details. The breasts are protruding and pointed. The attenuated waist line with or without a navel has been broadened towards the hip. The back is flat. The similarity of the shape and sex (female) of many figures may indicate that they represented female fertility cult. In animal figures, which are discovered from the region, bulls predominate. These are with the featureless mouth show in conical downward projection, the horns and legs worked out in masses. Some other forms like a tortoise with the legs shown by pinched masses and two tapering split projections for tail are also noteworthy. Such figures were found at Peddabankur (Sastry, V.V. K. 1983: 178-185), Kondapur (Yazdani, G. 1960: 775-76), Yeleswaram (Khan, M.A.W. 1963: 45-47), Nagarjunakonda (Murthy, K.K. 1977: 61), Dhulikatta (*AAR 1976-77:* 13-17), Kotilingala, etc.

5.2.1.2 Molded Figures - Single Mould

In case of molding, first the fuse of one mould was practiced. Mould which was also made of clay was prepared from taking negative impression form is the core model (Jayaswal, V. *et al.* 1986). After the mould is prepared or acquired, the clay strips are made from the prepared clay (details of the preparation have been elaborated in the section of pottery). These strips are flattened by dobbing into thick flat rectangular or square shapes. The mould is pressed against these strips which receive the modeling details as an impression. The composition thus prepared, acquires high or low relief and are generally of plaque category, the under surface of which is flat while the upper surface has carving in low to high relief.

Single molded form of terracotta was perhaps the intermediate stage between the primitive archaic form and the double molded sumptuous figures. For example, from Kondapur, Salihundam, etc., have yielded noteworthy finds of this category. The main composition made were Yaksha and Yakshi figurines in dancing posture.

5.2.1.3 Double Molded Specimens

Technique employed in the making of double molded figurines is very interesting and is highly specialized craft, which was probably inspired by the western artisans (Deshpande, M.N.1965: 604-05). There are two methods of manufacture of double molded clay figurines (Gupta, P.L.1972: 11-12). One the use of two moulds that means by pressing two moulds on a solid limp of clay and cutting off the surplus clay with a sharp instrument. In this case, figures are solid. Mostly Mother-Goddess figures were prepared from double moulds. They are in squatting posture with hair styles in two chignons and wearing profuse jewelry. In the second method, two thin layers of clay were pressed in the twin moulds. The casts recovered from the two halves were lusted together by pinching or applying a ribbon of clay with, in pre-firing condition. In some cases, the two moulds of the rear and front portions must have been tied with a thread outside and wet clay was pressed in through the hollow which is wide enough to allow the finger inside to oppress the clay over the negative. Similar technique was noticed at Yeleswaram in the case of a ram (Khan, M.A.W. 1963: 45-47).

The moulds were possibly made of terracotta. A considerable number of terracotta moulds have been recovered from

Yeleswaram excavation (Khan, M.A.W. 1963: 45-47) from the post-Andhra level. They included a double mould of ram, mother Goddess and a Scythian solder. Besides, moulds for making designed miniature post and stamps for making impressions on bigger pots have also been found. These moulds are made of finely levigated clay and were well fired for durability.

Double molded terracotta figures have been noticed profusely in the first three centuries of the Christian era, in the entire region. Made of both finely levigated clay as well as kaolin, these were well fired. These include males with elaborate hand dress, Yakshas and Yakshis in various standing postures, amorous couples, musicians, females in alluring posture, female with a child on her knee or *Ankadhatri,* Mother Goddess and other religions group of figures, etc. the male and female figures are characterized by bold physiognomy and extremely sensitive modeling and are also noteworthy for their vitality and plastic simplicity of form. The female figures are highly ornated with complicated jewellery, bangles, hand and ear ornaments, necklace composed of auspicious symbols, girdles and such. On the fore head is found a large circular beaded granulated ornament, etc., (Yazdani, G. 1941: 178, P1 IX). The hair dress shown in two chignons, three tired head gear with hair flowing on both shoulders. The frontally jotted hair was arranged in to an elaborate top knot fastened by a beaded band. The hair was made into a top double *makara* type of coiffure with a broad fillet embossed with lateral resettes tied around the forehead and the waving hair depicted with a knot at the nape of the neck. The style of coiffure resembled double *makara,* i.e., *makara* facing opposite sides with a central axis is a significant feature at this period. Through these figures are highly ornamented and jeweled, they are naked, exhibiting in most cases, their genital organs. These versions are frankly datable, stratigraphically speaking, in the early centuries of CE (Deshpande, M.N.1961). Similar type of figurines were unearthed from many archaeological sites of the entire region such as Anangi (*IAR 1977-78* : 1), Chandravaram(*IAR 1972-73*: 3), Dhulikatta (*AAR 1976-77*: 13-17), Gazulabanda *(IAR 1972-73*: 3), Kondapur (*ARN 1940-41*: 16-17), Kotilingala *(AAR 1982-84*: 37), Kandi (*AAR 1982-83*: 28-29), Mallipadu (*AAR 1987-88*: 20), Nagarjunakonda (*IAR 1954-55*: 22), Peddabankur (*AAR 1974-75*: 5), Rekulapadu (*AAR 1983-84*: 3), Salihundam (Subrahmanyam, R. 1964: 100-101), Satanikota (Ghosh N.C. 1986: 155-58), etc. Majority of these sites are located in the Telangana region.

Animal and bird forms in double molded terracotta appeared in a considerable good number. Among them, Kondapur, Yeleswaram, Peddabankur, Kotilingala and Dhulikatta collections are noteworthy. A gradual increase of this group of terracotta in noticed from the Andhra to post-Andhra levels but the proportion of these are lower then the human figurine category. Horse occurs in large proportion and the bull occupies the next place. The elephant, lion, ram and certain hybrid types with bodies of animals and the beak and head of birds were also found in the collections. These were made of fine levigated clay and also in kaolin in well fired.

Baking of these terracotta was made a closed or open kiln, but heat was never applied directly. The objects to be baked were kept in an earthen vessel which was covered from outside with charcoal and husk.

Most of the archaeological sites in the Telangana region appeared particularly useful for this section. The excavations from this region have yielded numerous terracotta figurines with elaborate typology and advanced technology. The artisans of this region were successful in the terracotta craft to produce highly skilled and sumptuous figurines. The terracotta craft is well documented in this region in both quality and quantity. The collections from Kondapur (Yazdani, G. 1960: 775-76), Yeleswaram (Khan, M.A.W. 1963: 45-47), Dhulikatta *(AAR 1976-77:* 13-17), Peddabankur *(AAR 1971-72*:12; 74-75:1-3) and Kotilingala, throw further light on the flourishing terracotta craft of the region. The present author got an opportunity to study these collection by the kind courtesies of the curator, Government of Andhra Pradesh Museum in Public Garden (for Kondapur collections), and the Director, Department of Archaeology and Museum, Government of Andhra Pradesh (for Yeleswaram, Kotilingala and Peddabankur), both in Hyderabad. The following description is based upon the observation made during the study of these collections.

Kondapur (Lat 17° 33' Long 78° 1') in Medak district of Telangana region, was a flourishing terracotta craft centre during Andhra and post-Andhra (*i.e.* 50 BCE-CE 200). It has not only revealed a good quantity of terracotta but also demonstrated a highly developed skill. The majority of the terracotta figurines at this site were made of kaolin and are the produced of double moulds. These are small in size, averaging 6.5 × 5 cm. Some of them have hollow interior while other are of solid variety. The solid variety of terracotta is made of soft clay mixed with sand. Usually, these were coated with a light red slip at pre-firing condition. The hollow variety of terracotta figures are made of kaolin and have been found in considerable quantities. Some of them were painted with green, red and yellow colors. These were either intact or in fragmentary condition and included human, animal, bird forms and other objects like toys. The present author had studied nearly 350 specimens from Kondapur collections. A few of these are, however, hand-modeled and some are also made of single mould (nearly 14%).

A small number (nearly 8%) of hand modeled figurines of archaic looking female forms were obtained from the early Andhra levels. These are characterized by prominent breasts, navel and the hands and legs were in the form of horizontal tapering projections without details. These figures could be compared to the figurines found at Ahichchatra (Agrawal, V.S. 1947-48: 104-79), Khairadih (Jayaswal, V. 1991: 12), Kolhapur (Sankalia, H.D. *et al.* 1952: 84-85), etc.

The female figurines (55% of the total) of secular nature can be differentiated from the religious ones on account of their ornamentation, prominent breasts and the hands raised up above the elbow in inviting posture and the legs stretched so as to display the pudenda which was strongly marked and often exaggerated in size. The second type (nearly 23%) demonstrated prominent features like heavy breasts, attenuated waist, profuse ornamentation, the posture of the hands which were kept on either side of the nevel with or without holding some objects, and legs with prominent nudity. The common and significant feature of the female figurines was the style of coiffure (Plate I). The hair was made into a to double *makara* style, i.e., *makaras having* opposite with a central axis. A broad fillet embossed with lateral rosettes tied around the forehead and the waving hair depicted with a knot at the nape of the neck. The figures representing conventional ringlets of hair with a flat nose, thick lips and oval face, show typical features of an indigenous ethnic type. Some figurines with a jewellery band round the forehead, heavy ear rings and mass of hair on the crown of the head and the ornamented plaits falling on the nape of the neck are only some of the characteristics, all of which show the particular care bestowed by the sculptor in the treatment of the coiffure. Besides, there are figurines meant to be joy objects depicting forms with dumpy noses and irregular features and peculiar hair style in which long hair are shown turned up at the end.

The typical religious forms which have been identified are the Yaksha and Yakshini, and a female with a child on her knee with a fan or an incense burner in her hand. A mutilated figure is sought to be identified as the Mother Goddess but the best figure is identified as a Bodhisattva (Sreenivasachary, P. 1953: 9).

The animal and bird figurines also appear in a considerably good proportion (18%). Majority of them are made of kaolin and are double molded. Horse, elephant, ram, bull, lion, dove, parrot, etc., are the identifiable animals and birds in which horse is the most common variety. All of these are decorated and artistically molded. The head stales of horses are composed of vertical check strap and face strap with horizontal front and nose bands. At the junction of the straps, there appears a boss medallion or rosette in most of the cases. Plumes were prominently showed. The eyes are made in circles or round pellets crossed by straight incision. Above the knee of the front legs, there is a thick circular boss. As these figurine's are lavishly ornamented (Yazdani, G. 1960:775-76, Pl LVa), it may be suggested that these were used as decorative pieces rather than toy objects.

The foregoing discussion reveals that though clay figures were made in limited number much earlier than the Andhra culture period, e.g., the Neolithic and the Megalithic periods, this craft received impetus only around the second half of the first century BCE. The earlier technique of hand modeling and the production of archaic forms were modified by the use of moulds. Introduction of mould, during Andhra culture, supports the general thesis that this technique is an urban trait where mass production of artistic forms can be done in short durations (Jayaswal, V. *et al.* 1986: 137). Besides, moulds which are prepared from the core models, also cast the figures in the same style which is borne by the stone sculptures of the period. In Andhra, during Andhra culture period, use of single mould is the chief characteristics of terracotta, in which low to high relief plaque or composition were produced. This category has correspondence with the Sunga terracotta clay art of North India (Verma, N, 1986). Though it may be difficult to ascertain at present, in which region the use of single mould was initiated first, yet there are evidences believe that casts of the single mould in view of their composition, style and the technique appear to be an Indian trait of the first century BCE.

The second stage of terracotta art of early Andhra is marked by the use of double moulds. The Satavahana period is significant for the imitation and mastery of this technique. It may be noted that the use of double mould, contemporary to that of Andhra region is not attested to in the Gangetic plains or the north India (Jayasawal, V.1991). It may, therefore, appear that this technique was a borrowing from non-Indian region. Usually smaller in size, about 10 cm high, the Satavahana clay figurines reflect sculptural aesthetics which are seen in the contemporary lithic icons. The stylistically reproduction in mass, is an urban requirement, which appears to reach its zenith during Satavahana times. In Ikshvaku period, around

3rd and 4th century CE deterioration in the terracotta craft can be seen in our area of study.

The above account of terracotta suggests that the Telangana region retained evidence of advanced stages of the terracotta art. The general proportions of figurines as well as other utilitarian items were comparatively very high in the collection of antiquities. The nature of this craft appears in very well advanced form. It was also noticed that the figures unearthed form such sites in the Telangana region, appear to have been cast out of one or two moulds only. These figures apparently appear to be manufactured at one place and were exported from the centre to other places. It may be put to record that the Telangana region appears to be the main terracotta producing region from where the product were taken to the rest of the State during the Satavahana times. It was also noted that the frequency of occurrence of clay figurines was very high in the Telangana region than rest of the region. Prolific terracotta craft centers in the Telangana region, which were the production centers of advanced techno-typological objects, recalled in innate nature and flourishing condition of the craft during the period under study. Further, the terracotta human figurines in the Coastal Andhra and Rayalseema region, through are of high artistic value, their meager proportion in these region is noteworthy. Terracotta objects of other daily utility were produced locally in the entire region. It may, therefore, be held that baked clay craft was mastered uniformly throughout Andhra during Early Historical period but the production of figurative forms were specialized in particular region like Telangana.

In contrast, Dharanikota excavations were bereft of any terracotta, which is rather strange in view of the fact that this site was an active and important trade as well as political centre during the second century CE. The double mould technique did not flourish in the region even though they had direct contact with the Mediterranean people. However, at Nagarjunakonda, excavations throw a light on the terracotta art of this region as well as their knowledge of the advanced technology in regard to this craft once under the school of the Satavahanas. Religious sites like Salihundam exhibit not only a considerable quantity but shows that they were more ritualistic than secular. Though there is a regional variation of occurrence or absence of typology, a similar technical trend has been observed in the entire region by the end of the second century CE.

Out study of terracotta collection from the important excavated sites of all the three regions, suggests that Telangana was the most prominent region during the Early Historical times for clay figure making. Not only the quantity of figurines and the other utility items have been reported in large proportion from this region, but the region is also significant for production of artistic composition and use of advanced technique of double mould casting. Particularly during Satavahana times, Telangana became terracotta producing region. It was also noted that for one type of composition, only one or two moulds were used. The finished products were distributed to the other regions from the Telangana. Not only the proportion of figurines is large in Telangana, but their occurrence is meager and restricted in number in the other two regions. Further, in spite of the small numbers, the compositions in Rayalseema and Coastal Andhra are of high artistic quality and have striking similarities with that of Telangana. All these facts put together, support the possibility of Telangana being the main region of molded terracotta production and the remaining State as the area of export of these clay sculptures.

Terracotta objects of daily utility were produced locally in the entire region. It may, therefore, be held that baked clay craft was mastered uniformly throughout Andhra Pradesh during the Early Historical period, but the production of figurative forms was specialized by particular regions like Telangana. Regional variation seen in the type of composition produce also at times depends on the nature of settlement. For instance, at the religious settlement of Salihundam, ritualistic compositions outnumber the secular ones. Another noteworthy site of this category is Nagarjunakonda, which too, is famous for its Buddhist establishment. But, there are some exceptions like Dharanikota, where use and production of terracotta are negligible. This feature is particularly important as Dharanikota as important trade as well as political centre in around *circa* second century CE.

It has been often suggested that terracotta figurative art developed in India as a parallel craft to the pottery tradition (Jayaswal, V. *et al.* 1986: 142-43). This observation is not repeated in our area of study. For, in the Early Historic remains from Andhra, the most developed stage for the clay potting craft was the Andhra culture period but for terracotta figures it was the Satavahana period which distinguishes itself as the period of classicalism.

REFERENCES

Ahmed, K.M. 1950. *Inscribed and Riveted pottery from Kondapur.* Kondapur Series. No 1. Hyderabad

Annual Administrative Reports (abbreviated as *AAR*). Government of Andhra Pradesh. Hyderabad.

Annual Report of Archaeological Department of His Exalted Highness of the Nizam's Dominion. 1940-41(abbreviated as *ARN*). Department of Archaeology. Hyderabad.

Begley. V. 1992. Ceramic Evidence for per-Periplus Trade on the Indian Coasts. *Rome and India:* The Ancient Sea Trade. (eds) Begley, V. & R.D. De Puma. New Delhi: 157-203.

Casal, J.M. 1949. *Fouilles de Virapatnam- Arikamedu.* Paris.

Chapekar, B.N. 1969. *Report on the Excavation at Ter.* Poona.

Dasgupta, C.C. 1961. *Origin and Evolution of Indian Clay Sculpture.* Calcutta

De Leeuw, V.L.J.E. 1987. What was the Purpose of the Terracotta Animal Figurines. Discovered at Kondapur. *Kusumanjali,* New interpretation of India Art and Culture, Sh.C. Sivaramamurti Commemoration volume. (ed) M.S. Nagaraja Rao, Delhi II: 369-371.

Deshpande, M.N. 1961. Roman influence on the Terracotta of the Satavahana period. *International Conference on Asian Archaeology.* 14th -20th December, 1961. Summaries of Papers. New Delhi: 70-71.

Deshpande, M.N. 1965. Classical Influence on the Terracotta Art. *Eighth international of classical Archaeology* (1963). Paris: 604-407

Fenwick, I.M. & B.J. Knopp. 1982. *Soils Process and Response.* London

Foote, R.B.1916. *The Foote Collection of the Indian Prehistoric and Protohistoric Antiquities: Notes on their Ages and Distribution.* Madras.

Garhwali, V.S. 1984 (reprint). The Terracottas of Ahichchatra, District Bareilly, U.P. *Ancient India.* Bulletin of Archaeological Survey of India. No 4 (1947-48). New Delhi: 104-179.

Garhwali, V.S. 1985 (reprint). *Terracotta Figurines of Ahichchatra.* District Bareilly , U.P. Varanasi.

Ghosh, A. 1953. A Remarkable Feature of South Indian Pot Making. *Man.* LIII, March: 39-48.

Ghosh, A. (ed) 1989. *An Encyclopedia of Indian Archaeology.* 2 Volumes. New Delhi.

Ghosh, N.C. 1986. *Excavation at Satanikota (1977-80).* Memoirs of the Archaeological Survey of India. No 82. New Delhi.

Gupta, P.L. 1972. *Gangetic Valley Terracotta Art.* Varanasi.

Gurumurthy, S. 1981. *Ceramic Traditions in South India.* Madras.

Indian Archaeology A Review (abbreviated as *IAR)* (eds) Director General of Archaeology in India. New Delhi.

Jaggi, O.P. 1981. *History of Science, Technology and Medicine in India, Technology in Ancient India*. Delhi.

Jayaswal, V. 1990. Kushana Clay Art of Khairadih. *Lalit Kala*. Journal of Oriental Art Chiefly India. (ed) Karl Khandalawala. 24: 61-69.

Jayaswal, V. 1991. *Kushan Clay Art of Ganga Plains*, A case study of Human Forms from Khairadih. Delhi.

Jayaswal, V. & Krishna. 1986. *An Ethno-Archeological view of Indian Terracottas*. Delhi.

Khan, M.A.W.1963. *A Monograph on Yeleswaram Excavations*. Andhra Pradesh Government Archaeological Series. XIV. Hyderabad.

Mahalingam, T.V. 1969. Ceramic Industries in south India. *Potteries in Ancient India*. (ed) B.P. Sinha. Patna.

Mahalingam, T.V. 1970. *Report on the Excavations in the Lower Kaveri Valley*. Madras.

Margabandhu, C. 1976. Some mother Goddess Plaques from west India. *Homage to a Historian, A Festschrift*. (eds) Jagadeesh, N. & S. Jayapragasam. Madurai.

Margabandhu, C. 1985. *Archaeology of the Satavahana-Kshatrapa times*. Delhi.

Marshall, J. 1951. *Taxila* (An Illustrated Account of Archaeological Excavation at Taxila between 1913-14). 3 Volumes. Cambridge.

Mehtha, R.N. & S.N. Chowdhary. 1966. *Excavations at Devisor*. Baroda.

Mishra, A.K. 1989. *The Indian Black Ware* (first millennium B.C.). Delhi.

Murthy K.K. 1965. Some Technical Aspects of the Indian Pottery. *Orissa Historical Research Journal*. XIII. 2: 29-42.

Murthy, K.K. 1971. The Pottery-Making Technique in Early Indian Literature. *The Andhra Pradesh Journal of Archaeology*. 1: 73-77.

Murthy, K.K. 1977. *Nagarjunakonda-A Cultural Study*. Delhi.

Noorjahan, B. 1979. A Unique storage Jar from Yeleswaram. *The Andhra Pradesh Journal of Archaeology*. 2: 15-17.

Pande, B.M. 1966. Ring well in Ancient India. *Bulletin of the Deccan college Research Institute*. XXV.

Patwardhan, N. 1984. *Hand Book for Potters*. New Delhi.

Peacock, D.P.S. Ed. 1977. *Pottery and Early commerce*. Characterization and trade in Roman and Later Ceramics. London.

Pisipaty, S.R.K. 1997. Some observations on ceramics of the Andhra and Satavahana cultures. *Ancient Ceramics: Historical Enquiries and Scientific Approaches.* (eds) Pant, P.C. & V. Jayaswal. Delhi.

Pisipaty, S.R.K. 2006. Ceramic traditions in early Andhradesa-an appraisal. *Mahasenasiri Riches of Indian Archaeological and Cultural Studies.* A Felicitation Volume in Honor of Dr. I.K. Sarma. (ed) Chenna Reddy, P. Delhi.

Rajan, K. 1991. Stratigraphical Position of Russet Coated Painted ware. *Indian Archaeological Heritage.* Sh. K.V. Soundara Rajan Felicitation Volume. 2 Volumes. (eds) C. Margabandhu, K.S. Ramachandran, Sagar, A.P. & D.K. Sinha. Delhi. II: 241-245.

Rao. B.K.G. 1972. *Megalithic culture in south India.* Mysore.

Rao. B.S. 1958. *Personality of India,* Pre and Protohistoric foundation of India and Pakistan. Baroda.

Rao, S.R. *1966. Excavations at Amreli.* Bulletin of Baroda Museum and Picture Gallery. No XVIII. Baroda.

Rawson, P.S. 1953. The Surface Treatment of Early India Pottery. *Man* LIII, March: 30-34

Ray, A. 1983. *Life and Art of Early Andhradesa.* Delhi.

Rice, P. 1987. *Pottery Analysis: A Source Book.* Chicago.

Rouse, V. 1989. *The Potters, Wheel craft specialization and Technical Competence.* New Delhi.

Roy, T.N. 1986. *A Study of Northern Black polished ware Culture,* An Iron Age Culture of India. New Delhi.

Sankalia, H.D. 1957. Imported Mediterranean Amphorae from Kondapur. *Journal of the Royal Asiatic Society*: 207-08.

Sankalia. H.D. & M.G. Dikshit. 1952. *Excavations at Brahmapuri (Kolhapur) 1945-46.* Poona.

Sankalia, H.D. & S.B. Deo. 1955. *Report on the Excavation of Nasik and Jorwa 1950-51.* Poona.

Sankalia, H.D., Subba Rao, B. & S.B. Deo. 1958. The *Excavation at Maheshwar-Navdatoli (1952-53).* Poona.

Sankalia, H.D., S.B. Deo, Ansari, Z.D. & S. Ehrhardt. 1960. F*rom History to Prehistory at Nevasa (1954-56).* Poona.

Sankalia, H.D. and M.K. Dhavalikar. 1969. The Terracotta Art of India. *Marg.* XXIII, l: 33-34.

Saraswati, B. 1979. *Pottery Making Cultures and Indian Civilization.* New Delhi.

Saraswati, B. & N.K. Behura. 1966. *Pottery Techniques in Present India.* Anthropological Survey of India. Memoir No 13 (1964). Government of India. Calcutta.

Sarkar, H. 1973 (reprint). Kesarapalli 1962. *Ancient India.* Bulletin of the Archaeological survey of India. No 22 (1966). New Delhi.

Sarma, I.K. 1977. *Religion in Art and Historical Archaeology of South India, Contact and correlations.* Madras.

Sarma, I.K. 1990. Ancient Andhra Ports Religious Centers and Seafaring. *Journal of Marine Archaeology.* I. Jan. 19-23.

Sastri, T.V.G., Bai, M.K. & V.J. Rao. 1984. *Veerapuram:* A Type site for cultural study in the Krishna Valley. Hyderabad.

Sastry, V.V. K. 1971. Terracottas from Peddabankur and Dhulikatta. *The Andhra Pradesh Journal of Archaeology.* I.1.

Sastry, V.V. K. 1983. The Proto and Early Historical culture of *Andhra Pradesh.* Government of Andhra Pradesh . Hyderabad.

Sastry, V.V. K., Subrahmanyam, B. & N.R.K. Rao. 1992. *Thotlakonda* (A Buddhist site in Andhra Pradesh. Government of Andhra Pradesh series No. 68. Hyderabad.

Subrahmanyam, R. 1964. *Salihundam-A Buddhist Site in Andhra Pradesh.* Andhra Pradesh Government of Andhra Pradesh series No 17. Hyderabad.

Thapar, B.K. 1985 (reprint). Maski, 1954 : A Chalcolithic site of the South southern Deccan. *Ancient India.* Bulletin of the Archaeological Survey of India. No 13 (1957): 4-142.

Verma, N. 1986. *The Terracottas of Bihar.* New Delhi.

Wadia, D. N. 1970. (reprint) . *Geology of India.* London.

Wheeler, R.E.M. 1983 (reprint). Arikamedu: An Indo-Roman Trading station on the East of India. *Ancient India.* Bulletion of the Archaeological Survey of India. No 2 (1946). New Delhi: 17-124.

Wheeler, R.E.M. 1984 (reprint). Brahmagiri and Chandravalli, 1947; Megalithic and other cultures in the Chitaldurg district, Mysore state. *Ancient India.* Bulletin of the Archaeological survey of India. No 4 (1947-48). New Delhi: 181-310.

Whilten, D.G.A. & J.R.V. Brooks. 1972. *The Penguin Dictionary of Geology.* London.

Yazdani, G. 1941. Excavation at Kondapur: An Andhra Town (200 B.C.-200 A.D.). *Annuals of the Bhandarkar oriental Research Institute.* XXII.

Yazdani, G. 1960. *The Early History of the Deccan.* London.

Chapter 6

METAL OBJECTS

Initiation of metal technology was a major break through in the history of mankind. Because the barbaric mode of living of the Stone Age had a turn towards successive stages of modification with the mastery over daily utility metals like copper/bronze and iron. Besides being technological attainment, the use of these metals improved general living patterns and also governed economic processes during the early history of man. In Andhra Pradesh, the early stages of metal technology are not well envisaged. As, the lithic based early food producing communities of the Neolithic times, appear to have suddenly came into contact with the iron users of the Megalithic phase. With the result, the succession of the lithic technology in terms of the use of copper and a successive later innovation of iron technology is not documented in this region. Iron and copper appear on the scene side by side during the first millennium BCE when the entire Andhra region came under the spell of Megalithism. These people were perhaps the immigrants who had mastered daily utility metal working before settling in this region. In

Andhra, they explored the native iron resources and also perhaps deposits of other metals. The metal technologies of the Megalithic times appear to have been transferred to the Andhra culture people as one of the basic culture trait. The skill and technological know-how inherited by the Andhra cultural group, was not only utilized extensively to facilitate their day to day activities, but certain new metals and their new combinations such as bronze, potin, etc., were also adopted for use. Following Andhra culture period, the same traditions were continued. By this time, use of metal became so much deep rooted in the society that large quantities of various types of utility items along with decorative and luxury goods were being produced in the region. The noteworthy metal objects of the Early Historical period of Andhra have been divided first into five groups, e.g., iron, copper, lead, precious metals, alloys. A brief account of the technology and typology of individual group is followed by the important archaeological remains of the region.

6.1 IRON OBJECTS

Iron is such a metal which is abundant in natural state and is readily obtainable from surface out crops and bog iron deposits. It is a more prosaic metal, lacking the lustrous color. However, it yields effective edges and drudge marking of implements and thus had a far more utility effect for man. Once its potentialities had been realized, and technology mastered, the use of this metal became indispensable.

6.1.1 Technology

Industrial production of iron, in the Early Historical period of Andhra appears to be a regional phenomenon. The ores used were extracted from the local deposits. Perhaps due to the limitation of long distance transportation facilities, the iron using communities inhabited the resource areas. The concentration of smaller settlements of the Early Historical period in the iron ore rich inland of Andhra, is noteworthy in this period. For instance, Tellakunta iron-working centers in Nizamabad district of northern region were the world famous steel swords production centers (Sastry, V.V. K. 1983: 213).

Iron ore deposits which were well know to the Early Historic people of the region, were Vizayanagaram, West Godavari, Krishna, Guntur and Nellore districts of coastal Andhra region; the entire hill range from Tellakunta to Bongathurthi in Karimnagar district, Konasamudram, Dindurthi, etc. had mines which were source of Damascus steel (Kuppuram, G. 1989: 235) and Jagtial, Warangal, etc., all in Telangana region; and districts Kurnool, Cuddapah in Rayalseema region (Krishna, M.S. 1954).

The frequent from of ore, which occur in this region, are Magnetite, a double oxide or iron (Fe_3O_4 or $FeOFe_2O_3$; Hematite, a sexnetite, a sexquioxide of iron ($Fe_2 O_3$); Limonite, a Hydrated from of Hematite ($2Fe_2O_3 . 3H_2O$), etc. (Kuppuram, G. 1989: 24). After extracting ores the iron, as is the indigenous way of the present day, these are smelted in furnace. The ores are first heated before they are actually put into furnace for smelting. The clay lined crucibles are arranged by negative iron smelter in alternate layers of charcoal and iron ore (Fagan, B.H. 1978: 358). The crucibles which are filled by ores and fuels are tightly packed with small pieces of iron booms together with charred rice husks, leaves of 'asclepias gigantean amiculata' as the carbonizing material. Such packed crucibles are kept in charcoal fire at very high temperature for about 24 hours. At the end of this period, the earthen crucibles are broken and lumps of heat iron / steel are obtained. In order to render their malleable, they are again covered with clay and annealed from 12 to 16 hours (Hussaini, H.A.G. 1962: 84). To remove impurities from iron ores, catalytics like lime, are also used at the time of smelting (Forbes, R.J. 1972: IX).

That the above mentioned technique of smelting iron was under practice during the Early Historical times in the Andhra region, is suggestive from the archaeological remains. For example, at Satanikota, an earthen crucible was discovered, which was placed / fused with slag and charcoal and put within a furnace (Ghosh, N.C. 1986). Besides, remains of furnace have been unearthed from industrial sites, which were built of circular clay bricks. The diameter of one such structure was 30 cm and its height 25 cm. The bottom of the furnace was also paved with bricks. A hole near the base was also paved with bricks. A hole near the base was also noticed (Sastry, V.V. K. 1983: 253). A comparable furnace which is used in *wootz* production has a temporary circular structure of clay of 5 to 6 feet in height and about 5 feet in diameter. It is usually sunk 2 feet below the surface of the ground (Kuppuram. G.1989: 331. 335).

The smelted iron lumps were marked out in various shapes and objects by hammering. On account of Archaeological finds from the region, it may be suggested that the blacksmiths after producing extracted bloom, forged these into strips while it was red. Evidence for forging has been reported from Kondapur (Diskhit, H.G. 1952: II-III), Tellakunta, Konasamudram (Sastry, V.V. K. 1983: 213) etc. of the Telangana region. All these evidence, together, testifies that the iron technology right from the selection of ores to the making of utility items was mastered in Andhra Pradesh during the Early Historical period.

In Andhra Pradesh iron technology appears in developed from around the second half of the first millennium B.C. The initial processes of various early stages of mastery is not demonstrated, nor do one finds prevalence of any other utility metal, e.g., copper or bronze , which could provide grounds for the negative origin of iron making tradition. The circumstantial evidence also indicates that iron technology came in the region in developed from with the advent and spread of Megalithic people. Due to the inherent qualities of this metal and the local rich resources, use of iron soon became an inseparable part of the Early Historical utility kit (Banerjee, N.R. 1965: 203).

6.1.2 Typology of Iron Objects

Large quantities of iron objects have been unearthed from various archaeological horizons of the region which are dated between *circa* fourth century BCE and third century CE. Elaborate functional classification of iron objects of this region have been done in this part. It was observes that most of the iron objects unearthed from almost all the archaeological sites of the region under study follow a uniform pattern. These implements could, thus, be classified broadly on the basis of their utility into the following heads, viz., 1. Household objects 2. Building materials, 3. Agricultural implements, 4. Implements of war and chase, 5. Miscellaneous, and 6. Unidentified.

6.1.2.1 Household Utility Objects

Household utility objects of iron dominated in the studied collection of our region. It was possible to identify the following fifteen types of this category.

Balancine Rods have been noticed in different lengths with or without perforations to string pans. At Peddabankur (Sastry, V.V. K. 1983: 164), seven balancing rods were noticed. Among them, five are 36 cm in length and rounded all over and thickened in the middle, and other two are 25 cm long. These resemble the carvings of sculptures at Nagarjunakonda (Murthy, K.K. 1977: 288) and Amaravati (Murthy, S.C. 1966), which are shown in use of balancing rod.

Bowls (?) Dishes/Lids group of pots and pans was found at ⟶ contd... page no. 136.

Table 10
Typology of Iron Objects

Types	Name of sites				
	Salihundam	Kotilingala	Peddabankur	Satanikota	Veerapuram
Household utility objects	P	P	P	P	P
Balancing Road	-	-	P	-	P
Bowls/ dishes/lids	-	-	-	-	P
Ferrules	-	P	P	-	-
Fish hook	P	P	-	-	P
Fork	-	P	P	-	-
Key	-	-	P	-	-
Knife	P	P	P	P	P
Ladles	-	P	P	-	P
Lamp	P	-	P	-	-
Needle	P	P	P	P	P
Razor	-	-	P	-	-
Ring	P	P	P	-	P
Spoon	-	-	-	-	P

Contd...

Types	Name of sites				
	Salihundam	Kotilingala	Peddabankur	Satanikota	Veerapuram
Stylus	-	P	P	-	-
Trowels (domestic)	-	-	P	-	-
Building Materials	P	P	P	P	P
Used in Construction					
Clamps	-	-	-	P	-
Hooks	P	P	-	P	P
Nails	P	P	P	P	P
Rings	P	P	P	P	P
Rivets	-	P	P	P	P
Staples	-	-	-	P	-
Carpenter's / Smith's tool					
Adzes	-	-	P	-	-
Borers	-	-	-	P	-
Chisels	-	P	P	P	P
Drills	-	-	-	-	-
Hammers	P	-	-	-	-
Scrapers	-	P	P	-	-
Mason's tools	-	-	-	-	-
Agricultural implements	P	P	P	P	P
Adzes	P	P	P		
Axe	P	P	P	-	P
Hoe	-	-	P	-	P
Plough Share	-	-	-	-	-
Sickle	P	P	P	P	P
Spuds	-	P	P	-	-
War and chase weapons					
Arrow – heads	P	P	P	-	-
Caltrops	-	-	-	-	P
Choppers	-	-	-	-	-
Dagger / sword	-	P	-	P	P
Javelin	-	-	-	-	-
Lance	-	-	-	-	P
Spear head	P	P	P	P	-
Spikes	-	-	-	-	-
Miscellaneous objects					
Cylindrical bars	-	P	P	-	P
Handles or fragments of tools	P	P	P	-	P
Indeterminate objects	-	P	P	-	-

Veerapuram (Sastri, T.V.G. *et al.* 1984: 149). There were nine objects out of which, two belonged to the Andhra cultural level and the rest were obtained from the post-Andhra cultural content.

Ferrules or casing are cylindrical rings, with are still commonly used as the hub of a wheel, which rotates around the axle. The other type of ferrules are a simple one which are used for strengthening the ends of mulller, pestle, sticks (walking), etc. At Peddabankur (Sastry, V.V. K. 1983: 164) two types of ferrules were discovered and had 5.5 cm diameter, while the other was almost half of the size of the former with 2.5 cm diameter.

Fish Hooks consist of a simple curved 'U' shaped ending in a sharp point. The rods may be rectangular, round or square in section. At Veerapuram, two hooks were noticed from Andhra level and one from post-Andhra level (Sastri, T.V.G. *et al.* 1984: 149) and similarly at Kotilingala (information from excavator) and Yeleswaram from Early Historical level (200 BCE-CE 400) (Khan, M.A.W. 1963: 54) such hooks were discovered. The occurrence of fish hooks ('U' shape) suggest that water animals formed part of the staple food during this period.

Fork consists of two prongs, riveted together at the butt end and separated below. The prongs are thick. These are reported from Peddabankur, Kotilingala, etc.

Key shaped objects (2 in number) were noticed in the antiquities of Peddabankur (Sastry, V.V. K. 1983: 163). One with disk handle had tail end missing. The other one had a round disk handle with a small round plate and was riveted at the other end. Unfortunately no lock has been noticed so far which could match these objects.

Knives have been found in various sizes and forms. On the basis of working edge, it could be grouped into: knives with straight back and straight edge, ending in a tang for handle. The first type may perhaps be related to the non-vegetarian kitchen. The other one with small size appear to be for table use. Other group of knives with the sharp edge with an upward curve, towards apex to meet the straight blunted back, is commonly useful for killing the fowl by cutting its neck. Another group of knives having curved cutting edge taking a backward sweep like an arc and forming a hook at the apex with flat ending in a tang for handle, is used in cutting twigs, leaves, fruits, etc. This type of objects was found in profuse from almost all the archaeological sites during the Early Historical period in good number. At Peddabankur, more than two dozen knives were noticed in different sizes and forms and similarly from Kotilingala also (information from the excavator). This group was obtained at Veerapuram, seven objects were found from Andhra phase whereas 13 were recovered from post- Andhra deposits (Sastri, T.V.G. *et al.* 1984: 149). Similarly, a good collection of knives were noticed from Dhulikatta (*AAR 1976-77*: 13-17) and Yapaladevipadu (*AAR 1976-77*: 13-17). In both Andhra as well as post-Andhra cultural levels the type is found in good propositions.

Ladles were noticed in Dhulikatta excavations. Two ladles were found, one with 6 cm diameter and 2.5 cm deep with horizontal handle, whereas other one is having very shallow cup with a diameter of 4.5 cm and a depth of 0.5 cm. Attached to it was a 18 cm long handle which is square in cross section (*AAR 1976-77*: 13-17; Sastry, V.V. K. 1983: 163). Similar type of objects was also noticed at Peddabankur (Pl IV B) and Kotilingala. These are very similar to those found at Nasik

(Sankalia, H.D. and Deo, S.B. 1955; Fig 52, No 11, 13, 52, Pl 771) and Pauni (Deo, S.B. & J. P. Joshi. 1972. Pl XVIII. No 10, Fig 17, 84) sites of Maharashtra.

Lamps have been noticed in many varieties. Among them, a shallow dish with vertical handle bent backwards at the top for suspension and a solid dish with an out-curved lip are important types. Both the varieties are found at Peddabankur. The hallow dish type has a diameter of about 4.5 to 7cm (*AAR* 1970-71: 1-3; 1971-72: 3; Sastry, V.V. K. 1983: 163). At Dhulikatta (*AAR* 1976-77: 13-17) a similar type of object was also noticed.

Needles were found in various sizes and lengths, throughout the region. A needle of 14.5 cm was noticed at Peddabankur (Pl III B) with one thickened and rounded end the other tapering and painted. At Peddamarrur *(AAR 1977-78*: 12) through type occurs in Megalithic context, in Kondapur *(ARN 1940-44*: 16-18) and Veerapuram (Sastri, T.V.G. *et al.* 1984: 149) it has been reported from the post-Andhra level.

Razor has a side tang which is parallel to the blunted edge. With hafted to a wooden handle, it therefore, can conveniently be used as a razor. At Peddabankur, these were noticed in two sizes. One with 8.5 cm long and the cutting edge at the bigger knife takes a backward sweep and widens at the curved top and other one has 1.5 cm broad cutting blade, which is damaged at the top. These are comparable with iron objects found at Taxila (Marshall, J. 1951: 454, No 122).

Rings of iron have been noticed in spherical and rectangular in shape. At Veerapuram, iron rings were found in both Megalithic (Sastri, T.V.G. *et al.* 1984 PL XXXVIIB, No 3) and post-Andhra levels (Sastri, T.V.G. *et al.* 1984. PL XXXIXA, No 5). But in Peddabankur *(AAR 1970-71*: 1-2) rings with diameters of one and half to two cm (Pl IVB) were found from Andhra cultural deposits.

Spons were unearthed at Veerapuram from post-Andhra levels.

Stylus with thick middle portion which is square in cross section and tapering pointed ends are reported from Ṗeddabankur. The single 12.3 cm long specimen from this site is comparable with Brahmagiri find of stylus (Wheeler, R.M. 1947. Fig 40, 47: 260).

Trowels which were also used in domestic activities are reported from Peddabankur and Dhulikatta (Sastry, V.V. K. 1983: 163).

6.1.2.2 Building Materials

The iron objects which were used for or in the construction of houses and other structures have been grouped in this category. The frequency of this category is next to the domestic objects in all over the region. These have been further divided into three groups, viz., 1. Used in construction 2. Carpenter tools and 3. Mason tools. Under each group, the following objects were noticed.

Used in construction are a group of six types of objects that were used for buildings.

Clamp in an appliance for holding things together tightly. These are found in different shapes. In this region, important finds were unearthed from Satanikota (Ghosh, N.C. 1986) and Dhulikatta (*IAR* 1974-75).

Hooks are curved or bent pieces of metal for catching or holding things. These were noticed at Satanikota, Dhulikatta (*IAR 1974-75*: 5) and Veerapuram. The two hooks from

Veerapuram were from Andhra level while one came from post-Andhra horizon of the same site (Sastri, T.V.G. *et al.* 1984: 149).

Naill is an essential component in building material. These are used predominantly for carpentry work. The tiles were fixed to the rafters of the houses with the mails. Several nails and tiles found together confirm the above point, for instance, Nevasa (Sankalia, H.D. *et al.* 1960: 435) and Devnimori (Mehta R.N. *et. al.* 1966: 96-97). Much of them are of round head. However, some are also found with flat square, rectangular and triangular heads. Their different sizes were noticed in almost all the archaeological sites region from the Megalithic period to the Satavahana times. At Peddabankur (Pl IV B), Kotilingala (Pl IV A), Veerapuram, Satanikota *(IAR 1974-75*: 5), Ghantasala (*IAR 1984-85*: 5), etc. for example good number and sizes of nail were retrieved from both the levels – the Andhra and the Satavahana.

Rines were used as hold for joints or supports for wooden end of implements. These rings were fastened to objects for giving them more strength and durability. Many rings in *in situ* positions have been reported from Megaliths of south India (Margabandhu, C. 1985: 313). At Peddabankur, Kotilingala, Veerapuram, etc., wider rings (6.4 cm diameter) were noticed (Sastri, T.V.G. *et al.* 1984. Pl XXXIXA, No 6)

Rivets are metal pins or bolts for fastening metal plates. The plain end is hammered flat after it is joined together with the plate to prevent slipping. At Peddabankur *(AAR 1970-71*: 1-2; 1971-72: 13), Kotilingala, Dhulikatta *(AAR 1976-77*: 13-17) and Veerapuram (Sastri, T.V.G. *et al.* 1984. Pl XXXIXA, No 1, 2) these objects were found. At Kondapur, it was observed that the potters also had used rivets in piecing together storage jars (Ahmad, K.M. 1950. Pl V. IX, X).

Carpenter's Tools are the other group of tools in building Material category, which were used for wood working. The following six types are grouped in this category.

Adze has a thin rounded or flat top and thick but sharply tapering blade. These were used for cutting wood and also used for shearing the skin by cobblers. At Peddabankur *(AAR 1971-72*: 1-3) similar type of objects were noticed.

Borers are a sharp pointed tool, which is used to make perforation in wood, metal plates, leather, etc. (Petrie, F. 1901: 52). These have been found at Yeleswaram (Khan, M.A. W. 1963: 54) from post-Andhra level and also from Satanikota. The type is also reported in copper from Ter (Chapeker, B. N. 1969: Fig 35, 4) and in bone from Prakesh (Thapar, B.K. 1985. Pl XXIX 4). C. Margabandhu (1985: 283) noticed that most of the iron borers belong to the early centuries of the Christian era.

Chisels are used for cutting metal, wood or stone. It is used in both carpentry and black smithy. The working edge is indifferent shapes such as beveled edge, sloping edge cut from both sides, etc. (Marshall, J. 1951: 553-54). Blacksmiths used a chisel of a very thick solid which withstand the direct and heavy blows in its shank (Coughlan, H.H. 1956: 113-14), whereas carpenters use it for monitoring work, which requires a long thin slender body and chisels with widely splayed blades. C. Margabandhu (1985: 281) has classified these into bare metal, sicketed handle and tang in handle with straight or curved cutting edge, etc. on the basis of the hafts. The type is reported from post-Andhra levels at Peddabankur *(AAR 1970-71*: 1-3; 1971-72: 1-2), Kotilingala, Satanikota (Ghosh,

N.C. 1986: 159), Veerapuram (Sastri, T.V.G. *et al.* 1984: 150) and Yeleswaram (Khan, M.A.W. 1963: 54).

Drills are primary tools of the carpenter, which are used along with chisels. Unfortunately, no such object has yet been discovered from this region. However, iron and copper drills were reported in the Deccan from Megalithic period onwards. For instance, at Nasik (*c* 400-200 BCE) drills which are found, have a round body and a sharp tapering point (Sankalia, H.D. & S.B. Deo. 1955).

Hammer is one of the oldest tools of the carpenter's kit. At Salihundam, a few hammer shaped bars of iron have been found (Subrahmanyam, R. 1964).

Scrapers consist of a widely splayed semi-circular edge with small tang to hold. It may be used by cobblers for cutting leather. At Peddabankur (*AAR 1970-71*: 1-2; 1972-73: 3), similar objects were found.

Mason's Tools like plummets, trowels wedges, etc., through are necessary in building activity, have not been reported from the area under study. It is particularly significant because in other regions, the group was in use from the Chalcolithic times (Roy, A.K. 1967) at Mohenjo-Daro and Taxila (bronze plumb *c* 300 BCE). This is in spite of the fact that in our region, much building activities such as, construction of palatial buildings, residences, fortifications, etc., were carried on during the Early Historic period. However, at Peddabankur (*AAR* 1971-72: 1-3), an object similar to trowel was noticed but the excavator (Sastry, V.V.K. 1983:163) has reported it as a domestic implement.

6.1.2.3 Agricultural Implements

Agricultural Implements occur in a considerable number throughout the region. Their frequency, however, occupies third position in the iron objects. The types in this category are as follows.

Adze is a long rectangular implement, the edge of which forms 90^0 to the handle. It has been reported in two varieties – in one, the butt is rounded and tangled, while in the other, the butt has shaft holes for hafting handles. The main function of the adze is to chip thin strips from large mass of wood. Noteworthy finds of this category are reported from Peddabankur *(AAR 1972-73*: 1-2).

Axe, a most common tool has wide occurrence in Andhra. This type is almost similar to the above except that its edge remains parallel to the handle. It is used primarily to cut and split wood. The group can be grouped into two, on the basis of the method of hafting and use, in one, the butt is left plain while in the other, a hole is provided to the butt for hafting. Sites of Peddabankur *(AAR 1971-72*: 1-3; 1972-73: 1-2), Kotilingala, Veerapuram (Sastri, T.V.G. *et al.* 1984: 154. Pl XLIB, No 7) and Dhulikatta (*AAR* 1976-77: 13-17) have revealed all the types of axes in good number.

Hoe is a generally made of thick and flat metal with round projection or flange on each edge of the butt - end and bent inward to from a hole for the handle. Its main function is hoeing and breaking the ground and digging light earth. These objects have been found from sites like Peddabankur (*AAR 1970-71*: 1-2; 1971-72: 1-3; 1973-74: 1-2), Kondapur (Dikshit, M.G. 1952: V), Yapaladevipadu (*AAR 1977-* 78: 13-21), Peddamarrur (*ARA* 1977-78: 12) etc.

Plough Share, a type of a sharp implement (17 × 3.5 cm) has been discovered from Veerapuram (Sastri, T.V.G. *et al.* 1984: 152, Pl XXXIXB, No 6), a fragment of plough from Dhulikatta (AAR *1976-77*:13-17), Kondapur (Yazdani, G. 1941: 18 Pl XVI) and Yeleswaram (Khan, M.A.W. 1962: 54).

Sickle, used for cutting crops from the agricultural fields, has a crescent shaped curved blade or a horizontal broad blade with a little curve at the end and long straight tang. These objects were noticed at Peddabankur (*AAR* 1970-71: 1-2, 1971-72:1-2, 1972-73:1-3), Salihundam (Subrahmanyam, R. 1964), Veerapuram (from Megalithic and post-Andhra context), Satanikota (Ghosh, N.C. 1986), Kondapur (Dikshit, M.G. 1952: V), Yeleswaram (Khan, M.A.W. 1963: 54), Peddamarrur (*IAR 1977-78:* 12), Yapaladevipadu *(AAR 1977-78*: 13-21) and Dhulikatta *(AAR 1976*-77: 13-17).

Spade is a tool for digging, which has been recovered from the excavations at Peddabankur *(AAR 1970-71*: 1-2).

6.1.2.4 Weapons

Weapons of war and chase (*cf* Table 10) occupies fourth position in order of utility of iron objects. The following types in this category have been reported from Early Historical period of Andhra Pradesh.

Arrow Heads are small pointed implement, which are attached to a shaft. This type has been divided into sub-groups on the basis of forms of handles and blades (Margabandhu, C. 1985: 303-304). The type has been reported from Peddabankur (*AAR 1971-72*: 1-3; *AAR 1972-73*: 1-2), Kotilingala and Veerapuram (Sastri, T.V.G. *et al.* 1984: 150,154) (Megalithic and post-Andhra levels), Peddamarrur (*IAR 1977-78*: 12) and Yeleswaram (200-100 BCE) (Khan, M.A.W. 1963: 54, PL XIIIB).

Dagger and Sward – though there is a structural difference between the two, this group practically belong to the same type. Dagger has two edges made of thin blades, tapering to a point with or without a medium ridge, whereas sword is composed of a long blade, sharp on one or both edges. Both are undoubtedly fighting and mostly a thrusting weapon. J. Marshall has suggested that daggers of Taxila may be copies of or influenced by the Greco-Roman types (Marshall, J. 1951. II : 544-55) but, it is very clear that similar daggers were well known during the Megalithic period from as early as the 5th or 4th century BCE in south Indian. At Yeleswaram (Khan, M.A.W. 1963. Pl VIII & XIIe) a dagger was unearthed from Megalithic burial (200-100 BCE). A portion of sword with prominent curve at top 13.0 × 2.4 cm size was recovered from Veerapuram (Sastri, T.V.G. *et al.* 1984. Pl XXXIX B, 5) while excavations of Andhra levels were conducted.

Javelin is a thin spear-shaped weapon with sharp point. These are not a complete weapon by itself as it is hafted lengthwise to a wooden handle. The weapon is used by throwing. Remains of Javelin are found in different shapes right from the Megalithic period to the Satavahana times. At Yeleswaram, a unique javelin was found from Megalithic cists burial of Andhra Cultural period (*c* 200-100 BCE). It is studded with spikes perhaps to be used as an effective weapon (Khan, M.A.W. 1963. Pl VIII).

Spear Heads comprise a leaf-shaped and triangular blade ending in short point with a tang. It is reported from Megalithic to the later periods in Andhra. At Nagarjunakonda, for instance, spear heads occurred from Megaliths whereas at Kondapur (Dikshit, M.G. 1952: V) (*c* 2nd century BCE), the type was obtained from the deposit of Andhra level. The discoveries made at Peddabankur (*AAR 1971-72*: 1-3; 1972-73: 1-2), Veerapuram (Sastri, T.V.G. *et al.* 1984. Pl XXXIXB, No 4-5) and Satanikota (Subrahamanyam, R. 1974. Pl LVI) belong to the Andhra and post-Andhra levels. The typology of this weapon remained unchanged from Megalithic time onwards.

6.1.2.5 *Miscellaneous and Indeterminate Objects*

Broken parts of objects are grouped under this category. Many such objects were found at almost all the excavated sites. However, in certain cases undetermined shapes were noticed. Among them, Peddabankur indeterminate use of iron objects (Pl IVB) is interesting. It is 58 cm long which is curved like 'S' at one end. Two holes were perforated near the top and one hole below these perforation resemble like eyes and mount on a snake hood. The back of the curve is flat (Sastry, V.V.K. 1983: 165). Similar type of perforated objects was also used as rivets to the door and has been reported from the same site.

The iron objects recovered from the region, throw ample light on the flourishing iron industry throughout the region in the Early Historical period. Table 10 & 11 presents the iron objects recovered from different sites of the region, the analysis of which show the following tendency.

Table 11

6.1.3 Frequency of Iron Objects

Name of site	Culture	Types *					
		1	2	3	4	5	6
SALIHUNDAM	Andhra	10	5	N.K	N.K	N.K	22
	Post-Andhra	22	12	N.K	N.K	N.K	62
KOTILINGAL	Andhra	18	9	11	5	31	74
	Post-Andhra	54	24	10	9	41	138
PEDDABANKUR	Andhra	21	10	8	6	28	73
	Post-Andhra	64	30	9	11	42	156
VEERAPURAM	Andhra	14	5	11	4	44	78
	Post- Andhra	66	17	8	17	127	235
SATANIKOTA	Andhra and Post- Andhra	N.K	N.K	2	4	N.K	88

N.K. = not known; 1.* Domestic or Household; 2. Building material; 3. Agricultural implements; 4. War & Chase weapons; 5 . Miscellaneous & indeterminate objects; 6. Total objects

Religious site like Salihundam, in the Coastal Andhra region, has revealed a good collection of iron objects (84 in all). The proportion of objects varies from Andhra to post-Andhra phase, which increases almost three times in the later phase. The above table further demonstrates that household or domestic and building objects predominate in both the phases e.g., Andhra and Satavahana culture, which are followed by agricultural and war-chase implements. Urban and political centers of Telangana region are represented by the selected sits of Peddabankur and Kotilingala. The iron objects from these sites are also present in considerably good amount in the Andhra and post-Andhra periods. Typology of the assemblage is marked by a dominant proportion of the objects of domestic building and industrial uses. However, the agricultural and war-chase implements also have been recovered in considerable number and variety. Large number of collection of iron objects from these confirms the utility and industrial activity and production of the objects at these sites. It may be noted that the iron ores are abundant in the neighborhood areas.

Royalseema region is represented by Satanikota and Veerapuram. The collection from the second named site was found particularly useful for this section. As Veerapuram has not only revealed good quantity of iron objects but also variety of typologically advanced tools are reported from here (Sastri, T.V.G. *et al.*1984 : 147). The total number of objects unearthed at Veerapuram was 313, among which 78 came from Andhra phase and 235 from post-Andhra phase (Table 11). Like the above sites, in this case also, iron was utilized mostly for household purposes, and carpentry and building construction activities. The agriculture and war-chase implements were comparatively less (Table 11). From the first phase (Andhra), more then 80 per cent (61 out of 78) objects are classified as household objects. Among these, nails and rivets were many (44 in all). A total of 15 per cent objects were used for building, agricultural and weapons. The proportion of war and chase is very low (6 per cent). The specimens of lances, swords occurred in this cultural context. The rest 5 per cent objects go to the miscellaneous and unidentified categories.

In the next phase (post-Andhra phase), the quantity of iron objects was increased by almost three times more then the former phase. But the similar typological trend to the phase I was noticed in the types of objects used in this phase also. A good number of objects (66 in all) were of indeterminate nature as their actual use could not be ascertained.

Satanikota (Ghosh, N.C. 1986: 159) too has revealed the collection of iron objects in a good number (88 in all). Though the category wise number of objects is not available, it appears that a good number of objects belong to household or domestic use and building material. The offensive weapons were negligible in number (only two varieties). The agricultural implements also appear in very low frequency (only two specimens). In the absence of detailed published report and also non-availability of the collection for examination, the phase and category wise distribution of the objects was not possible to make.

The foregoing account of iron objects suggests that all the thirty-seven types indicate multifarious use of iron in various activities of the Early Historical period of the Andhra Pradesh. Most of the types particularly the carpenter tools and war weapons were adapted from megalithic times to the Andhra and Satavahana periods in almost unaltered forms. But may be noted that the proportion of iron objects remains somehow restricted during the Andhra cultural phase. At almost every site, increase in the number of iron objects was observed during Satavahana times. Iron appears to be an important medium for day to day life in both the periods of the Early Historical times. For equipments of domestic use, building activities invariably dominate in Andhra and Satavahana times. In comparison to this the lower proportions of agricultural tools and weapons are noteworthy.

6.2 COPPER OBJECTS

Copper (cuprum-Cu) is reddish, glittering metal. The metal is normally but not invariably alloyed with tin. The alloys are more extensively used then the pure metal. It has been suggested that in the history of south India, there was not a single period when copper was not used in good quantity. However, we have evidence for the use of copper objects from the first millennium BCE, which was basically the time for the use of iron implements in our region. Similar to iron, copper technology also appears to have entered Andhra Pradesh in developed from. Use of copper in our study period got confined to the monitory unit. For, plenty of coins were made of copper. Avadhanulu, A.B. (1981) has analyzed some coins of Satavahana and is of the opinion that the metal used for these were extracted from the ore deposits of the neighborhood. This would obviously suggest that of copper smelting and casting were performed locally.

6.2.1 *Technology*

Capper workings of the ancient time in Andhra Pradesh was similar to the ones followed in the other parts of the country. For example, the miners used to tap surface lodes under the ground. Some such ancient quarries have been dated by Radiocarbon dating. Bandalamattu hill in Guntur district gives 800 $\pm$ 90 and 650 $\pm$ 90 BCE date brackets whereas Mailaram mines in Khammam district shows 535 $\pm$ 90 BCE (Kuppuram, G. 1989. Vol I: 84). The important ore deposits in this region are found in the form of Chalcopyrite ($Cu_2SFe_2S_2$), Chalcocite (Cu_2 S), and Bromite (Cu_3 FeSO).

Smelting of copper, one of the ancient processes have been recorded from central Africa (Michall, S.B. 1974: 242-247), which might be the same in all over the ancient world. The ore was placed in a small furnace with the alternating layers of charcoal and smelted for several hours at high temperature. The molten copper was dripped on top of a sand-filled pot buried under the fire. Two processes were employed for manufacturing copper objects. There were hammering of metal into appropriate shape and casting. Hammering was done by repeatedly heating the bars or slags, while for casting, earthen moulds were used. In casting, both hollow casting by *cire perdue* process and solid casting technique were found to have existed during Early Historical period (Margabandhu, C. 1985: 324).

Utility of copper metal in the region was low and was relegated primarily to ornamental as monetary units. However, utilitarian like domestic, toy objects, etc., were also noticed but in a very low proportion. Table 12 presents the frequencies of objects in the important reported sites. It reveals that the sites like metal, whereas at Salihundam and Satanikota (only one specimen) copper use was in very low proportion. The details of coins and ornaments made of copper have been incorporated in the preceding chapter. The following description enumerates the other copper objects, which have been reported from the region.

Table 12

6.2.2 Typology of Copper Objects

Sl .No.	Type	Name of site*				
		1	2	3	4	5
I.	**Ornaments**	P	P	P	P	P
II	**Coins**	P	P	P	-	P
III	**Utilitarians**	-	P	P	-	P
	1. Ear cleaner	-	P	P	-	-
	2. Needle	-	P	P	-	-
	3. Spindle	-	-	-	-	P
	4 Spoon	-	-	P	-	-
	5. Tooth picks	-	P	P	-	P
IV	**Games & Toy objects**	-	P	P	-	P
	1. Gamesman	-	P	P	-	P
	2. Rattles	-	P	P	-	P
V	**Miscellaneous**	-	P	P	-	P

1*. Salihundam 2. Kotilingala 3. Peddabankur 4. Satanikota 5. Veerapuram

6.2.2.1 Utilitarian copper objects through have restricted types, are marked by advanced technology. The following types have been noticed from this region.

Ear Cleaner is a small pin with one end flattened like the snake's hood or clubbed and other is pointed. At Veerapuram, similar object was noticed from post Andhra level, which is in 3.5 cm long. Pin and prick is broken (Pl VIIIB). Such objects were also noticed from Peddabankur and Kotilingala.

Needle has been noticed from Peddabankur (Sastry, V.V. K. 1983: 165). It is a semi-circular rod with pain pointed at both the ends like a suturing needle of a surgeon. Functionally, it appears to be used for sewing leather pouches.

Spindles found in half broken and circular in shape (with 3.6 cm diameter) belong to post-Andhra level at Veerapuram.

Spoon, a small cup of 3.8 cm diameter and 6.5 cm long handle of square section, has been found at Peddabankur from post-Andhra level (Sastry, V.V. K. 1983: 167). The excavator suspects that it was used by the apothecary for mixing ingredients or herbs.

Tooth Picks were noticed from post-Andhra level at Peddabankur (Sastry, V. V. K. 1983: 166). Noteworthy example is a 4 cm long with one pointed end the other is thickened with loop.

6.2.2.2 *Games and Toy Objects*

Games And Toy Objects of copper: Under this category, only two types of objects have been found.

Rattles have been found at Peddabankur from post-Andhra level. One of it is a beautifully molded specimen in the shape of a frog have two circles central pellets, resembling the eyes and a banded line in the middle. It has a lifted mouth and hollow body where a small copper ball was put for producing rattling sound. Through similar in shape, the Peddabankur find is more artistic then Maski (Thapar, B.K. 1957: 115, Fig 34, 7).

Gamesman / Hopscotch is a circular or almost round flat disc shaped object are found with or without being pierced. The excavations at Peddabankur have Yielded hopscotches (*AAR* 1970-71: 1-3).

The use of copper in the Early Historical period of Andhra Pradesh was much restricted in comparison to iron. It utility was confined primarily to decorative objects and coinage. In the daily utility items too, only luxury items have been reported in restricted number. It may also be noted that copper was more in use during Satavahana times and was quite sparingly used in the Andhra culture stage. It may further be suggested that more of the objects in this metal were produced locally.

6.3 LEAD OBJECTS

Lead is dull and metal, which was also utilized in Andhra Pradesh in the Early Historical times. Its density is 11.33 and is easy to work. This metal is found in fairly high concentration in many parts of the State. 'Galena' is the most important ore of lead and was possibly exploited by ancient man. Smelting of the ores and extraction of this metal is one of the simplest metallurgical operations. In ancient times, metallic lead could be obtained by simply heating the ores. A heap of lead ores was placed on ground or in a pit. Fused metal, which melts at 327° C, could be taken out and collected from the bottom of the heap, after heating them. The crude lead as obtained above was repeatedly melted and crystallized. The remnant of lead was removed by the cupellation process. The most common use of lead in the region under study, was for coin. Besides, some ornaments were also produced with this metal. Both of these categories have been described in the other chapter under miscellaneous collections.

6.4 PRECIOUS METAL OBJECTS

Precious metals such as gold and silver were sparingly used in the entire region for ornaments. Gold is the most precious of all metals, sought after due to its international and intrinsic value since its advent. Pure gold is yellow in color and of a glittering nature. It has a pleasing color, luster, resistance to atmospheric and chemical. It is not affected by most of the acids except Acqua Regia (i.e., a mixture of hydrochloric acid and nitric acid) which is an additional horizon in the preservation of gold objects in archaeological horizons. Its melting point is 1065° C, which is comparatively low to the other metals like copper and iron. In the region under study, frequent use of gold can be seen from the Neolithic and Megalithic periods.

The early traces of gold working have been found in the districts of Cuddapah, Kurnool in Royalseema region and Palnadu area of Guntur district. Besides, the well known Kolar, Wondapalli, Maski and other mines in Karnataka and Hatti in Tamil Nadu states were noticed as the ancient gold mines. These are situated in the neighborhood areas of Andhra Pradesh on the western and southern sides, respectively and were important resources of raw metal in the Early Historical times. A number of crucibles of terracotta, which were used for melting of this metal, have also been noticed from several sites. The archaeological discovery of traces of gold objects mostly comprises jewelry, ornaments and coins. They were made by dices and moulds. The technique adopted, include granulation, filigree, etc. At Dharanikota (Ramachandran, K.S. 1975: 35), a goldsmith's mould was reported from Andhra level (200 BCE).

Silver (*Argentums*-Ag) is another noble metal, which is beautiful white in color. It has a melting point of 960^{0} which is comparatively lower then gold. It has to be noted that silver dose not occur in India as primary mineral source but is suggested to be associated to either of the following secondary sources, *viz.*, a silver of light color in combination with gold from Kolar gold mines in Karnataka state, or associated with galena (*argentiferous*) which is a primary one of the lead.

The Precious metals are used primarily for jewellary, ornaments and coins. Therefore, detailed typology of these metal objects have discussed in miscellaneous collection.

6.5 OBJECTS OF ALLOYS

The alloys, bronze and potin have been used during the Early Historical period of Andhra Pradesh. Bronze is an alloy of copper and zinc (60: 40). Utility of this alloy in the region appears in a very low proportion. Through the utility was limited, the technology in the manufacture of objects were found to be considerably high quality (Srinivasan, P.P. 1973).

Casting of Bronze object: the process which was employed for the craftsmanship is known as '*cire perdue*' or 'lost wax' technique. This is an ancient method which was employed by the Chinese and the Greeks. It was also skillfully practiced in India since the Harappan culture (Srinivasan, P.P. 1963). In this process, the wax model which served as core of operation, was lost or drained out before the actual casting took place. But in hollow image method, the subject would be first modeled in clay, and then coated with wax. Thus after the casting of an image, its mould is destroyed with the result that no two specimens of the south Indian bronzes are alike even if they are made by one and same hand. Each item is characterized by a rare individuality of its own.

From Dhulikatta excavations (Pl V), a unique figure of bronze was found. It is an image of the mother-and-child *(amkadhatri)*. On the basis of stratigraphic position, the figure might be dated to *circa* second century BCE. The mother is seated on a pedestal with dangling legs. She holds a baby in her left hand, while the right hand rests on her knee. The baby flexes its left hand to touch the mother's left breast. The mother's hair, eyes, mouth and ornaments such as ear-rings, torque around the neck, necklace, armlets, bracelets, waist band, etc., were crudely made in appliqué. The crude modeling of the figure is in conformity with archaic terracottas found in the same level at the site as well as the finds of the region and north Indian settlements of the Mauryan time (Jayaswal, V. 1991: 11).

Metal objects in the entire region under study, are marked by a number of similarities in the form of strong prevalence of both typology and technology. The foregoing account of the techno-typology of the were metal objects of the region suggests that the iron objects were profuse and retain advanced technology with elaborate typological variation. Next in the sequence of utility of metal, is copper and then precious metals, lead and alloy metals.

Table 13
Metals and Forms

S. No.	Metal	Equipment*			Coin	Pot	Ornament	Figure
		1	2	3				
1	Iron	H%	H%	H%	-	S%	S%	-
2	Copper	H%	M%	-	H%	S%	H%	-
3	Lead	-	-	-	H%	-	S%	-
4	Gold	-	-	-	H%	-	H%	-
5	Silver	-	-	-	M%	-	M%	-
6	Bronze	-	-	-	-	-	-	S%
7	Potin	-	-	-	H%	-	-	-

Note * 1. Agricultural 2. Domestic 3. War & Chase weapons
H% = High percentage M% = Medium percentage
S% = Small percentage

Iron object, on a close security, and account of the typological consideration, are marked by occurrence or absence of some specialized types like agriculture and war and chase categories and varying frequencies of some implements like household and building objects in the entire region. The working spots and production centers, which produced export quality with advanced technology, were noticed in the north-western region. Damascus steel and production of export quality high technique swords were one the famous export item from the north western side of the region in Andhra culture period. Besides, slags and crucibles also could be seen in certain industrial sites like Satanikota, Konasamudram, Kondapur, etc., which further attest to the industrial activity of iron working in this region. The general proportion of the copper objects through is comparatively very low in this, yet utility of this metal appears to have aristocratic value (ornaments, coins and special purpose utilitarians). A somewhat similar trend was also noticed in the case of lead and precious metals. The circulation of precious metals, during third century BCE to third century CE seems to have been intense in the entire region. As the use of coins (Roman), bullions and ornaments, appears to be especially widespread in the coastal Andhra and other trading routes of this region. Lead and alloy potin also played important monetary role and were used side by side copper and precious metals like gold and silver. Alloy bronze had restricted utility, mostly in the from of figurines, etc., and was perhaps non-indigenous medium of craftsmanship.

In the second half of the first millennium BCE, the extent of utilization of the metal by Andhra settlers was invariably low through they had the knowledge of metals and the relevant metallurgy. The frequency of metals and their utility and typo-technology are remarkably increased from the end of the first millennium BCE. By the end of the second century CE, the metals occupied significant role in their daily utility items and appear to have replaced the lithic medium in this region. Through use of various metals was initiated during Megalithic times, it was only in the Satavahana period that their quantities increased considerably. With regard to the typology and even technology, the Andhra culture phase does not seem to lag behind, but general, the proportion of individual metal objects in particular and groups of various metal items in general are lower in this periods in comparison to the Satavahana times.

REFERENCES

Agrawal , B.P. 1971.*The Upper Bronze Age of India*. New Delhi.

Ahmed, K.M. 1950. Inscribed Riveted Pottery from Kondapur. *Kondapur Series.* No 1. Hyderabad.

Allchin, B. & F.R. Allchin. 1968. *The Birth of India Civilization.* Harmondsworth.

Annual Administrative 1970-71;1971-72, 1972-73 and 1976-77 *Reports* (abbreviated as *AAR*). Department of Archaeology and Museums. Govt of Andhra Pradesh. Hyderabad.

Annual Report of Archaeological Department of His Exalted Highness The Nizam's Dominions. 1940-41 (abbreviated as *ARN)*. Hyderabad.

Banerjee, N.R. 1965. *Iron in India*. Delhi.

Bhardwaj, H.C. 1979. *Aspects of Ancient India Technique*. Delhi.

Chapekar, B.N. 1969. *Report on Excavations at Ter*. Poona.

Coughlan, H.H. 1960. *Notes on the Prehistoric and Early Iron in the old World.* Oxford.

Dikshit. H.G. 1952. *Some Beads from Kondapur*. Hyderabad Archaeological Series. No 16. Hyderabad.

Fagan, B.M. 1978 (3rd edn). *In the Beginning*, An Introduction to Archaeology. Boston.

Forbes, R.J. (ed). 1964-66. *Studies in Archaeology*. 9 Vols. Leiden. IX.

Ghosh, A. (ed). 1989. *An Encyclopedia of Indian Archaeology*. 2 Vols. New Delhi.

Ghosh, N.C. 1986. *Excavations at Satanikota* (1977-80). Memoirs of the Archaeological survey of India. 82. New Delhi.

Husain, H.A.G. 1962. *The Economic History of India*. Calcutta.

Imperial Gazetteer of India. 1909. Provincial Series. Hyderabad State. Calcutta.

Indian Archaeology-Review (abbreviated as *IAR*). (ed) Director General of Archaeology of India. Archaeological Survey of India. New Delhi.

Jaggi, O.P 1981. History of Science, Technology and Medicine in India. *Technology in Ancient India*. Delhi.

Jayaswal, V. 1991. *Kushan Clay Art of Ganga Plains*. A Case stuffy of Human Forms From Khairadih. Delhi.

Khan, M.A.W. 1963. *A Monograph on Yeleswaram Excavations*. Andhra Pradesh Archaeological Survey. XIV. Govt of Andhra Pradesh. Hyderabad.

Krishna, H.S. 1954. *Iron ore and Iron and Steel*. Calcutta.

Kuppuram, G. 1989. *Ancient Indian Mining, Metallurgy and Metal Times*. Delhi.

Margabandhu, C. 1985. *Archaeology of the Satavahana- Kshatrapa Times*. Delhi.

Marshall, J. 1951. *Taxila*. (An Illustrated Account of Archaeological Excavations at Taxila between 1913-41). 3 Vol. Cambridge.

Marshall, J. 1973 (reprint). *Mohenjo-Daro and the Indus Civilization*. 2 Vol. Varanasi.

Mehta, R.N. & S.N. Chowdhary. 1966. *Excavations at Devnimori*. Baroda

Michael, S.B. 1974. Prehistoric Copper mining in North-Western Zambia. *Archaeology*. October.

Murthy, K.K. 1977. *Nagarjunakonda -A Cultural Study*. New Delhi.

Murthy, S.C. 1966. Sculptures in Madras Govt Museum. *Bulletin of Madras Government Museum*. New Series. Madras. IV.

Noorjahan Begum. Ankadhatri from Yeleswaram. *The Andhra Pradesh Journal of Archaeology*. I.1.

Petrie, F 1901. *Tools and Weapons*. London.

Ramachandran, K.S. 1975. *Radiocarbon Dates of Archaeological sites in India*. Archaeological Series. No 42 Government of Andhra Pradesh. Hyderabad.

Roy, A.K 1967. Ancient Survey Instruments. *The Journal of the Institute of Surveyors*. VIII, 5: 367-74

Sankalia, H.D. & S.B. Deo. 1955. *Report on the Excavation of Nasik and Jorwa* (1950-51). Poona.

Sankalia, H.F., Deo. S.B., Ansari, Z.D. & S. Ehrhardt. 1960. *From History to Prehistory at Nevasa (1954-56).* Poona.

Sastri, T.V.G., Bai, M.K. & J.V.P. Rao. 1984. *Veerapuram, A type site for Cultural study in the Krishna Valley.* Hyderabad.

Sastry, V.V. K.1983. *Proto and Early History of Andhra Pradesh.* Govt of AP. Hyderabad

Singh, R.N. 1988. Ancient South Indian Metallurgy-A Reappraisal. *Studies in Ancient Indian History* (D.C. Sircar Commemoration Volume). (ed). Gupta, D.K.K., Bhattacharyya, .P.K. & R.D. Choudhury. Delhi.

Sreenivasachar, P.R. 1953. *Kondapur*. Govt of AP. Hyderabad

Srinivasan, P.R. 1963. Bronzes of South India. *Bulletin of Madras Govt Museum*. Madras. VIII.

Subrahmanyam, R. 1975. *Nagarjunakonda* (1954-60). Memoirs of the Archaeological Survey of India. No 13 (1957). New Delhi.

Warmington, E.H. 1928. *The Commerce between the Roman Empire and India.* Cambridge.

Wheeler, R.E.M 1984 (reprint). Brahmagiri and Chandravalli 1947: Megalithic and other cultures in the Chitaldurg District, Mysore state. *Ancient India.* Bulletin of the Archaeological survey of India. No 4 (1947-48). New Delhi: 181-310.

Yazdani, G. 1941. Excavations at Kondapur: An Andhra town (200 B.C.-200 A.D.). *Annals of the Bhandarkar Oriental Research Institute.* XXII.

Chapter 7

STRUCTURES

Structural activities in the region under study stared in the Neolithic period. During this period, huts circular, oval, oblong and irregular shapes were constructed, evidences for which are found in the form of post-holes, reed impressed clay lumps, etc. Remains of huts have been reported from Veerapuram, Ramapuram, Nagarjunakonda, etc.

In the Early Iron Age, architectural activities were increased in the region also. The small settlements of the period had agricultural based economy and rural bias. Along with simple settlements, funerary monument was made in the form of megaliths. Building of Megaliths was made in the form of megaliths. Building of structures for after death appears to be more popular during the beginning of the Early Iron Age then the constructions of residential areas. However, habitation *debris* at Veerapuram indicates use of circular and rectangular huts at the pre-Andhra cultural level.

During the Andhra and Satavahana periods, progressive growths of settlements into large habitational centers are envisaged. The development of cities and towns along with many small satellite settlements was a noteworthy feature of the period. In constructional activities permanent and durable materials like brick and iron were also used. Besides, various types of secular and religion buildings were constructed during this period. Details of building activities of the Andhra and Satavahana levels are described below.

Structural activities of the Early Historical period of Andhra have been discussed with the help of the excavated remains of the region. It may be mentioned that the observations are based primarily on the excavator's reports and personal communications. Details of the structures of the Andhra and Satavahana periods are as follows.

Salihundam, the selected religious site of coastal Andhra has revealed many interesting structures of the Buddhist *Sangharama* on the top of hill. It was also found that there were distinct phases of structural activities here. In each phase, the builders had adopted their different plans. Natural contours of the rock outcrop were an additional advantage at this site, which governed the general plan of structures. Majority of the structures of the early Andhra phase are of mud bricks. In the later phase, burnt brick structures with lime plaster and lime flooring were built. It was noted that walls retained rows of well-aligned bricks of different sizes, which, perhaps, is indicative of the use of bricks of different dates in the constructions. The structures thus made, are identified as *stupas, votive stupas, viharas, chaitya grihas*, etc. It may be noticed that the stupa here exhibits some difference of details of plan as compared to the other sites in the region like Nagarjunakonda. Through it had a plan with wheel and central hub, radiating spokes and rim, the *ayaka* platform and the *stamba* are absent here. The flooring was furnished by line mortar mixed with pebbles. Many of the post-Andhra or

Satavahana period structures appear to have been destroyed (Subrahmaniyam, R. 1964).

Besides the above site, remain of many other religion (Buddhist) establishments were found from the coastal Andhra region. Interesting among them are, Bhavikonda, Thotlakona (Sastry, V. V. K. *et al.* 1991), Goli, Amaravati, Bhattiprolu (Rea, A. 1984: 7-16), Chandavaram (Murthy, P.R. 1972), etc. Through these were constructed in almost the same period (around third century BCE) a few variations are noticed between the stupa of the Northern Coastal Andhra and Southern Coastal Andhra. The early stupas of the Northern coastal Andhra, for instance, have brick rims at the periphery wile the inner walls are filled with clay and rubble but those of the south were initially solid brick construction, which were later on turned into wheel pattern. The other important feature is the establishment of the drum with finely carved *vedika* or *ayaka* slabs as found at Amaravati, Nagarjunakonda, etc., in the lower Krishna valley. But this feature did not appear in the northern stupas of the region. However, the other surface of the drums has been plastered with fine lime.

Amaravati in Guntur district of the middle Coastal Andhra region is the great Mahachetya site of the southern region of India. The foundation remains are said to have been raised during the early Andhra period (*c* 4th century BCE). The stupa during the Andhra period was a single hemispherical dome flattened at the top. The drum of the stupa is 35 m. In diameter and rose to a height of 6 m. with a diameter of 27 m at the top in late Andhra period. During the Satavahana, the drum was faced with sculptured slabs representing richly carved *dagabas, chaityas*, etc. The Satavahana period witnessed not only increased architectural activities but also reared up a large number of stupas all over the region (Sitapati, P. *et al.* 1980). In Chandravaram of Prakasham district, the stupa consisted of two terraces. The stupa was surrounded by a double railing almost 4 m in height and 133 m in circumference at the base. The railings were most richly ornamented and 59 m in diameter, which is almost double to that of Bharhut stupa.

Apart from the religious structures, many other constructions have come to light in the region during the study period. Among them, Dharanikota fort-cum-port is a significant building of this region (Ramachandran, K.S. 1975: 35). It may be mentioned that Dharanikota was a busy trading as well as political centre of the period.

In Telangana region, the selected sites, Peddabankur and Kotilingala have revealed settlements with town planning of a developed order. The structures in the Andhra phase at Peddabankur are represented by brick structures, walls, cisterns, etc., and continue further to the Satavahana period. Brick houses were built over rubble foundations. It may be noticed that there are three huge brick structures, two of them measuring 30 × 40 m and the third one 16.80 × 15.80 m. It is also found that the enclosures appeared like castles (Pl VII) and have only single gateway either in the north-east or north-west corner. The entrances which were very broad (upto 3 m) and evidently intended to allow vehicular traffic. Inside these enclosures traces of houses, wells, cisterns, etc., came to light. It has also been reported that some enclosures have two to three wells, most of which are near to the walls. The entire complex looks like a self-sufficient unit. These were evidently occupied by wealthy individual families. The size of the brick of the enclosure is 35 × 28 × 9 cm. The house planning was either rectilinear or elliptical. From enclosure

II, several thousands of Satavahana coins were unearthed (Sastry, V.V. K. 1983: 134). It was also found that the common people had their residences, outside the enclosures. They are built of mud wall with rubble basement and the roof was either made of thatches or tiles. There were 22 wells exposed during the excavations. Out of these, one is in square plan and the remaining others are round. It is also noticed that one well is lined with terracotta ring and the others are constructed with square or wedge shaped baked bricks. The bricks were well burnt and measured 30 × 20 cm long (wedge shaped) and 90 × 90 cm (square shaped). Closed drains (11.15 cm long) also came to light. It was constructed of bricks (57 × 27 × 9 cm) laid in 3 courses with a middle space of 12 cm. The drain was covered with brick to the full length. Many brick built cisterns were unearthed. These are either in perfect square (1.10-0.75 × 1.10-0.75 m) or rectangular (2.37 × 1.45 cm) in plan. Some of these had floors rammed with *morrum* and then paved with bricks to prevent percolation. It may be mentioned that none of these cisterns are near the well but found to be located at a considerable distance. The cisterns are one of the features of civic life. All these structures are datable around second or first century BCE, i.e., Andhra Phase (Sastry, V.V. K. 1983: 139). The entire complex continued to be used during Satavahana times. A shrine with a stone built platform of an elliptical plan has also been noticed. The temple like brick cells (5.30 × 4.90 m and 2.00 × 2.50 m) was noticed. Blacksmiths' workshops are also found. In all probability, the three cisterns or troughs and a hearth (22 cm broad) and the working platform studded with slag, are the remnants of a blacksmith's workshop.

Kotilingala excavations have also revealed a settlement with planning of a developed order which was protected by a defense wall. The area of settlement was divisible by roads and streets into rectangles, and the buildings were located on both the sides of roads. The early Andhra phase (upto second century BCE) is represented by the remains of dwellings and an extensive mud defense wall with bastions. Besides, a few religious and secular structures also to be used in the Andhra period. It was reinforced by bricks during the matured Andhra period. It was roughly oblong in plan and was surrounded by the river Godavari on the north and by the Kapparaopetvagu (*nullah*) on the east and south. The entrance through the fortification was available only on the western side. Thus, it seems to be a *jaladurga* (Murthy, R.N.S. 1979) and stands in close parallel to Pataliputra (Yusuf, S. 1936-37: 39-42), which stands on the confluence of river Ganga and Son. The total length of mud rampart is 1055 m from the surrounding level with a basal width of 70 m filling material revealed a total of 9 layers comprising black alluvial silt and grayish yellow *morrum* mixed with *kankar* in alternate layers. There were watchtowers or bastions on four corners (south west, south east, north east and north west). This, incidentally, is the first evidence so far known for the construction of bastion in Andhra culture level. The present temple of Koteshwara Swamy stands on the north-eastern tower. The other important structural remains unearthed were houses build of bricks (56 × 30 × 11 cm) and rubbles, stones with rubble foundation, which were rectangular (4.40 × 5.60 m) in plan. The rubble stones are arranged in rows and the gap is filled with chips. Two circular (2.58 m in diameter) brick built platforms with a central hole (1.30 m in diameter) were noticed in this phase I (second century BCE). Two storage jars with some portion completely crushed were found in the centre. Possibly, these platforms were either pounding or house of grain storage jars. Besides the above secular structure, there also existed a few religious structures. A circular wedge shaped brick built structure of 2.25 m diameter had been found. The size of the bricks varied from 32-28 × 20 × 7-6 cm. Its functional could not be ascertained. However, the excavator had compared the votive stupa, found at Salihundam (Subrahmanyam, R. 19: 32, Pl XVIII & XIX). In the next phase, i.e., Satavahana, increase in structural activities was evident. Complete brick fortification wall was built over the mud rampart with a brick revetment wall as its foot and a bastion on four corners. The bricks used are of 59-56 × 29 × 8 cm size. Besides the defense, there were many secular structures and a stupa. A circular well (2.48 m diameter) built of wedge shaped brick (25 × 18 × 71 m) was also noticed. It was connected to a drain. The northern side of the fort adjacent to the water course of the river Godavari, the brick structures in a long row which were either square or rectangular in plan, are identified as remains of a wharf. The brick structures near the water course are reminiscent of a once commercially and politically important town. It compares well with wharf-cum-navigational channel that find at Dharanikota (Raghavachari, K. 1972-73: 1-3) in the Coastal Andhra. The gate in the centre of the rampart encircling the river side at this site was built to facilitate the merchandise traffic to and from the township. The stupa in this phase was completely destroyed without leaving any traces of foundations. But a large number of stone slabs unearthed during excavations used for veneering the *vedika*, contain illegible inscriptions in *Brahmi* (second century BCE), which are beyond decipherment (Information from the excavator, Department of Archaeology and Museums, Hyderabad).

Besides the selected above sites, there are many significant structural remains in the entire region. Among them, Dhulikatta palace complex needs to be mentioned (Pl VI). A mud brick fortification belonging to the early Andhra level (around third century BCE) was unearthed here. The structural plans of the buildings inside this enclosure were beyond surmise as they were all covered by buildings of successive phase. Four cardinal points of the fort with a flight of steps and a number of rooms possibly identified as guard rooms prefaced by a gate house. Pathways were also traced, which were made of rubble *morrum* and silt (15.13 × 14 m with 4.40 m width). The structures in the fort were characterized by spacious halls with brick-paved floors, granaries, wells, buildings provided with sewage, etc. The plan of main palace building resembles that of a quadrangular building known as *chatussala*, with four rectangular halls (9.35 X 4 m) on four sides and a central open courtyard. The entire edifice forms into a square plan. In many chambers on the walls, marks of wooden beams were noticed which evidence installation of beams in masonry. Covered drains (nearly 71 cm broad) were also noticed. There are brick built granaries, which measured 1.20 × 1.35 m with a depth of 4 m; 1.35 × 1.45 × 1.60 m and the other 1.25 × 1.35 × 3 m. These are in the shape of an inverted pyramid and taper towards the floor. The bricks were laid in receding layers so that one can easily get down to the floor. The buildings were plastered with lime and burnished to smooth surface. Lime concrete was also used for paving the floors. Besides these secular structures, a stupa was also exposed. The original stupa (*c* 3rd century BCE) at Dhulikatta was enlarged and the *ayaka* platforms were embellished with a series of *ayaka* slabs during second century BCE. It is likely that the stupa at Bhattiprolu (Rea,

A. 1989: 7-16) and Chandravaram (Murthy, P.R. 1972) both in Guntur district of the Coastal Andhra region were also constructed during Andhra Period. Yeleswaram (Khan, M.A.W. 1963) in Nalgonda district is another interesting religious (Brahmanical) site in the Telangana region. The structures include bathing ghats with flight of steps, a huge *mandapa*, votive shrines, etc., during the period of study. Majority of these constructions are in Cuddapah sand stone slabs. The *mandapa* (148.80 × 40.3 m) was supported by lime stone columns. Many brick built votive shrines were also traced.

Satanikota and Veerapuram, the selected sites of Royalseema region, structural remains from the first named site is a typical example of the Andhra town. As Satanikota (Ghosh, N.C. 1986) has not only revealed a defense wall (*kota* means fort or defense wall in local language) with moat and gateway but also it is well documented as a township or administrative center of Andhra period. The fort was almost elliptical on plan and built on a promontory in an area of about 300 sq m. The main wall of the rampart was built of irregular and thin cuddapah stone slabs laid in mud mortar. The stone used was quarried from the neighborhood. The rugged external face of the wall was built with baked bricks. The elaborate gateway complex, facing south, has a flight of five steps with a width of 3 m. These were flanked by a brick wall (0.30 m thick). On either side of the third step from the bottom, there was a socket with iron casing on each side, probably meant for the two door leaves. Two pairs of post holes (about 1.80 m in diameter) were identified on the southern and northern sides at the lower steps. These post holes were probably meant for erecting heavy wooden posts which carried pullies on the top and were instrumental in flowering or lifting up the draw bridge over the moat. A deep rock cut moat (4 m wide at top and 2 m at the bottom and 3 m deep) with steep sides was defending the fort from all the sides except the parts of the north and north-west where a natural channel worked as a moat. This cutting itself was a great engineering feat at that time. Between the moat and the base of wall, was an open gallery or berme. It is the first time that the berme was noticed in an early Andhra fort (probably in India). Inside the fort, the major portion of the mound is now under occupation. A very limited area was available for excavation. However, the stables are still mentioned by their traditional names. A series of granaries (Ghosh, N.C. 1986. Pl XXXIX) with the major portion below the ground level were traced. These were rectangular (2.10-1.10 × 1.60-1.20 m) in plan. The floor as well as the walls was not plastered but the joints between the bricks were very nicely finished. It was covered by a tiled roof. Similar structures found from many other sites have been referred to in Andhra as *pataras*. A few such *pataras* have been recorded from the village Satanikota itself. Besides the above, a few chambers designed in series and adjacent rooms and had common walls in two sizes (7.50 × 3 m and 2.50 × 2 m) have also reported. Brick (57-50 × 28-25 × 8-7 cm) and Cuddapah stone slabs (both dressed and undressed) are the main building materials of this region. The foundation was filled with *morrum* and small pellets of *kankar*.

Veerapuram is another excavated site in the Royalseema region. The structural remains here are dated from the Neolithic period to the Early Historical times. An intensive building activity has been noticed from Andhra and post-Andhra periods. During the Andhra phase, floors were similar to those of the Megalithic in comparison, *i.e.*, made up of calcareous nodules. The top portion of the floor was plastered with fine earth and lime. It may be mentioned that the structure remains during this period was rural in nature. Many post-holes (nearly 11) were traced. A group of these make a circular alignment of a diameter (6 m). The post-holes also contained disintegrated wood remains, suggesting that the house was built on wooden posts. Many fire places and hearths were traced. There is a structure with three vertical slabs (60 × 40 cm) arranged like in a rectangle plan. The excavator is of the opinion that it may be the arrangement for the burial with orthostats and klinostats. But there is no evidence of bones. In the western mound, there is long charred wooden log (beam) (1.35 × 1.15 m and 1.25 × 0.12 m) with ashes of grass found *in situ*. It may be suggested that the house was constructed with wooden beams and rafters, and that the roof was covered with wild grass, which was locally available. This type of houses is still in practice in the rural areas of Andhra Pradesh. The structural activities were quite significant in the post-Andhra level. The Cuddapah stone slabs (20 × 10 cm to 90 × 40 cm range) were in use extensively. The significant construction of this phase was a massive fortification wall (20 extant courses of Cuddapah slabs), which was 23.6 m long east-west direction. Abutting it, an apsidal structure, possibly a watch tower was built. Besides, many structures like stairway, houses, floors, etc., were also traced (Sastri, T.V.G. *et al.* 1984: 32-44).

According to occidental travel accounts, the Andhra domain possesses thirty fortified town and many villages and ports and harbors at the end of first millennium BCE. Some of these towns may be identified with modern towns, such as Dharanikota (*EI* XV: 263), Gaṅtasala (Luder's No 1303), Kudura (Luder's No 1295), Kondapur, Peddabankur,

Kotilingala, Sattenapalli, Satanikota (Mangalam, S.J. 1986), etc. The *Gatha Saptasati* by Hala is a veritable literary mine of information in respect of early villages, towns and their planning of the Andhradesa. Amaravati and Nagarjunakonda sculptural art provide another evidence of urban sophistication and courtly elegance in Andhra during that time.

Table 14
Structural Activities in Early Andhra

Site	Phase	Secular	Religious	Commercial Nature and others
Salihundam	I	-	Stupas, Votive Stupas, Viharas, Chaityas, Votive Platforms, Chambers, etc.	-
	II	-	Destroyed	-
Kotilingala	I	Defense wall With bastions and town planning	Stupa	Wharf and embankment
	II	Continued	Continued but damaged	Continued
Peddabankur	I	Town planning, Brick enclosures, well & cisterns, etc	Votive shrines	Blacksmith's forge
	II	Continued	Continued	Continued
Satanikota	I	Fort, moat, gateways, etc. along with town planning	-	Furnace with iron slags
	II	Graneries, Stables etc. besides phase I	-	-
Veerapuram	I	Port-holes, houses, hearths, etc.	Votive shrines	-
	II	Fortification, Wall, housses, etc.	Temples	-

Note : Phase I - Andhra, Phase II – post-Andhra/Satavahana

The structural remains discussed above, can broadly divided into three categories, *viz.*, I Secular II Religious and III Structures of commercial nature (*cf* Table 14). Besides, good evidence for the use of building materials has also been obtained. All these categories are summarized below.

7.1 SECULAR STRUCTURES are further divisible into two groups, *viz.*, defensive or protective structures and civil constructions. The former group of structures consist of fortifications, ramparts (for defense), ditches or moats, bastions, guard rooms along with other establishments such as gateways, draw bridges, etc. It may be mentioned that town or village, which was politically or commercially important, were provided with fortification during the Andhra period. Some of these are Dharanikota, Dhulikatta, Budigepalli, etc. In case of settlements of political importance, elaborate defense devices were made, such as ramparts with bastions, ditches or moats, guard rooms, draw bridges, etc. For instance, settlements like Kotilingala and Satanikota were protected by defense wall. It may also be noticed that the fortification or defense structures appeared only in a few centers in the Andhra level. But in the late Andhra period, most of the urban as well as the rural settlements were fortified with a defense wall having two or four huge gateways, rows of guard rooms, pathways, gate houses, etc. The capital township was encircled by a fort like defense such as that of Satanikota. Elaboration of defenses, therefore, appears to be related to the political power.

Civil constructions during the period of our study include various types of houses, roads, drainage system, wells and cisterns, storage rooms (underground), granaries, etc. The Andhra period, in the entire region has revealed many centers with developed system of town planning. The houses found in this period, were built over rubble foundation, which were rectangular or square in plan. Majority of the houses were enclosed by compound walls. In general, rooms are arranged in one alignment along with common *verandah*. The walls are usually made of clay or mud bricks during the Andhra period. However, some important structures were constructed with burnt bricks also. The palace complex and residential quarters evidence spacious rectangular halls along with many rooms which were constructed over rubble foundation, such as at Dhulikatta (Sastry, V.V. K. 1983: 136-138). At Peddabankur, many wells (22) and cisterns were exposed. Majority of the wells were paved with brick platforms and were connected with drains. Besides, closed drains were provided with sewage. Long broad roads were intercepted by cross roads and bylanes, some of which were paved. At Satanikota and Dhulikatta, brick built rectangular granaries were also unearthed. From Kondapur excavations, underground chambers (6 in all) were found. Some of them (3 out of 6) are double chamber with a partition wall in the center, ranging in depth from 5 to 25 feet. The floor is paved with bricks and laid flat. Many new settlements grew up in the post-Andhra level. Burnt bricks, lime, brick and rubble floors are the main features of most of the houses. The rooms with central courtyard were rectangular or square in plan. Drains with ring and brick walls are also evidenced.

7.2 RELIGIOUS STRUCTURES are further regrouped into two, *viz.*, Buddhist and others. Majority of the structures of the Andhra level are Buddhist. It may be mentioned that there are more than five dozen sites recognized as Buddhist establishment in the entire region. Some of the important sites among these are Amaravati, Salihundam, Thotlakonda, Bhattiprolu, Kesarapalli, Gantasala, Bhavikonda,

Chandravaram, Goli, Jaggayapeta, Kondapur, Kotilingala, Vatakapura and many others. Majority of them were located in the Coastal Andhra region. Buddhism, particularly Hinayana, laid great stress on the veneration of the stupa along with *chaityas,* votive stupa and platforms. In the post-Andhra period, these were geared up by some developments including secular structures such as viharas, congregation halls, *bhandagaras,* refractory *(bhojanshala*), etc., along with civil constructions like cisterns, stone pathways and drainage.

Kappiyabhumi are kitchen complex (Upasak, C.S. 1975) and is a place outside the actual dwelling in which the provisions could be kept or cooked. The separation of *kappiyabhumi* from the main complex was probably intended to preserve the tranquility and sanctity of the *vihara*. The *kappiyabhumi* at Thotlakonda appears to have been built in this area as it lies at a lower gradient and adjoins a big water tank. The complex consists of rectangular halls varying in dimensions, some of which might have been used as store rooms while others as refractories (Sastry, V.V. K. 1992, Fig 11).

The *Bhandagara* or store room was meant for keeping the precious material and the robes (*civara*) of the monks. At Thotlakonda (Sastry, V.V. K. *et al.* 1992. Pl XXV), it is situated on the lowest terrace of the complex in a rectangular hall facing north (12.25 × 5.15 m) had a finely plastered floor.

Though the other group of structures in this religious category also appeared during the Andhra level, yet its proportion is very low and in primitive stage. A few votive shrines are noticed. In this regard Guddimallam Shivalingam in Chittoor district is noteworthy (Sarma, I.K. 1974). But in the post-Andhra level, this category (other than the

Buddhist) of structures appears in a great number in the entire region. Many new structures such as temples, bathing ghats, *mandapas* (pillared halls), etc., were constructed during the post-Andhra period. It may be mentioned that though both of the structures were found in the post-Andhra period, the new constructions belong to Brahmanical group, which were more than the Buddhist structures. However, the former building type of Buddhist pantheon continued with some new extensions and additions. Moreover, during the study period, Buddhist establishments were large in number than others.

7.3 STRUCTURE OF COMMERCIAL NATURE: In this category of constructions, wharfs, navigational channels and embankments in port or navigational related structures, and other craft related constructions like furnaces, workshops (smith), etc., were also noticed. Wharf is a brick built platform along the river bank or the seashore for the loading and unloading of ships. At Dharanikota (Margabandhu, C. 1990) a brick built wharf-cum-navigational channel was noticed, which was in use in both the phases, the early Andhra and the Satavahana. Similarly, a brick construction of wharf has been noticed from Kotilingala, which was dated to early Andhra period. Brick built smith's workshops have been noticed not only from the craft centers like Kondapur, but also in the large settlement areas like Satanikota, Dharanikota, etc.

7.4 BUILDING MATERIALS are grouped into four categories depending upon the function in the construction, *viz.*, materials used in foundation, material used in structure, plastering material and roof material.

Materials used in foundations are generally rubbles. In some cases, it was found as baked bricks or stones. Mud mortar is common. In some cases the foundations were filled with *morrum* but some pieces of *kankar* were used as filling material in all the cases. These were common foundation materials during the Early Historic period, which have been found in all categories of structures. But the material used in the body or walls, differs in categories and phases. Mud, mud bricks, baked bricks and undressed and dressed stone slabs were the main construction material during the period of study. However, mud and mud bricks are in general, common materials in the early Andhra level. The baked bricks were used for some specific purposes. Majority of the defense or fortification walls and religious structures were initially made of mud but were rebuilt or reinforced by bricks or stones in later times. In mature Andhra period, the baked brick was the main building material for all the secular as well as other constructions. It may be mentioned that the bricks was carefully prepared out of moulds with sharp edges. It was also found that bigger size (57 × 28 × 7 cm) bricks were used in fortification walls and religious structures (stupas) while the smaller (50 × 20 × 4 cm) size were found to be used in secular buildings, in general. Cuddapah stone slabs were another popular building material during the period of study, particularly in the Coastal Andhra and Royalseema regions. These were used with baked bricks as well as independently. Their major use was however, confined to the fortifications, floors and stair cases, and religious establishments. Undressed boulders were used mainly in the repairs of fortifications and in raising the heights of the outer embankments of the moats or such similar heavy and rough works. Mud was used in building as well as plastering material in the early Andhra constructions. But it was replaced by lime in the early centuries of present era. The material remains probably which were used in roofs, help us to trace out the types of the roof. The carbonized material remains of thatches, grass, bamboo or wooden pieces, etc., and tiles along with a large number of nails are found in many archaeological sites. Occurrence of these materials suggests that the roofs were not only having various types, but also made of various materials. It was a general practice in the humblest of dwellings to use broad and wide leaves of trees, evidently of palm and coconut, woven into a pattern, on bamboo and reed frames. Similar type of roofed houses is quite common in the Andhra Pradesh villages even now. In this context, the earliest circular houses are found even today among the Boyassemi and Chenchu nomadic tribes (Ray, A. 1983: 177). Considerable number of tiles are found in most of the archaeological sites in the entire region during study period. These are found in different shapes such as perforated, convex, concave, etc. Sites of Satanikota, Peddabankur, Kotilingala and Dhulikatta have yielded considerable number of tiles in different shapes along with iron nails, suggesting use of tiles for covering roofs.

In the Andhra phase, large and small settlements, in general, were protected by the fortification wall. Some of them which were politically important were provided with elaborate defenses which included deep moats, bastions, guard rooms, gate houses, etc. Well established town planning with intersecting streets and roads have been noticed during this period. The houses were constructed in a regular plan along with roads, streets and narrow lanes. Burnt bricks were molded in standard size. Lime, rubble floors, tiles, etc., were used in the constructions. Drains with terracotta rings, brick wells, soakage jars and pits were also noticed. These settlements developed into townships, which were politically important as well as trade, and craft centers in later period and many of them are still important centers in the region. Many religious establishments, primarily Buddhist, were noticed during this period, especially in the coastal Andhra region. Besides, many port towns and port-cum-fort towns were also established in the Coastal Andhra region and on the banks of large rivers. A development of such urban centers appears to be due to two factors, *viz.* accessibility of transportation by the rivers and the sea and surplus production of export items such as species, precious stones and other luxury items. Navigation and mechanization were important modes for the exchange of goods. The architecture and the other antiquities, indicate urbanization of the Andhra region during the period under study. However, there also existed a number of rural settlements like Veerapuram, which though was using permanent materials for buildings, could not develop into a real township.

In the next phase, *i.e.*, under Satavahanas, growth of urbanization was very pronounced. For, besides the expansion of the early cities, some of the villages also became towns along with a few urban settlements. The establishments of new towns were due to mostly for administrative and political reasons. In architecture, massive strong building reflecting elaborate defenses and imperial power is evident. For example, establishments of forts, structures inside the fort included palaces, dormitories for Royal retinue, stadium, stables, barracks, etc., were made. The most noteworthy feature of the Satavahana period is the demarcation of the residential area. Within a township of political nature, there was the fort area, which was utilized by the Royal persons and which included massive and elaborate residential building of the king and his courtiers. This area was well protected. Contrary to this, the residences of common people were confined to the outer periphery of the township. All the dwellings of this category were located outside the fortified fort area. But this area had all civic amenities such as well planned residences, drainage system wells, cisterns, etc. It was further noted that role of religion to the building activities was at the minimum during Satavahana times. Only some of the earlier Buddhist structures were renovated or enlarged. However, the sumptuous sculptural embellishments on stupas were extensively enlarged under the school of Satavahanas. Besides, though the earlier ports and port townships continued to exist, there were no new important settlements, which were established during this period. It may be noted that the long distance trade had almost lost its grounds during Satavahanas times.

REFERENCES

Ghosh, N.C. 1986. *Excavations at Satanikota* (1977-80). Memoirs of the Archaeological Survey of India. No 82. New Delhi.

Khan, M.A.W. 1963. *A Monograph on Yeleswaram Excavations*. Andhra Pradesh Archaeological series. No XIV. Government of Andhra Pradesh. Hyderabad.

Luders, H. 1912. A List of Brahmi Inscriptions from the Earliest Time to about A.D. 400 with the exception of those of Asoka. *Epigraphica Indica*. Appendix. Calcutta.

Mangalam, S.J. 1986. *Historical Geography and Toponomy of Andhra Pradesh*. New Delhi.

Margabandhu, C. 1990. Material culture during the Early Historic period (C. 300 BC-300 A.D.) (As revealed from excavated remains). *South Indian Studies*. Dr. T.V. Mahalingam commemoration volume. (eds) Nayak, H.M. and B.R. Gopal. Mysore: 53-69.

Murthi, N.S.R. 1979. Forts in Andhra Pradesh. Unpublished thesis. Karnataka University. Dharwar.

Murthy, P.R. 1972. *Excavations at Chandravaram, Prakasham district*. Unpublished. Hyderabad.

Raghavachari, K. 1972-73. Dharanikota and its western contacts. *Quarterly Review of Historical Studies*. Calcutta. XII, 3: 1-3.

Ramachandran, K.S. 1975. *Radiocarbon Dates of Archaeological Sites in India.* Archaeological series. No 42. Government of Andhra Pradesh. Hyderabad.

Ray, A. 1983. *Life and Art of Early Andhradesa*. Delhi.

Rea, A. 1989 (reprint). *South Indian Buddhist Antiquities including the stupa of Bhattiprolu, Gudivada and Gantasala, and other Ancient sites in the Krishna district, Madras presidency*. Archaeological Survey of India. New Imperial series Vol. XV. (first published in 1814). New Delhi.

Sarma, I.K. 1974. Gudimallam–Sivalayam. *Bharati* (in Telugu). Hyderabad. 51, 8, August: 7-11.

Sastri, T.V.G., Bai, M.K. and J.V.P.R. Rao. 1984. *Veerapuram*, a type site for cultural study in the Krishna valley. Hyderabad.

Sastry, V.V. K. 1983. *The proto and Early History of Andhra Pradesh.* Government of Andhra Pradesh. Hyderabad.

Sastry, V.V. K., Subrahmanyam, B. & N.R.K. Rao. 1992. *Thotlakonda* (A Buddhist site in Andhra Pradesh) Andhra Pradesh Government Archaeological series. No 68. Hyderabad.

Sitapati, P. & V.V. K. Sastry. 1986. *New Satavahana Sculptures from Andhra Amravati*. Archaeological Series. No 54. The Government of Andhra Pradesh. Hyderabad.

Upasak, C. 1975. *Dictionary of Early Buddhist Monastic Terms*. Varanasi.

Yusuf, S. 1936-37, Paithan Excavations. *Annual Report of the Archaeological Department of His Exalted Highness the Nizam's Dominions*. Hyderabad.

Chapter 8

MISCELLANEOUS OBJECTS

In order to assess the potentiality of the culture of the region, other categories of objects such as ornaments, weights and measures, stone objects, coins, etc., were also studied, details of which form subject of the present chapter.

8.1 ORNAMENTS AND LUXURY ITEMS

This category of objects are diverse in nature and varied in forms. They are grouped into beads, bangles, rings and ear ornaments. Luxury or toilet objects comprise combs, antimony rods, skin rubbers, caskets or jewellery boxes, nail parers, etc. All these items were found to be made in various materials like metal, stone, ivory, bone, terracotta, etc.

8.1.1 BEADS are one of the major antiquarian wealth of all the Early Historical sites in general and in the case of Andhra Pradesh too. The word bead is derived from the saxon verb 'biddan' meaning 'to pray', and was originally associated with the 'beads' on rosary. In the present context, it means almost any pierced object which can be strung. Majority of archaeological excavations have yielded a large number of beads in the entire region, especially in Telangana, *i.e.*, Kondapur. It is also noticed that nearly two dozen types of materials were used for the preparation of beads during this period. They include stone (both precious and semi-precious), metal, bone, shell, coral, glass, terracotta, etc. were noticed in the collections.

Materials used in the bead craft may be noted with interest because all materials were not locally available. Amethyst was an indigenous product in the Deccan whereas lapis lazuli was an imported item and thus, very sparingly used. It was probably obtained mostly from the Persia and Afghanistan. The nearest source where beryl was available may be at Gudur district of the southern Coastal Andhra. For carnelian, the principal source was the Ratnapur deposits in Gujarat. Another interesting material used for beads was faience. It is a product of fine powdered quartz mixed with a small quantity of flex material. A small amount of alkali might have been added in many cases to enable the quartz to fuse together at a low temperature. It is a material best known in Egypt.

In the Early Historic period of Andhra Pradesh, the use of raw material for making beads in the selected sites (*cf* Tale 13) indicates that glass was the most common medium. Next in popularity were shell and terracotta. All other medium were used sparingly in low to very low production.

Table 15 shows that beads were common to both the cultural periods but their proportion was very high in the post-Andhra or Satavahana period. Along with increased quantity, materials as well as typological variations were also vast in the post-Andhra phase. Terracotta beads, however, appear in very high proportion, in all the levels. Majority of them were wheel made as indicated by the close grooves on the exterior of many of the beads. However, hand made beads were also traced in low proportion.

Table 15
Materialwise Distribution of Beads

Type	Salihundam	Kotilingala	Peddabankur	Satanikota	Veerapuram
Agate	-	P	P	P	P
Amethyst	-	P	P	-	P
Bone	-	-	P	-	P
Baryl	-	-	P	-	-
Carnelian	-	P	P	P	P
Chalcedoney	-	P	P	-	P
Crystal	-	P	P	-	P
Faience	-	P	P	-	P
Garnet	-	P	P	-	P
Glass	-	P	P	P	P
Gold	-	P	P	-	P
Jasper	-	P	P	P	P
Lapis Lazuli	-	P	P	-	P
Oyster	-	P	P	-	-
Opaque	-	P	P	-	-
Oyster Pearl/ Quartz	P	-	-	-	-
Shell	-	P	P	P	P
Silica	-	P	P	-	P
Steatile	-	P	P	-	P
Terracotta	P	P	P	P	P

* The date bracket of these objects is c 400 BCE to CE 300

Table 16
Frequency of Beads

Type	1		2		3		4		5	
	I	II	I	II	I	II	I	II	I	II
Terracotta	40%	38%	46%	30%	31%	30%	40%	36%	95%	92%
Semi-precious Stones	10%	12%	7%	12%	10%	12%	-	2%	-	-
glass	5%	15%	2%	19%	2%	19%	N.K.	40%	-	-
Faience	8%	10%	3%	10%	0.2%	05%	-	-	-	-
Metal	2%	10%	1%	6%	.02%	.02%	-	-	-	-
Shell	5%	10%	5%	9%	30%	38%	N.K.	5%	-	-
Others	30%	5%	36	12%	27%	11%	N.K	18%	5%	8%

N.K. = Not known

1. Paddabankur 2. Kotilingala 3. Veerapuram 4. Satanikota

5. Salihundam I - Andhra Culture II - Satavahana Culture

Similarly, many technical advances and artistic expressions have appeared in the bead craft of the region like the other parts of the Indian sub-continent (Kenoyer, J.M. 1986: 18-23). For example, many geometrical designs, etched on natural stones by chemical application in required designs, metal foils in glass, millefiore and several other techniques in the mode of glass fabrication (Francis, P.J. 1982), faience material preparation, etc., are noteworthy.

From Pedddabankur and Kotilingala, a considerable number of beads in different materials have been noticed. The gold beads were made of thin foils of the metal which included tabloid and octagonal shape. It was noticed that to prevent the bead from squeezing by threading, a cylindrical glass bead was inserted into the hollow spaces formed by foil cover. At Peddabankur, a complete necklace (43 beaded) was found. It was composed of amethyst (24), lapis lazuli (7), gold (2), jasper (1) and other beads. Besides, many hundreds of beads (Sastry, V.V. K. 1983: 219) were found in different materials and shapes (more than 100 beads have been studied by the present author). Majority of them in this case also are of terracotta (nearly 45%). Next to the terracottas were the semi-precious, shell and glass beads. Similar tendency has been seen at Kotilingala also (nearly 100 specimens have been studied). Among them, a necklace of beads, shaped like sub-disc with radiating lines, *Nandipada*, frog, tortoise, gadrooned cylinders, etc. is noteworthy (Pl VIII B). These beads are made of think foils of gold, made into two separate facets and pressed together. The necklace resembles like a '*Grahamala*' (representing the planets) (Sastry, V.V. K. 1983: 219).

In the case of Veerapuram, the glass beads were found to be predominating in the post-Andhra level, but their proportion was very low in the Andhra level (less than 5%). The high proportion of the glass beads in the post-Andhra level indicates that the glass technology was mastered and that the medium had gained popularity in the later time. Similarly, the shell and jasper also appear in good percentage in the Satavahana levels. The limited number of metal beads particularly gold (5 in all) are noticed during the period under study. It is quite possible that the settlements survived under rural condition in Andhra level and became an urban centre in later period.

Beads obtained from Salihundam not only appeared in meager quantity but also only two mediums were used. Majority of them in this case were also made of terracotta.

At Satanikota, the beads were found in good quantity but their shapes and materials were of limited nature. Here also, terracotta was the most preferred medium.

Among the selected sites of the Telangana region, Kondapur, Dhulikatta and Yeleswaram have yielded a very good number of beads. Among them, the collection from the first named site was found particularly useful for this section. Kondapur (Dikshit, M.G. 1952; Margabandhu, C. 1978: 35-46) not only revealed good quantity (23, 391) of beads but the group also shows use of different variety of materials and production of varied shapes. The bead craft appears to be well developed here as was unearthed at Paithan (Yusuf, S. 1936-37: 39-42, Pl XIX, XX) and Maski (Thapar, B.K. 1985: 4-142) in the Deccan.

Clay medium for making beads dominated at Kondapur also. Next to the terracotta were Glass (700), faience (200), Amethyst (200), Chalcedony (90), Crystal (60), Shell (60), Carnelian (30), Lapis lazuli (25), Garnet (8), Jasper (70), Bone (3), Agate (3), Quartz (3), Jade (1), Beryl (1), etc. Gold beads were reported with enamel work. It is also noticed that some of the Buddhist symbols were reported in the bead forms such as *triratna*, the pippal leaf, the *harmika* of the stupa, the altar, etc. Quite a large number of bull amulets were found in terracotta. The *swastika*, the *srivatsa* and the *Gajalakshmi* motives are among the other symbols represented in the beads. Clay medallions and imitation of Roman coins were also noticed. Another interesting specimen is the glass bead containing an amount of gold foil and a Ruby red bead over a opaque necklace. It seems that Kondapur had also developed as a bead craft centre during the period of study.

Materials used in the manufacture of beads show the significance and importance attached to this craft. The semi-precious stones including some of the non-indigenous sources were in use on a large scale in the region under study. Some materials like lapis lazuli were imported. Another interesting material used for beads, is faience which is found in colors. Glass in multi-colors was used much widely during the late Andhra level. It was used not only as a single item but also used in and along with the metal beads. The technique of mixing metal foils (gold and Silver) with the glass, seems to have been perfected and probably inspired by the western countries. It is also found that carnelian was another favorite material. Materials like terracotta and shell are found very extensively in the entire region. Metals like gold, silver and copper were found fairly in a considerable frequency.

Certain shapes provided a clue to relative dating and the characteristic features of the bead craft. For example, collared grooved and lug and gadrooned were found much popular during *circa* 200 BCE to CE 200. Similarly, circular beads, barrel-shaped beads with lug collar and lenticular section, etc., typical forms were found in between first century BCE and third century CE. Areca nut shaped terracotta beads were predominantly found from *circa* 200 BCE to CE 200 these shapes are comparable with similar beads from Taxila (Beck, H.C. 1941 : 38), Ahichchatra (Dikshit, M.G. 1985 : 33-63), Maski (Thapar, B.K. 1985 : 32), etc. Among the elaborated bead types, the most characteristic form is the lenticular colored bead, which is repeated in almost all materials. Most of the general geometric shapes have been found in semi-precious like Carnelian and Agate. Among them, bicone-square and hexagonal, long and short barrel square, circular tablet, gadroon, etc. are noteworthy. The *triratna*, pippal leaf,

Swastika, *Gajalakshmi*, bull, etc., religious symbols are also frequently found in the form of beads from many sites like Kondapur. The tablet bead is also a common type during the period of study. Majority of terracotta beads were in an areca nut shape. It is a very common type and occurs over a wide area during Early Historical period.

8.1.2 Bangles

Bangles and rings are another common ornament from very ancient time. The material used was diverse out of which glass and shell were used on a large scale for bangles and the rings during the period of study. A few terracotta bangles were also noticed. Besides, metal bangles such as gold, silver, copper and lead were also recovered from Andhra and Satavahana level. Glass became a common material for fashioning bangles and rings from the second century BCE onwards. However, prolific use of glass for manufacture of bangles is attested from the first century CE. The polychrome glass bangles also appeared from the first century CE (Dikshit, M.G. 1969: 34-35). The most popular colors were blue, green, red and black with various shades and combinations. Majority of bangles from Veerapuram are black. Different shapes of bangles were found such as round, rectangular, etc. The shell bangles are not perfect circular in shape since these were cut from conch shell and retained the basic morphology of the present media. Majority of them are devoid of any decoration. Metal bangles, many of them were also plain without any ornamentation. Other materials like ivory and bone were also used for bangles and rings, but their use was very restricted.

From Peddabankur and Kotilingala, a considerable number of bangles were traced in different materials. Copper and lead bangles were found with simple ornamentation. A lead bangle (4 cm in diameter) from Peddabankur is decorated with peripheral serration like the cogs of wheel. From Kotilingala, a copper bangle of spherical thin wire was noticed. Besides, many glass and shell bangles have been reported. At Veerapuram, shell bangles dominate in both Andhra as well as post-Andhra phases. The monochrome and bichrome glass bangles were found from *c* 50 BCE onwards. Similar trend has also been found at Satanikota. Some of them are similar to those found at Nevasa (Sankalia, H.D. *et al.* 1960: 459).

8.1.3 Ear Ornaments

Ear Ornaments of various shapes and materials were also noticed in the excavated remains of our region. Chronologically the early forms are know from about third century BCE in the entire region. From Peddabankur and Kotilingala, the ear ornaments like spools, lobes, etc., were noticed both the copper as well as lead. These are in different sizes (8.2-2.8 cm in length and 1.2 cm in diameter). In contrast, a glass ear ornament perhaps Greeko-Roman in origin, was the noteworthy finds of Andhra level (first century BCE) at Dharanikota (Raghavachari, K. 1972-73: 1- 3).

Many types of ornaments in different materials were traced during the period of study. Among them, some of the Kondapur finds are interesting. A number of crescent shaped terracotta pendents (16) from Satavahana level (c 2nd CE) were found. They appear to have been worn on the forehead (Dikshit, M.G 1952: 252, Pl V). Similar objects were also discovered from Satavahana levels at Brahmapuri (Sankalia, D.D. *et al.* 1952: 96, Pl XXVI B-2).

Among the toilet objects, a copper jewellery box from Peddabankur is noteworthy. It consists of shallow dish and knobbed lid. The dish has a prominent cord at the rim to hold the lid. The rim of the lid is decorated with stepped moldings and a prominent cord around the knob. Similar type of jewellery boxes is represented from the sculptures of Nagarjunakonda (Murty, K.K. 1977: 156).

Another interesting object is ivory comb of Dhulikatta. It has been carved on both sides. One of the sides has the figure of a woman holding a mirror in her left hand and combing her hair with the right hand. The hair is plaited the coiled. On the other side, she appears with finished hairdo with coiffeur. Unfortunately, it was found in a damaged condition. Similar type of ivory combs with carved figures was noticed from Sircap (Ghosh, A. 1947-48: 79-80). Sculptures at Amaravati (Murty, K.K. 1977, Pl XXVIII b & XXXII a) and Nagarjunakonda (Murthy, K.K. 1977) also present the use of similar type of combs and hair dressing scenes.

The ornaments and luxury items unearthed from the Early Historical levels of Andhra indicate over all affluence of the societies. Bead craft and ornaments were present in developed forms which indicate local production as well as import. It was observed by the present researcher that though Satavahana period appears to be richer in ornaments and the luxury items. It was the Andhra Culture period where in foreign goods were more in fashion. Illustrative examples of this tendency can be seen in the form of Roman gold coins used as pendants during the Andhra period. Besides, these coins were imitated in clay and were also used as pendants perhaps by common folks during this period.

8.2 WEIGHTS AND MEASURES

Many such objects have been found from the excavations which were prepared from terracotta, metal and stones and were presumably used as weights (Margabandhu, C. 1977: 15-25). For example, copper and stone like granite and horn blende-gneiss objects are found as heavy weights, while jasper and chert were used as small weights. Jasper weights are found in spherical shapes. These were also polished and their sides were rubbed off for affording base. Spherical granite stone weights were also noticed in different sizes. All of them fall into a regular binary sequence or ratios. Besides, terracotta objects which appear to have been used as weights occur in the entire region in good quantity. These are in different shapes and sizes. For example, from Salihundam, crescent shaped terracotta objects were found while at Peddabankur, these are in spherical shapes of various sizes. Stone weights in many sizes were traced from the entire region, such as Satanikota, Peddabankur, Kotilingala, etc.

Many measuring pots in different shapes and sizes were also noticed from Peddabankur, Dhulikatta and Kotilingala. From Dhulikatta, a large number of globular shaped measures have been discovered from the palace complex. They are in different sizes and compares well with the description found in Kautillya's Arthashastra (Kangle, R.P. 1992: 134, 136-137). The literary references of Arthashastra are equivalent to modern measurements of *saravas* or *kumbhas* (nearly 4 kg), half-*saravas* and quarter *saravas*. These were used as a measure of grains. From Peddabankur straight sided measuring vessels have been found in a good number. Similar type of vessels made of iron shuts are very common measures in present rural areas which are known as *addas* or *manikas* (nearly one kg). Comparable measuring pots are reported from Peddabankur and Dhulikatta, which were stamped with *Nandipada* or trident. The excavator has suggested that the *Nandipada* was another Royal standard mark (Sastry, V.V. K. 1983: 2008), used during Andhra and post-Andhra periods, and perhaps could be associated to the system laid down by the imperial administration.

Both weights and measuring pots which are found from the Andhra and Satavahana cultures suggest a marketing system governed by established administration and systematic trade.

8.3 COINS

Coins are reported extensively from the entire region of our study. These could broadly be divided into two categories, viz., local and foreign issues (*cf* Table 17).

Metal employed in the locally issued coins were copper, lead, potin and silver. Majority of them are made of lead and potin. In the absence of silver in south India, lead was the only alternative with which the early Andhras maintained the monetary balance between the two currency systems, *i.e.*, copper in the north and silver in the west (Srivastava, B. 1968: 178). Silver coins were introduced in the region from the time of Gautamiputra Satavahana (Smith, V.A. 1972: 208).

The foreign currency in the region was obtained especially from the Roman traders in the form of bullion, besides some authorized issues. Hence these coins were either melted for making ornaments or were hoarded as gold and silver bullions (Srivastava, B. 1968: 191). Besides, many local as well as north Indian minted copper and silver Punch Marked coins were also found in use in this region.

In the collections of coins, early ones belonged to the punch marked variety. In excavations, punch marked moulds and casts of coins have been discovered from Andhra. For instance, punch marked moulds from Dhulikatta (Pl IXA) and similar coins from Peddabankur (Pl IXB) provide a clue to the fact that these were locally minted coins. However, the north Indian types (Gupta, P.L. 1965) Punch Marked coins (pre-Mauryan and Mauryan types) were also noticed in the stratified layers (of Andhra level) as well as in the form of hoards in almost the entire region. This group can be associated with the import of coins from the north and north-west, the nuclear region of Mauryan empire.

The second group belongs to the un-inscribed coins which were found from several places in the region such as Kondapur, Kotilingala, Phanigiri, Nandalpur, Veerapuram, etc. Chronologically they may be assigned to a period between fourth/third and second century BCE. Generally, the obverse symbols include elephant, bull, camel, lion, arched hill, *swastika*, bow and arrow, etc., while the reverse is either blank or contain *ujjaini, swastika, Naga* or *damaru*, etc. These coins have been ascertained as issues small regional local dynasties of the beginning of the Early Historical period in India.

Inscribed coins during the period under study have been divided into two groups, *viz*., issues by Andhra chiefs and the Satavahana Royal persons. Kotilingala excavations have yielded the earliest inscribed coins of the region (Gupta, P.L. 1979: 17-28; Reddy, R.D. *et al.* 1991). In fact, the coins of Gobadha, Kamvyasa, Naranasa and Samagopa are known only for the first time from the site which is dated from third to first century BCE. Gobadha (layer 6, 3 and 2; 16 coins from surface) coins are copper issues. The obverse symbols include, bow-arrow, arched hill, variegated lines with dots on either side besides the authority name such as Gobadha while the reverse is invariably blank. Samagopa coins are obtained from the same site and Peddabankur (Rao, M.R. 1961) and Dhulikatta (Sarma, I.K. 1978: 66), all in Karimnagar district of Telangana region. They are made of copper and in shape range from square, oblong or rectangular. On the obverse, these bear multiple symbols like *swastika*, trident, *ujjaini* symbols, *sadara chakra*, bow and arrow, tree in railing and bull. On the reverse, all coins bear only one symbol, *i.e.*, *Triratna* or *Nandipada* around a circle in double line.

The second group of coins belongs to the Satavahanas and their feudatories (Rapson, E.S. 1989: XV; Sarma, I.K. 1980: 126-27). The coinage of the Early Historical period of Andhra, particularly that of the Satavahana times is marked by more than one types of coin were, however, issued during this period reflecting multipurpose monetary systems such as the local use, and money for long distance trade. Sea route long distance trade is also reflected by a group of coins. The issue of ship type coins by the Satavahana rulers, *viz.*, Vasistputra Pulamavi and Yajnasatakarni (Mirashi, V.V 1941) are of particular significance. Further, the occurrence of Yajna Satakarni coin at Chebrolu in the middle Coastal Andhra region (Reddy, R. *et al.* 1991: 50) supports this presumption.

Wide occurrence of Roman coins (*c* 50 BCE-CE 217) is attested to from this region. This group (*cf* Table 18) indicates the vast sea bourn long distance trade contacts of Andhradesa during early centuries of the Common Era. Majority of these were Augustus to Nero (*c* 50 BCE-CE 50). It may be mentioned that there appear to be a large demand for Indian luxuries by the Roman aristocrats who was traded. The coins hoards are found from those areas which were centers for the production of luxury goods. Besides, cotton growing areas were also suitable for trading items (Satyanarayana, K. 1975: 147). It has also been noticed that a large extent of coin bulla have been found with objects of Roman character. These consist of copies of imitations in clay media of Roman coins with similar symbols. In contrast, Roman imitation silver coins (55) from Akkenapalle hoard (Singh, A.K. 1981: 35) are noteworthy. However, majority of imitation coins were made of terracotta composition. Most of them have been pierced at top suggesting their use as ornaments, e.g., Kondapur (Dikshit, M.G. 1952. Pl VI), Nagarjunakonda (*IAR* 1956-57. Pl LXI), etc.

All these evidences put together, would suggest the flourishing long distance trade between the Andhra region and the Western world, in which Roman coins appear to have played a significant role. Prevalence of Roman coins appears to be a characteristic feature of Andhra Period. Besides, issue of coins by Andhra chiefs is also noteworthy. Similarly, use of Punch Marked coins, both the local variety and the imported ones, were also another noteworthy feature of this period. In contrast to this, most of the coins in circulation in the succeeding phase were issues of the Satavahana kings suggesting Royal hold on the monetary transactions. However, the earlier varieties such as Punch Marked and Roman coins also continue side by side.

8.4 OTHER OBJECTS

Many stone objects were recovered from the region during the Early Historic period. Among them, millers, querns, flat stones, spherical balls, hammer stones, rubber stones, etc., were important. Majority of them are constituents of the kitchen equipments. Though most of them were of earlier origin, quite a few were further improved during the Early Historic period (Sankalia, H.D. *et al.* 1957: 209-212). For example, from Veerapuram, Peddabankur, Kotilingala, Satanikota and Nagarjunakonda good quantities of stone objects were unearthed.

The other materials like bone, shell, horn, ivory, etc., were also used for different purposes during the period under study. The horn objects mainly consisted of arrow heads. Many dice or game objects have been noticed from the sites like Peddabankur in bone and ivory (Pl II B).

The study of the above miscellaneous objects further attests the artistic expression and technical developments in the different crafts of the Early Historic Andhra Pradesh people. For example, adoption of glass technology, preparation of new materials like faience and luxury goods, etc. are some of the noteworthy features which can be related to the mastery of various types of technologies.

Among the ornaments, the bead making craft was very developed. The technology of making beads out of different materials was highly advanced. Imported materials and techniques indicate the craftsmen's inter-regional contacts and adoption of non-indigenous techniques and material. The artistic caskets, combs and skin rubbers show that even the small objects were so much minutely decorated. All these rich repertoires of ornaments and toilet objects indicate the trend towards luxurious items. The affluence of the contemporary society is reflected by this group and also the import of foreign items of decoration.

The use of coins in Andhra Pradesh was introduced for the first time during the Andhra Period. This feature appears to be the import of idea, technology and some of the actual coins from the north, e.g. Gangetic plains. For, the earliest group of Punch Marked coins of this region was in circulation in North India at least a couple of centuries before it appears in Andhra. However, a few local issue authorized coins have also been found in restricted areas. Also a little later, another variety of foreign coins viz., Roman coins as a local politico-economic trade came into being in full developed form. For a number of Satavahana rulers and their feudatories issued quite a few varieties of coins for various purposes of money transactions.

Table 17
Early Coinage in Andhara Pradesh

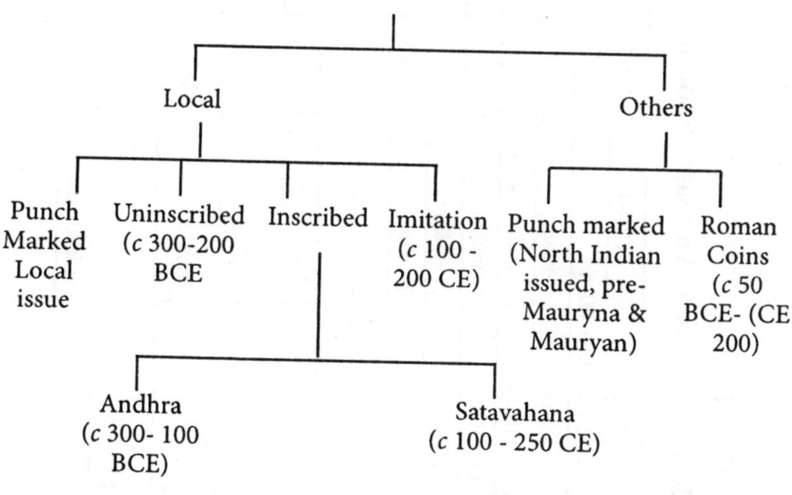

Table 18
Roman Coins in Andhara Pradesh

Site	District	Metal	Total	Provenance	Authority	Reference
COASTAL ANDHRA						
Amaravati	Guntur	Silver		STL	N.K.	*IAR 1973 –74* :4
Bhavikonda	Vishakhapatnam	Silver	2	STL	Tiberius	*IAR 1983 –84* :20
Bhavikonda	Vishakhapatnam	Silver	1	STL	Augustus	*AAR 1985-86* :15
Chandravaram	Prakasham	Silver	1	STL	Augustus	*IAR 1972 –73* :3
Gantasala	Krishna	Gold	N.K	Surface	N.K	*IAR 1984 – 85* :5
Gumda		Gold	23	N.K		Gupta, P.L 1965 :45
Kotapad			4	N.K	Augustus & Tiberius	Gupta, P.L 1965 :45
Nagarjunakonda	Guntur	Gold	4	N.K	Tiberius etc.	Khan, H.H.1990 :64
Nellore	Nellore	Gold	N.K.	Hoard	Ending with Antonius	Wheeler, R.E.M.1983:118-120
Mallayapalam	Guntur	Gold	4	N.K.	-	Wheeler, R.E.M.1983:118-120
Ongole	Ongole	Gold	2	N.K	Nero& Hadrian	Wheeler, R.E.M.1983:118-120
Salihundam	Srikakulam	Gold	2	Hoard	Tiberius	Gupta, P.L.1965 :45

Contd...

Vijayawada	Krishna	Gold	N.K	Surface	N.K.	Wheeler, R.E.M.1983:118-120
Vinukonda	Krishna	Gold	15	Hoard	Vespalian etc.	Wheeler, R.E.M.1983:118-120
TELANGANA REGION						
Akkenpalle	Nalgonda	Silver	153	Hoard	-	Singh, A.K. 1988 :35
Gaiparti	Nalgonda	Gold	3	N.K	-	ARN 1933 ; 7
Kondapur	Medak	Gold	1	STL	Augustus	Dikshit, M.G.1952
Nasthullapur	Karimnagar	Gold	3	N.K	Augustus & Tiberius	Gupta, P.L.1965 : 44
Peddabankur	Karimnagar	Silver	1	STL	Augustus	*IAR 1968* :1
Yeleswaram	Nalgonda	Gold	1	STL	Septimus	Khan, M.A.W. 1963 :63
ROYALSEEMA REGION						
Athirala	Cuddapah	Gold	1	N.K.	Trajan	Gupta, P.L.1965 :43
Nandyal	Kurnool	Gold	52	Hoard	Ending with Antonius	Gupta, P.L.1965 :43

Note : STL – Stratigraphical Position N.K. – Not known

REFERENCES

Annual Administrative 1983-84 and 1984-85 Report (abbreviated as *ARR*). (ed) Director of Archaeology and Museum. Government of Andhra Pradesh. Hyderabad.

Annual Report of Archaeological Department of His Exalted Highness of the Nizam's Dominion. 1933. ((abbreviated as *ARN*). Department of Archaeology. Hyderabad.

Beck, H.E. 1941. *The Beads from Taxila.* Memoirs of the Archaeological survey of India. No 65. New Delhi.

Dikshit, M.G. 1952. *Some Beads from Kondapur.* Hyderabad Archaeological Survey. No 16. Hyderabad.

Dikshit, M.G. 1964. *History of Indian Glass.* Bombay.

Dikshit, M.G. 1985 (reprint). Beads from Ahichchatra, U.P. *Ancient India.* Bulletin of the Archaeological Survey of India. No 8 (1952). New Delhi: 33-63.

Francis, P.J. 1982. *Glass Beads of India.* The world of beads Monograph Series. No 7. New York.

Ghosh. A.1984 (reprint). Sirkap (1944-45). *Ancient India.* Bulletin of the Archaeological Survey of India. No 4 (1947-48). New Delhi: 45-84.

Gupta, P.L. 1965. *A Catalogue of Roman Coins in the Andhra Pradesh.* Government Museum. Museum Series. Government of Andhra Pradesh. Hyderabad.

Gupta, P.L. 1979. Kotilingala find of post-Mauryan coins. *Numismatic Digest.* 3:17- 28.

Kangle, R.P. 1992 (reprint). *The Kautiliya Arthasastra.* 3 Volumes. First Edition 1963. Delhi: 134, 136-137.

Kenoyer, J.M. 1986. The Indus Bead industry: Contributions to Bead Technology. *Ornament.* 10, 1: 18-23.

Khan, H.N.1990 (reprint). Excavations in Southern Circle. *Archaeological Survey of India Annual Report 1936- 37.* (ed) K.N. Dikshit. Delhi.

Khan, M.A.W.1963. *A Monograph on Yeleswaram Excavation.* Andhra Pradesh Archaeological Series XIV. Government of Andhra Pradesh. Hyderabad.

Margabandhu, C. 1977. Evidence of Weights and Measures during the Early Historic Period. *Itihas.* IV, 1: 15-25.

Margabandhu, C. 1978. Some etched beads and pendants from Kondapur. *Journal of Indian History.* LVI: 35-46.

Mirashi, V.V. 1941. A Ship coin of Yajna Satakarni. *Journal of Numismatic Society*. VII.

Murthy, C.S. 1956. Amaravati Sculptures in Madras Government Museum. Bulletin of Madras Government Museum. New Series. Madras. IV.

Murthy, K.K. 1977. *Nagarjunakonda-A Cultural Study*. Delhi.

Raghavachari, K. 1972 –73. Dharanikota and its Western Contact. *Quarterly Review of Historical Studies*. Calcutta. XII, 3: 1-3.

Rao, M.R. 1961. *Satavahana Coins in the Andhra Pradesh Government Museum*. Andhra Pradesh Government Series. No 2. Hyderabad.

Rapson, E.J.1975. *Catalogue of the Coin of the Andhra Dynasty the Western Ksatrapas, the Trikutaka Dynasty and the Bodhi Dynasty*. New Delhi.

Reddy, R.D. and S.P. Reddy. 1991. Unpublished Satavahana coins from Kotilingala and Sangaredy. *Numismatic studies*. (ed) D. Handa.

Sankalia, H.D. and M.G. Dikshit. 1952. *Excavations at Brahmapuri* (Kolhapur) 1945-46. Poona.

Sankalia, H.D. and S.B., Ansari, Z.D. & S. Ehrhardt. 1960. *from History to pre- History at Nevasa (1954-56)*. Poona.

Sarma, I.K. 1980. *Coinage of the Satavahana Empire*. Delhi.

Sastry, V.V. K. 1983. *The Proto and Early History of Andhra Pradesh*. Government of Andhra Pradesh. Hyderabad.

Satyanarayana, K. 1975. *A study of the History of Andhra Pradesh (from Stone Age to feudalism)*. New Delhi.

Singh, A.K. 1988. *Indo- Roman Trade*. New Delhi.

Smith, V.K. 1972. *Coins of Ancient India*. Catalogue of the Coins in Indian Museum. Calcutta.

Srivastava, B. 1968. *Trade and Commerce in Ancient India*. Varanasi.

Thapar, B.K. 1985 (reprint). Maski, 1954: A Chalcolithic site of the Southern Deccan. *Ancient India*. Bulletin of the Archaeological Survey of India. No 13 (1957). New Delhi: 4-142.

Wheeler, R.E.M., Ghosh, A. & Krishna Deva. 1983 (reprint). Arikamedu: An Indo-Roman Trading Station on the East coast of India. *Ancient India*. Bulletin of the Archaeological Survey of India. No 2 (1946). New Delhi: 17-124.

Yusuf, S. 1936-37. *Paithan Excavations*. Annual Report of the Archaeological Department of His Exalted Highness the Nizam's Dominion. Hyderabad.

Chapter 9

DISCUSSION AND CONCLUSION

The Early Historical remains of Andhra region are dated between 400 BCE and CE 300. This entire span of about seven centuries can be grouped between two stages i.e., the Andhra culture stage which can be dated around 400 BCE to CE 100 and the Satavahana culture stage having the date bracket of 100 to 300 CE. The account of archaeological remains of both these stage, which have been elaborated in the preceding chapters, throws light on the various aspects such as craft, technologies, structural activities, settlement patterns, etc., the main features emerging from it can be woven together for interpreting the socio-cultural personality of the twin cultural stages of the early Andhradesa. The same has been attempted in the following.

9.1 ANDHRA CULTURE

The cultural trait of the Early Iron Age Megalithic period, i.e., *circa* 800 to 400 BCE appears to undergo changes during the second half of the first millennium BCE. These change are reflected in the collection of antiquities as developed craftsmanship and technologies on one hand and extension of internal and international trade on the other. The basic tribal elements of the Megalithic period appeared to have transformed into a systematic and complex socio-economic structure of the urban character under this process. This changed culture could be recognized as Andhra culture.

In the first part of the present volume has discussed about the relevance for the use of the term Andhra Culture for the time span of *circa* 400 BCE to CE 100 which post dates the Megalithic culture and is of pre-Satavahana period. It was also noted that ' Andhra' is used in the ancient literature both for the people and the region. Because the period under consideration was identified as such an important stage which laid the foundations for almost all the culture traits which continued for a number of centuries and was responsible stages of Andhra Pradesh, the proposed terminology was found suitable.

The early Megalithic socio-economic structure of the region appears to have experienced change the second half of the first millennium BCE. This change can be seen in the form of developed crafts, advanced technologies, extension of the internal and international trade, formation of political organizations and religious institutions. It is also evident that this period was under many pretty chiefs of *ganarajyas* during this period. Though they were politically insignificant, they were strong and powerful like the Mauryas in the northern region of the Indian sub-continent. They had introduced coins for the first time in the Deccan, which further facilitated the trade and commerce. Simultaneously, metal exploration and the technologies have also been popularized. They started to produce in large scale commercial based items, which attracted not only the Indian but also the foreign traders. The natural water and caravan routes were additional advantage of the region which promoted sea and land route trade during this period. Along side with expansion of Buddhism in this region not only there was a spread of the religious ideology but trade activities and culture interactions too had intensified. All these features together with urban sophistications appeared in the form of towns, cities and metropolis centers around *200* BCE.

Iron technology has been regarded as one of the important aspects for the sophisticated way of living. The use of this metal was initiated in the region by Megalithic folks. Andhra culture inherited this technical knowhow from their ancestors. It may be noted that during the fifth / fourth century BCE a wave of high technical skill penetrated in the region which boosted the existing primitive iron technology to a great extent. Some ancient working spots have also been noticed at Warangal, Konasamudram, Dindurthi, etc. Majority of them are located in the north-western region which has rich iron deposits. A few of these later became production centers of the famous *Damascus* steel.

The knowledge of iron working and its further exploitation for manufacturing objects on a mass scale had progressively increased during Andhra period. The unearthed evidences such as the number of furnace, crucibles along with slags and unfinished objects from smiths' workshops like at Kondapur, Satanikota, etc., suggest that the process of smelting, forging and forge- welding objects were well known to Andhra people. The knowledge of carbonization and thereby production of steel was thoroughly known to the Andhra smiths by this time. The famous Damascus steel production during this period is noteworthy. The wootz or *ukku* (means cast iron or steel in local language) was another variety of iron which was under production and is a preferred form till today. The utility of iron was extended to a variety of items comprising household or domestic objects, building materials and agricultural implements. But the general proportion of iron object was lower in the Andhra phase in comparison to the succeeding period *viz.*, Satavahana.

Most of the objects are indigenous in nature and represent the creations of the time as and when the need arose. Profuse occurrence of carpentry and building materials indicates construction·of carpentry and building materials indicates construction with permanent building materials. Widespread use of iron equipments with advanced techno-typologies demonstrates the urban sophistication of the early Andhra. It was a prevalent craft producing tools and equipments in the region and was catering to the need of major urban centers throughout the region. It may also be noted that some of the export quality products like *Damascus* steel swords were produced in the north-western part of the region and were exported not only to the other parts of the Indian sub- continent but also the Western countries as well (Satyanarayana, K. 1975). Some of the objects tend to show foreign influence in the method of manufacture or direct import from other regions. They included spade, javelin, double-tongued arrowheads, etc. At Yeleswaram, some of these were found from Early Historic Megalithic (*c* 2nd century BCE) burials (Khan, M.A.W. 1963). These evidently attested to the trade and regional contacts.

Besides the iron, the utility of other metals like copper, gold, silver, lead and alloys such as bronze, potin, etc. were also noticed. During this period, lead appeared for the first time in the form of coins as well as ornaments. Majority of the precious metals were found in the form of ornaments and others decorative items. Besides, gold appeared in the form of foreign currency (Roman) and bullions. Copper was found in restricted forms such as ornaments, objects for special purposes and coins. Bronze figures from Dhulikatta and Nelakondapalli (dated around *c* 2nd century BCE), were noteworthy finds of Andhra Culture period. Currency in Potin is another significant feature of this culture. It may be mentioned that different metals and its varied products in the Andhra Cultural period indicate changes in the value of the social matrix and economic conditions.

Ceramic industry is another major and prevalent craft during the Early Historic period. Pottery was the only media to satisfy the daily need of any category of people during this period because the metal pots were not much popular at that time. It was found that this craft was developed extensively during Andhra period. Through pottery of Megalithic period in the form of Black and Red ware, Black ware and Red ware continued, many new types were also being produced during this period. For example, Russet Coated Painted ware, which was called by R.E.M. Wheeler as 'Andhra ware' (Wheeler, R.E.M. 1947-48:181-310), was one of the characteristic and thus diagnostic ceramic type of period. In the present state of our knowledge it is difficult to ascertain whether this pottery was of Andhra origin or an adoption of a foreign tradition. But it is clear that it mark an evolutionary stage over the Megalithic Black and Red ware industry. Because, majority of this pottery type had a base of Black and Red ware, russet coated paint with kaolin designs were the significant new additions in this ceramic tradition. Besides, a few imitation of the foreign wares like Rouletted ware, Red Polished ware, Mould made ware, etc., were also adopted by the Andhra phase potters. The possible explanation for their occurrence is that it might have been to satisfy the needs of foreign traders or to reduce the demands for imported goods. The former explanation seems to be more appropriate because after diminishing the long distance trade, these imitation ceramic traditions had lost their grounds. On the basis of shapes and decorations, the Rouletted and Red Polished ware appeared more as an indigenous ceramic form (Rao, S.R. 1966: 51-59). However the little existing remains could be construed as imported 'table wares'. In this context K.W. Slane's opinion that 'table ware were not luxurious enough to be traded' (Slane, K.W.1990:204-215), seems to be more appropriate. Occurrence of foreign ceramic such as Arretine ware and Amphorae in meager quantity show that they might have been for the personal use of foreign merchants rather than meant for export.

During this period, majority of the post were wheel made with a few exceptions like storage jars, troughs, etc. Out of the total collection of the pots, utilitarians (domestic) were recovered on a large scale. These were used for different domestic purposes like cooking and other kitchen need, table serves and storage. Dominant shapes noticed in different forms and sizes were dishes, bowls, vases, lids, storage pots, etc. Besides, a few new shapes like hour glass stands, tulip shaped vases, brazier, etc., which were the rare and non-indigenous shapes, were also noticed. Majority of the non-indigenous shaped post were associated with grave goods.

Terracotta figurative form also evidence stages of development. From archaic hand modeling to the use of single and double moulds were the main stages of the development of this craft. The use of double moulds for the production of highly artistic terracotta compositions is noteworthy which was initiated in the last stage of the Andhra Culture. Use of mould has also been associated with mass production and urban features. It has been suggested that use of double moulds in the craft was possibly due to the influx of long distance traders, because the double mould technique of clay sculpturing was Mediterranean in origin (Deshpande, M.N. 1961). In this context, it may be mentioned that some of the figurines produced by this technique are marked by foreign facial feature. It may also be noted that this non-Indian technology of terracotta making was well adopted by the artisans of the Andhra culture period for indigenous themes like Buddha figures and other compositions. Evidence for this has been obtained from Kondapur. It was noticed by this researcher that either moulds or figures themselves appears to have been at one or two centuries from where these were distributed to the other regions. A similar trend was observed by V. Jayaswal (1991: 108) in case of the Kushana terracotta of the Ganga plains.

Bead making in India has always been a specialized craft. For centuries, their existed craftsmen experts for specific raw materials like precious metals and stones, faience, steatite, shall, ivory and terracotta. It was noticed that the bead technology had particularly developed by the second century BCE. Production of high quality and large quantities of bead during Andhra period was perhaps due to trade activities. As beads was also one of the trade items from the very beginning. P.J. Francis (1982: 4) has mentioned that many Agate localities and bead craft centers exist in India from the very beginning. Some of them were export centers. Perhaps the best evidence for trade between the region and the western countries was the etched carnelian beads and glass with metal foils. These were probably made with similar techniques and sometimes displayed identical patterns (Dubin, L.S. 1987: 181-200). It may also be noted that the craftsmen collected the raw materials not only from the local deposits but also from very long distances. For example, Lapis lazuli and Carnelian which were used during the Early Historical period in Andhra were not locally available. The later was imported from Gujarat and the former from West. However, the unfinished objects and raw materials indicate their local manufacture. Further, the metal beads with enamel work show the advanced artistic expression. Some auspicious symbols like *Triratna*, pippal leaf, *harmica* of the stupa, *Swastika*, etc., in the form of beads indicate the religious influence on their craft as well as local production of the category.

Glass was the new material adopted during the Andhra period for luxury items. The history of glass technology in India, through commences from the middle of first millennium BCE (Dikshit, M.G. 1969), yet in Andhra, this technology was in evidence only in the matured Andhra culture period. It my also be noted that the glass beads were one of the trade items probably for the Far East countries. They have been referred to as 'trade wind beads' since they were carried by ship via routes determined by the seasonal ocean currents and the directions of monsoon (Francis, B.J. 1982). The glass industry during the period under consideration includes beads, bangles, pendent, etc. Majority of them are bangles. Technical advancement such as metal in glass, in this industry was also noticed. Probably, these might have been adopted from the Roman world. In contrast, a few fragments of ribbed bowls from Dharanikota and glass pendent *(IAR 1962-63*: 1-2) are noteworthy. As ribbed bowls were produced both in the western and eastern parts of the Roman empire and reached India through the Red Sea route (Stern, M.E.1992:

117). However, local expertise in glass technology is also attested to by the production of multi colors and different shapes.

The foregoing discussion evidence a strong influence of long distance trade on the artifacts of the Andhra Culture. It is therefore, necessary to examine the nature of trade and their possible routes. On the south-east coast, large scale maritime activities flourished during the Early Historic period. The trade route, says the author of the *Periplus,* started from Machilipatnam and went across the Bay of Bengal to the Eastern Peninsula. This was the direct route Yavadvipa (Java), Suvarnadvipa (Sumatra) and Kamboja (Cambodia) (Sarma, I.K.1990: 551-560). The west ward movement from the Andhra coasts, perhaps via Ter and Paithan, was to Barygaza (Broach) from where the ships sailed directly to the western countries. H.W. Schaff observed that Machilipatanam had the best anchorage in the Bay of Bengal (Schiff, H.W. 1974: 252). Probably it was the only place at the time from where vessels sailed for Dsiam, Cochin, China, Mecca, Madagascar, Sumatra, Manila, etc. Ptolemy mentioned that Kantakosala (Gantasala), Koddur (Gudur), Allosygne (Avanigadda), etc., were ports in Maisolia (Machilipatnam) region.

The recent interest in 'water front archaeology' has revealed a growing number of places where boats could berth. Many ports, port towns and commercial towns had developed alongside the rivers, which were capable of receiving sea-going vessels (Sarma, I.K.1990). In contrast, the wharf found at Dharanikota was probably a typical one out of the many places where ships could transfer their cargoes. It is also evident that rivers played their part in providing a means of transporting goods to the inland regions. Undoubtedly sea-going vessels could enter some rivers and sailed upstream to docks and wharfs such as those on the banks of the Dharanikota and Kotilingala.

Besides water routes many caravan routes were also established in the region from the very beginning connecting the rest of the Indian sub-continent. The geographical features of the region which provide natural routes further facilitated the trade. For example, the breaks in the Eastern Hills might have provided natural passes which connected the plateau and the coastal region. J.F. Fleet traced two ancient caravan routes which went through the coastal Andhra region (Fleet, J.F.1901: 548). One of them started from Machilipatnam while the second one from Vinukonda proceeding through Kalyan, Ter, Paithan, Ajanta hills and finally reaching to Broach. The road from Machilipatnam took not only the local traffic from the coastal district, but also the sea-borne traffic from the Far East.

There were two another ancient routes to the Far East. The land route, commonly called the 'silk road' and the maritime route called the 'southern sea route' or 'spice road' (De silve, A. 1970). All these routes were traversed through the southern coast. The recent evidence also shoes that during the third or second century BCE the ancient port towns like Dharanikota (Andhra Pradesh), Arikamedu (Tamilnadu), *etc.*, were humming with oversea trade (Sarma, I.K.1987:7-9, 13). It is well known that these trading communities took to Buddhism prevalent in the region. It also appears that the region had been a very potential transmitter of cultures and relics to south-east Asia, south China, Korea and Japan. The archaeological finds include iron objects like knives, axes, daggers, spear points and other objects such as glass bangles, beads, semi-precious stones, etc., all of which bear close resemblance with the objects unearthed from the settlements located on the above mentioned routes (Chaudhuri, K.K. 1990 : 217-222). The Nagarjunakonda inscriptions of the Ikshvaku king (second half of third century CE) speaks of the fraternities of the foreign Buddhist monks, thus, confirming the movement of people from one to the other foreign region. Also, *Gatha saptasati* of Hala, descriptions further indicating the conditions of trade and communication facilities in the Deccan (Basak, R.D. 1971). According to early inscription like found at Amaravati, Dharanikota (Dhanya Kataka), Kevarura, Vijayapura, Narsala, Gantasala, etc., these were places where merchants used to reside (Satyanarayana, K.1975). Further, the abundant inscriptions from Amaravati, Bhattiprolu, prove the existence of organized guilds *(qosthis)* and co-operations *(nigamas)* in Andhra Culture time (*c* 4th / 3rd century BCE) (Sarma, I.K. 1988: 7). This, in itself is a determinant trait of urbanism (Joshi, M.C. 1974). *Periplus* describes that from Machilipatnam, immense quantities of fine muslins were exported (Majumdar, R.C.1960: 307). According to R.C. Majumdar, large vessels were loaded with timbers of teak wood to Oman. Further, the best iron and the famous *wootz* steel was produced in present Hyderabad region and exported to the West countries (Satyanarayana, K. 1975). In contrast, W.H. Manning speaks about the trade and trade routes to discuss here. According to him, the Romans imported the pure steel with great expense from India (Manning W.H. 1990: 595). Similarly, E.H. Warmington (1974: 257) also pointed out that the swords made of fine Indian steel have been very famous since the time of Ctesiss. He further mentioned that the Indians sent their steel in their own ships, probably to keep the secret of its production. Besides the above exported goods, precious stones like diamonds, agate, carnelian, etc., were also noteworthy exported item (Daniels, C. 1990: 225; Lahiri, N. 1992: 352-360).

Andhra not only exported the above mentioned objects during Early Historical period but it also imported many items either directly or indirectly from foreign countries. For example, many imported objects have been unearthed from the archaeological excavations like pottery, glass objects, coins, metal objects, etc., which were appeared to have been imported from the West. W.H. Manning (1990: 600) observed that Arretine pottery was exported through Red sea to India. We have noted occurrence of this ware primarily in coastal areas as Salihundam collection has this ware, which was acquired from Rome as a trade item. Profuse occurrence of Roman gold coins further attests the direct trading contacts with the Roman country. Besides, many infusions of techniques such as the use of double moulds, glass technology, preparation of faience, construction of amphitheaters like building are such noteworthy features which can directly be related to interaction between the Andhra and the Western world through trade. That this trade was gone through sea route is evident from the large and extensive Coramondal coast. Many ports and anchorages where vessels could berth were also noted during this period all along this coast. In addition to this, the coins of Yajnasri Satakarni, which frequently bear the symbol of a ship with two masts, may further indicate the full fledged trade through navigation. The large number of early imperial Roman coins, contemporary pottery and other imported datable objects indicate that the *circa* 50 BCE to CE 50 was the main period in which the long distance sea trade was at its peak. It was noted by us that by the second century CE the trade had considerably declined.

Settlements in the proto stage of the Early Historic period of the region under study were inhabited by some tribal communities. These settlement were in the from of self-sufficient villages. We have archaeological evidences to believe that a little later, i.e., around third century BCE, some large settlements based primarily on agriculture and specialized crafts like smithy came to exist. Meanwhile, some settlements of political nature like Kotilingala also were established. From the beginning of the second century BCE to the early centuries of the present era, a progressive growth of these settlements took place particularly at places where the location was at the nodal point and on the trade routes which helped in the cultural interaction between the regions. The trade, both inland and long distance, helped not only the development of commerce *vis-à-vis* material affluence, but they also were responsible for the growth of cities. Urbanism in Andhra region may have been a borrowing culture trait from the Gangetic plains. As, in the later region earlier glimpses of urbanism was seen around fourth/ third century BCE. There are archaeological evidences to show that both the region, e.g., Andhra and Gangetic plains were in close contact with other. The archaeological clues for urbanism in Andhra appear to be later than Gangetic plains, but earlier than its Roman contact. It may, therefore, be logical to presume that the formation of cities during the Early Historical period of Andhra was perhaps inspired by the north-western part of the Peninsula.

It may also be noted that a number of settlements of Andhra culture period has been located from the entire region. The location of these sites in this region reveals occupation of different types of geographical zones and pattern of settlements. That is to say, the agrarian based villages were located along the fertile alluvial plains of the lower Krishna and Godavari valleys and their tributaries such as Tungabhadra, Gundlakamma, Manjeera, Peddavagu, etc. They were favorite habitations of the early Andhra people. Besides, the entire coastal belt of Andhra is also dotted with several ports and port towns such came up a little later in the period under consideration. The small industrial settlements were located around the areas where raw material was available. For example, settlements of Konasamudram, Dindurthi, Komarapalli, Warangal, Erannapalli, Tellakunta etc., are noteworthy for iron smithy and location of iron resource of the neighborhood. It my also be pointed out that some settlements were found in Eastern Hill area. Majority of these settlements appear to be favorable avenues for religion establishments like at Salihundam and Sankaram. Besides, localities with political importance, such as, Kotilingala, Dhulikatta and Satanikota also were established as cities during this period. These were located either in the vicinity of fertile lands or natural resources. Further, V.V. K. Sastry discovered hundreds of habitational sites in the Karimnagar region, which were located in almost every alternate village (Sastry, V.V.K. 1983: 123) of the modern settlements. According to him, it might have been a political locality of the Early Historic people and appears to belong to the late Andhra phase. The unearthed finds from the excavations such as authorized issue coin, seals and sealing, structures with elaborate defense, palace complexes, etc., are also support his hypothesis. In this context, K. Satyanarayana's (1975: 110) argument that the Satavahana established their hegemony first in the Telangana region and then spread their regime towards the west and north supports the above view.

The settlements during this period were marked out by the natural boundaries like forests, thickets, rivulets and hillocks. However, a considerable number of sites were enclosed by the fortification along with gateways at the cardinal points. A large spread of urbanism has been found during this period. The urbanization can be seen in terms of high civic sense in the planning of the settlements. Planned fortified towns with high engineering skill displayed in the construction of buildings, huge religious establishment, water supply and storing as well as the disposal systems, transport facilities such as paved roads and streets, ports and anchorages, etc., indicative of the comfortable living and urban sophistication of the Andhras. Permanent building materials such as kiln baked bricks (in standard size), rubble foundations, lime plasters and utility of iron in carpentry and masonry employed in the constructions, are noteworthy. Houses followed a linear pattern in their arrangement and that they were constructed along broad roads intercepted by cross roads and by-lanes. Besides, elaborate defense system which included deep moats, draw bridges, bastions, guard room, gateways, gate houses, etc., show the high security and protection to the settlements. The technical skill of erecting huge wooden reinforcements (at Dhulikatta), massive protective embankments with laterite blocks (at Dharanikota), imposing gateways (at Satanikota), wharf-cum-navigational channels (from Dharanikota and Kotilingala), etc., spear of the technical superiority and ingenuity of the builders. Wells, cisterns, closed drains, sewage, attached baths and other standard domestic conveniences were also common in these settlement.

It is evident from the archaeological record that during the Andhra period, the settlements with sophisticated town planning were marked by such features as standard domestic conveniences, elaborate defense, etc., the forts, places, port-cum-forts, etc., were some other significant features of this culture. In this context, Pliny (1st century CE), who is said to have utilized the information recorded by Megasthenes (3rd century BCE), speaks of a powerful Andhra domain having thirty walled towns (Majumdar, R.C. 1968 : 194) is worthwhile to note. Some of these have been identified by the scholars with the modern towns of Kondapur, Peddabankur, Kotilingala, Satanikota, Sattenapalli, Dharanikota, etc. (Mangalam, S.J.1986:128). Machilipatnam, Gantasala, Guduru, Avanigadda and Calingapatnam were great ports and port towns of the Andhṛadesa (Sarma, I.K. 1990). The archaeological finds from these sites also attest to the above settlement.

Monastic establishments also thrived during this period under discussion in the entire region (Sarma, I.K. 1987: 17-22), which were located either in the vicinity of urban centers or in the rich agricultural regions. Majority of them are in the Coastal Andhra which had the double advantage of surplus commodities to support the monks and of easy accessibility to the sea through rivers. These places became favorite avenues for the Buddhist establishments like Jaggayapeta, Goli, Thotlakonda, Salihundam, Bhavikonda and Gudivada (Sarma, I.K. 1988: 11-112). The sculptural art (at Amaravati, Nagarjunakonda, etc.) of these establishment are particularly noteworthy (Narla, V.R. 1956; Srinivasan, P.R. 1956). Monolithic stupas at Bojjannakonda, Lingalametta, and rock cut stupas in the *caitya*-halls of Guntupalli and Ramatitham are unique examples of the Andhra art tradition (Rao, N.A. 1956).

Buddhism seems to have its beginning in the region at a very date. From the Buddhist records, we find that on the right bank of the Godavari, there is a tiny village, known as Andhagoan. This could have been a very holy city and many Buddhist missionaries are said to have visited this place from Magadha and Central India. V.V.K. Sastry (1983) has identified this site with the modern Andhergoan in Karimmagar district. This seems quite logical since the entire region is dotted with Buddhist and antiquities. Amaravati, on the river Krishna, was a famous as Sanchi, Sarnath and Bodhgaya in north India form the pre-Mauryan times (Sastry, V.V. K.1988). It may also be noticed that the maritime traffic was also responsible for the flourishing state of Buddhism in this region. Buddhism and Buddhist establishments received the patronage of the merchant class, who had close and intimate contacts with this region. It is also evident that the wealth of the merchants was utilized for the establishments like Amaravati and Nagarjunakonda stupa. It may be noted that the art of the Andhra spread in most of the area in Central Asia, perhaps due to the religious and merchants influx into this region from all corners (Rao, R.C.P.R. 1956: 71).

Further, a few regional variation have been noticed in the early settlement pattern of Andhra Pradesh during this period. For example, the north-western region had appeared more technically developed then the other region. By the end of the first millennium BCE, it became the nucleus for the artisans who specialized in the metal, clay and stone craftsmanship. There are sites for special smithy, in terms of steel iron object producing center, which attracted not only Indian traders but also trades from the foreign countries (Satyanarayana, K. 1975). Their produce of tools and equipments were catering to the need of major urban centers throughout the region. At the same time bead making craft was also specialized by the artisans of some of these settlements, who had mastered in stone working (various types of beads in precious and semi-precious stones) as well as clay modeling. Besides, these were certain settlements, which appear to be art centers, where particularly terracotta compositions, were made in larger quantities. The use of moulds for the production of these highly artistic terracotta compositions is noteworthy which was responsible for mass production of elaborately decorated compositions. In contrast to the north-western region, which held artisan, based settlements the eastern region had rich fertile lands and the long sea coast. This stretch thus attracted not only the merchants and trading communities but also the religious establishments. Through trade and religious contacts not only prevailed affluence in this region but also impetus was formed for the growth of cities. This is testified by the concentration of monastic establishments and the urban centers in the coastal region of Andhra.

It may, therefore, be suggested that through there was a cultural uniformity in the entire region, there existed regional variations, which were influenced by the geographical factors during the Andhra culture period.

9.2 SATAVAHANA CULTURE

The term Satavahana appears as the name of a royal family of the Deccan in the epigraphic record in a cave in Nasik (Sircar, D.C. 1991: 189-190) and inscriptions of Balasri (Bhandarkar, R.C. 1929: 17). The territorial concentration of the Satavahana to this region is suggested by the later Satavahana inscriptions found at Myakadoni (Sastri, K.A.N. 1957: 296) and Hirahadagalli (Sircar, D.C. 1991: 463). In Archaeological records only the later Satavahana level can be identified as authorized are found in the region. This event is dated to the end of the first century CE. Moreover, we have no evidence of the rule of the Satavahana in the Andhradesa before Gautamiputra Satakarni (Dutta, M.1990: 5). According to inscription and other evidences Satavahana ruled the region probably with Dharanikota as a metropolis center. It appears that after the decline of the long distance trade on the west coast, *i.e.*, somewhere in the last few decades before the end of the first century CE, the Satavahanas migrated towards the east, and found the new region where rich in fertile lands and natural resources. The powerful Andhra chief probably accepted the hegemony of the Satavahana (evidence of political conflict are not found in the history of the early Andhras) because the Satavahanas were probably a clan of the 'Andhras' or 'Andhra Bhrtyahas' (Bhandarkar, R.G.1960: 41), who migrated and started their hegemony a few centuries before the Christian era in the western region of the Deccan plateau. It may also be noted that they occupied the Andhra region gradually from the northern side. Telangana region was first occupied and then the spread was towards the east. The archaeological remains also illustrate this pattern. For example, in the Telangana region the Satavahana coins appear in earlier horizons and belong to the Gautamiputra Satakarni and his immediate successors, along with the remains of the first century CE (Sastry, V.V. K. 1983: 122). In this context, profuse occurrence of Satavahana coins from ancient towns like Kondapur, Kotilingala, Dhulikatta, etc., are particularly noteworthy. Contrary to this, in the other parts of the Andhra Pradesh, the Satavahana appendage are dated after the second half of the second century CE *i.e.* from the time of Yajna Sri Satakarni (*c* 174-203 CE) onwards.

During the Satavahana period, through administrative set up might have changed in the region, there was no striking cultural change. It was noticed that the former culture traits of the Andhra phase more or less continued in this phase also with a little variation here and there. For example, the Black and Red ware, which survived as a long ceramic tradition, show deterioration during this phase. Similarly, the characteristic ceramic type of Russet Coated Painted ware had also last its popularity. It may be noted that the imported and imitation wares also ceases to exist, which might have been due to the decline in the long distance trade and foreign traffic. In contrast, the Red Polished ware and the non-specific ceramic types such as Grey ware and Red ware gained importance.

The Satavahana domain in the region is marked by art activities, which increased tremendously. A number of religious establishments show a spurt of imposing architectural activities including great quantity of sculptures during this period. For instance, at Amaravati, Nagarjunakonda, Jaggayapeta, etc., finely carved sculptures and architectural components were added to the existing building (Srinivasan, P.R. 1956: 55) in the coastal Andhra region. These remains diverted for art and architectural activities. This feature appears to be related to the strong royal domain and thus compares well with the Maurya trait of earlier period, which was also responsible for the imposing art and architectural constructions in the northern region. The art and crafts during Satavahana time attain the status of Royalty from the small scale cottage industry of the previous culture phase.

Change in the urban set up can also be noticed during Satavahana period. This change is again marked by Royal domain, which may be referred as political based urbanism.

Many new settlements grew up into township of political importance. It is noteworthy that with the stabilization of political power, construction of massive palaces, dormitories, stadiums, stables, barracks, chapels, etc. were done. The protective devices attained the nature of strong forts with elaborate defense walls with bastions guard rooms, gate houses, moats and draw bridges. It may be mentioned that there was a demarcation in the residential areas of the Royal and the common people within the township of political nature. The residences of important personnel such as the Royal family members, the defense staff and the nobility lived within the fort area, which was well protected, while the dwellings of common people were confined outside the citadel. However, many buildings outside the citadel too were imposing. It may also be noted that the Mediterranean influence of building construction may be seen in the some of the buildings of this period. For example, amphitheatre type of buildings in the metropolitan cities like Nagarjunakonda is noteworthy example. This type of theatre was in use in the Western countries during the contemporary times (Armit, I. 1990: 439).

The foregoing study reveals that material remains of the Andhra culture were varied, diverse and sumptuous. It also represents a stage in the urbanization which was ushered in with the development of iron technology. These technical factors helped rapid progress in the fields of agriculture and industry. It is also evident that agriculture and animal husbandry as well as mining and smelting became important occupations during the period under consideration. Agriculture and animal husbandry were the main stay of the economic life of the people, which still continues in certain parts. The presence of cereals like rice and wheat (Kajale,

M.D. 1984) shows the knowledge of double crop system, i.e., the *rabi* and *kharif*, which speaks of a distinct advancement in farming. It may be presumed that the surplus food production and the exploitation of metal and other mineral resources on a commercial basis, promoted trade and commerce. The trade, particularly with foreign countries, not only made the people rich and affluent but also helped cultural transactions, which provided impetus to the formation of cities and metropolis centers.

The rapid growth of urban life, which usually comes with the development of trade and commerce, is the most important characteristic of the socio-economic life of the Andhra. Through the urban centers emerged in the region a couple of centuries before the trade with the Romans, the cities were further enriched by such a contact. It may, therefore, be held that two processes appear to have been responsible for the formulation of the Andhra Culture. One, the continuation and innovation of the local culture traits and the other the adaptation of non-indigenous ideas, technologies and articles. A balanced mixture of both of these traits in the process of acculturation appears to have constituted the Andhra culture stage, in which each of the elements played important role.

By the end of the second century CE the region was politically consolidated under the Satavahanas. A large number of crafts, which had already reached, advanced stage continued in this period in somewhat similar manner. This includes ceramic, textile jewellery, metal objects, which are found in increased number during Satavahana levels. There appears to have a general decline in the long distance trade, particularly with Rome. This was due to unsuitable political conditions of Rome. In Andhra, the vigour of the Royal personas helped concentration of wealth to the Royal treasuries and select few related personnel. As per archaeological evidence, the general economy of the people appears to have declined. As there to be a dearth of decorative pots and *deluxe* ware and some other daily utility items. The wealth appears to have accumulated more with the Royal people and was channelized for specific uses such as constructions of fort and Royal buildings, religious establishments thriving under their patronage, etc.

REFERENCES

Armit, I. 1990. Broch Building in Northern Scotland: The Context of Innovation. *World Archaeology*. 21, 3: 439.

Basak, R.D. (ed). 1971. *Gatha Saptasati of Hala.* Calcutta.

Bhandarkar, R.G. 1929. *Early History of the Deccan* (Collected works of Bhandarkar). Poona.

Chaudhuri, K.K. 1990. South India's Contact with China: A study in the Earliest Phase from Chinese Sources. 2 Vols. (eds) Kuppuram, G. & K. Kumudmani. Delhi. I: 217-222.

Deniels, C. 1990. Africa. *The Roman World.* 2 Vol. (ed) J. Wacher. London.

Datta, A. 1992. Early stages of Iron Technology and the Development of Regional pattern in India. *Man and His Culture, A Resurgence.* (ed) P.S. Bellwood. New Delhi: 293-308.

Deshpande, M.N. 1961. Roman Influence on the Terracotta of the Satavahana Period'. *International conference on Asian Archaeology*. 14-20 December. 1961. Summaries of Papers. New Delhi.

De Silva, A. 1970. The spice and silk Roads. *India 's contribution to World through Culture.* Vivekananda Commemoration Volume. Madras: 229-231.

Dubin, L.S. 1987. *The History of Beads from 30,000 B.C. to the present.* London.

Dutta, M. 1990. *A Study of the Satavahana Coins*. New Delhi.

Eggeling, J. (translated). 1990 (reprint). *Sacred Books of the East,* The Satapatha Brahmana. (ed) F. Maxmuller. New Delhi.

Fleet, J.F. 1901. Tagara, Ter. *Journal of the Royal Asiatic Society:* 548.

Francis, P.J. 1982. *Glass Beads of India.* The World of Beads Monograph Series. No 7. New York.

Francis, P.J. 1982a. *Agate Beads of India.* The World of Beads Monograph Series. No 6. New York.

Jayaswal, V. 1991. *Kushan Clay Art of Ganga Plains. A Case Study of Human Forms from Khairadih.* Delhi.

Kajale, M.D. 1984. New Light on Agricultural Plant Economy During the First Millennium B.C. Palaeobotanical Study of Plant Remains from Excavations of Veerapuram, district Kurnool, Andhra Pradesh. Veerapuram, district Kurnool, Andhra Pradesh. *Veerapuram A type Site for Cultural Study in the Krishna Valley.* (eds) Sastri, T.V.G. , Bai, M.K. & J.V.P. Rao. Hyderabad.

Khan, M.A.W. 1963. *A Monograph on Yeleswaram Excavations.* Andhra Pradesh Archaeological Series. No XIV. Government of Andhra Pradesh. Hyderabad.

Lahari, N. 1992. *The Archaeology of Indian Trade Routes* (upto *c.*200 B.C.). Delhi.

Mahning, W.H. 1990. Industrial Growth. *The Roman World.* 2 Vols. (ed) J. Wacher. London. II: 586-600.

Mangalam, S.J. 1986. Historical Geography & Toponomy of Andhra Pradesh. New Delhi.

Narla, V.R. 1956. Buddhist Art in Andhra - the Pride of India. *Buddha Jayanti souvenir.* (ed) P. Srinivasachary. Hyderabad.

Rao, N.R. 1956. Monolithic Stupas in Andhra Desa. *Buddha Jayanti Souvenir.* (ed) P. Srinivasachary. Hyderabad.

Rao, N.R. 19567. Asia – Wide influence of Andhra Art. *Buddha Jayanti Souvenir.* (ed) P. Srinivasachary. Hyderabad: 71.

Rao, S.B. 1958. *Personality of India*; Pre and Proto Historic foundation of India and Pakistan. Baroda.

Rao, S.R. 1966. Excavations at Amreli: A Kshatrapa-Gupta Town. Bulletin of Baroda Museum and Picture Gallery. No XVIII. Baroda.

Sarma, I.K. 1977. *Religion in Art and Historical Archaeology of South Indian contracts and correlations.* Madras.

Sarma, I.K. 1990. Ancient Andhra Ports, Religious centers and Sea-faring. Journal of Marine Archaeology. I: 19-23.

Sarma, I.K. 1990a. Ancient Port Towns of South-East India: Their Role in the spread of Buddhist Art and Religion to China and Japan. *Researches in Indian History, Archaeology, Art and Religion* (Prof. Upendra Thakur

Felicitation Volume). 2 Vols. (eds) Kuppuram, G. & K. Kumudamani. Delhi I: 551-560.

Sastri, K.A.N. 1939. *Foreign Notices of South India*. Madras.

Sastri, K.A.N. (ed). 1957. *A Comprehensive History of India*, the Mauryas and the Satavahanas, 325 B.C.-A.D. 300. Calcutta. II.

Sastry, V.V. K. 1983. *The Proto and Early History of Andhra Pradesh*. Govt of Andhra Pradesh. Hyderabad.

Sathyanarayana, K. 1975. *A Study of the History and Culture of the Andhra (From Stone Age to Feudalism)*. New Delhi.

Schoff , H.W. 1974 (reprint) .*The Periplus of the Erythrean Sea* (Travel and Trade in the Indian ocean by a merchant of the Ist century A.D.). first published in 1912. New Delhi.

Sircar , D.C. 1991 (reprint). *Select Inscriptions bearing on Indian History and Civilization.* first edition in 1942. Delhi.

Slane, K.W. 1991. Observations on Mediterranean Amphoras and Table wares in India. *Roman and India*, the ancient Sea trade. (eds) Bengle, V. & R.D. De Puma. New Delhi: 204-215.

Srinivasan, P.R. 1951. Early Buddhist Andhra Art-Mother of South Indian Architecture. *Buddha Jayanti Souvenir.* (ed) P. Srinivasachary. Hyderabad.

Suthankar, V.S. 1955. *Cambridge History of India.* (ed) F.J. Rapson. Delhi.

Wheeler, R.E.M. 1947-48. Brahmagiri and Chandravalli, 1947 : Megalithic and other Cultures in the chital Durg district, Mysore State'. *Ancient India*, Bulletin of Archaeological Survey of India No 4. New Delhi: 181-310.

Warmington, E.H. 1974 (2nd edn). The commerce between the Roman Empire and India. London.

Yazdani, G. 1960. *The Early History of the Deccan*. London.

BIBLIOGRAPHY

Agashe, K.S. (ed). 1986. *Aitareya Brahmana*. Poona.

Agrawal, D.P. 1982. *The Archaeology of India*. London.

Agrawal D.P. & A. Ghosh. (eds) 1973. *Radio carbon and India Archaeology*. Bombay.

Agrawal D.P. & C.Margabandhu. 1978. Ancient Gold Workings : Some New 14C dated. *Puratattva*. Bulletin of the Indian Archaeological Society. No 8. (ed) B.K Thapar. New Delhi: 139.

Agrawala, V.S. 1985 (reprint). *Terracotta Figurines of Ahichhatra* (District Bareilly, U.P). Varanasi.

Ahmad, K.M. 1950. *Inscribed and Riveted Pottery from Kondapur* (*circa* 200 B.C. – Cir. 200 A.D.). Kondapur Series. No 1. Government of Andhra Pradesh. Hyderabad.

Allchin, B. & R. Allchin. 1968. *The Birth of Indian Civilization*. Harmondsworth.

Allchin, B. & F.R. Allchin. 1983. *The Rise of Civilization in Indian and Pakistan*. New Delhi.

Allchin F.R. 1957. Poor Men's Thalis: A Deccan Potter's Technique. *Bulletin of the School of Oriental and African studies* XXII: 250-257.

Allchin, F.R 1960. *Piklihal Excavations*. Andhra Pradesh Government Archaeological Series. No 1. Hyderabad.

Allchin, F.R. 1961. *Utnur Excavations*. Andhra Pradesh Government Archaeological Series No 5. Hyderabad.

Allchin, F.R. 1962. Upon the Antiquity and Methods of Gold Mining in Ancient India. *Journal of Economic and social History of the orient*. V.

Altekar, A.S. 1952. Society in the Deccan during 200 B.C.-A.D. 500. *Journal of Indian History*. XXX, 1.

Annual Administrative Report (abbreviated as *AAR*). (ed) Director of Archaeology and Museums. Government of Andhra Pradesh. Hyderabad.

Annual Report of Archaeological Department of His Exalted Highness of the Nizam's Dominion. 1938-39, 1939-40 and 1940-41. (abbreviated as *ARN*). Department of Archaeology. Hyderabad.

Armit, 1990. Broch Building in Northern Scotland: The context of Innovation. *World Archaeology*. 21, 3:439.

Baden Powell, B.H. 1897. A Study of the Deccan Villages, their origin and Development. *Journal of the Royal Asiatic Society of Great Britain and Ireland*. London : 239-280.

Basak, R.D. (ed).1971.*Gathasaptasati of Hala*. Calcutta.

Batanton, R.1982. Urban Beginnigs: A View from Anthropological Archeology. *Journal of Urban History*. 8:447-446.

Beck, H.C. 1941. The Beads from Taxila. *Memoris of the Archaeological Survey of India. No 65*. New Delhi.

Begley, V. 1986. From iron to Early Historical in South Indian Archaeology. *Studies in the Archaeology of India and Pakistan*. (ed) J. Jacobson. New Delhi: 297-319.

Begley, V. & R.D. De Puma. (eds). 1992. *Rome and India, the Ancient Sea Trade*. New Delhi.

Bhandarkar, R.G. 1985. The *Early History of the Deccan* (collected works of Bhandarkar). Bombay.

Bhardwaj. H.C. 1973. Aspects of Early iron Technology in India. *Radio Carbon and Indian Archaeology*. (eds) D.P. Agrawal and A. Ghosh. Bomay: 391-400.

Bhattacharya, N.N.1991. *The Geographical Dictionary*, Ancienty and Early Mediaeval India. New Delhi.

Bray, W. & D. Trume. 1988 (second edition). *The Penguin Dictionary of Archaeology*. first published in 1972. London.

Brown, J.C. & A.K. Dey. (eds). 1955. *India's Mineral Wealth*. London.

Buhler, G.1 894. The Bhattiprolu Inscriptions. *Epigraphia Indica*. II: 323-339.

Burgers J.1887. *The Buddhist Stupas of Amaravathi and Jaggayyapeta*. Archaeological Survey of South India. London.

Cammiade ,L.A and M.C Burkitt.1930. Fresh Light on the Stone Age of South-east Asia. *India Antiquity*. IV: 327-339.

Campbell, J.H. 1874 .*Specimens of Languages of India including those of Aboriginal Tribes of Bengal, the central Provinces and the Eastern Frontier*. Calcutta.

Caspers,C.L.D.E. & E.A. Kuijper. (eds). 1984. *Annual Bibliography of India Archaeology* 1970-72. Derdrelh (Holland).XXII.

Çhakravarti, N.P.1984 (reprint). The Minor Rock Edicts of Asoka and some connected problem. *Ancient India*. No 4 (July 1947-January 1984). New Delhi.

Champion H.G. & S.K.Seth (eds) .1968. *A Revised Survey of the Forset Types of India* .New Delhi.

Chanda, R.P. 1919-20. Some unpublished Amaravati Inscriptions. *Epigraphica Indica*. XV: 258-278.

Chanda, M.1977. *Trade and Trade Routes in Ancient India* .New Delhi.

Chang, T.T. 1992. Rice and Asian Civilization. *Mand and His Culture, A Resurgence*. (ed). P.S.Bellwood. New Delhi.

Chapekar, B.N.1969. *Report on the Excavations at Ter.* Poona.

Chaplin, J.H.1962. Notes on Traditional smelting in Northern Rhodesiah. *South African Archaeological Bulletin.* 16, 63: 53-60.

Chattopadhyaya, D. 1986. *History of Science and Technology in Ancient India-The Beginnings.* Calcutta.

Chaturvedi, S. 1985. *Foreign Influx and Interaction with Indian Culture* (6th cent. B.C. to Ist Cent. A.D.). Delhi.

Chaudhuri, K.K. 1990. South Indian's contacts with china: A study in the Earliest phase from Chinese Sources. *Researches in Indian History, Archaeology, Art and Religion* (Prof. Upendra Thakur Felicitation Volume). 2 Vols. (eds) Kuppuram, G. & K. Kumudamani. Delhi. I: 217-222.

Chopra, P.N., Ravindra. T.K. & N. Subrahmanium. 1979. *History of South India.* New Delhi.

Clarence, M. 1976. Archaeology in south India: Accomplishments and Prospects *Essays on South India.* (ed). Burton stein. Bombay: 1- 40.

Coomaraswamy, A.K. 1930. *Early Indian Architecture. Eastern Art.* Madras.

Coomaraswamy, A.K 1989. *What is Civilization ?* New Delhi.

Cowell, E.B. (ed) 1990. *The Jataka or stories of the Buddha's Former Births.* 6 Vols. New Delhi.

Cunningham, A. 1871. *The Ancient Geography* of India. London.

Datta, A. 1992. Early Stages of Iron Technology and the Development of Regional pattern in India. *Man and His Culture*, A Resurgence. (ed). P.S. Bellwood. New Delhi.

De Leeuw, V. L.J. 1987. What was the Purpose of the Terracotta Animal Figuriness discovered at Kondapur ?. *Kusumanjali* New Interpretation of Indian Art and Culture. Sh. C. Sivaramamurti Commemoration Volume. 2 Vols. (ed). M.S.Nagaraja Rao. Delhi. I. 369-371.

De Silva, 1970. The spice and silk Roads. *India's Contribution to world Thoughts and Culture* : Vivekananda Commemoration Volume. Madras: 229-231.

Deo, S.B. 1969. Megaliths in Maharashtra. *Seminar Papers on the problem of Megaliths in India.* Memoris of the Department of Ancient India History, Culture and Archaeology. No 3. Banaras Hindu University. Varanasi.

Deop, S.B. 1976-77. Satavahana Anrchaeology. *Bulletin of the Deccan College Research Institute.* XXXVI: 37-41.

Deo, S.B. 1985. The Megaliths: Their Culture, Ecology, Economy and Technology. *Recent Advances in Indian Archaeology.* (eds) Deo, S.B. & K. Paddayya. Poona.

Deshpande, M.N. 1961. Roman Influence on the Terracotta of the Satavahana Period. *International Conference on Asian Archaeology.* Summaries of Papers. New Delhi.

Deshpande, M.N. 1965. Classical Influence on Terracotta Art. *Eighth International Conference of Classical Archaeology* 1963. Paris: 604-605.

Dikshit, K.N. 1969. Megalithc Typology and chronology–A Restatement. *Samskrit*: 85-89.

Dikshit, K.N. 1992. Iron Age and Peninsular India. *Puratattava.* Bulletin of the Indian Archaeological Society. No 22 (1991-92). (ed). K.N. Dikshit. New Delhi.

Dikshit, M.G. 1952. Some Beads from Kondapur. Hyderabad Archaeological Series No 16. Hyderabad.

Dikshit, M.G. 1969. *History of Indian Glass.* Bombay.

Dikshit, M.G. 1985 (reprint). Beads from Ahichchhatra, U.P. *Ancient India.* Bulletin of the Archaeological Survey of India. No 8 (1952). New Delhi.

Dubin, L.S. 1987. *The History of Beads* from 3000 B.C. to the Present. London.

Dubreuil, J.L. 1981 (reprint). *Ancient History of Deccan*. first publication in 1920. New Delhi.

Dutta, M. 1990. *A study of the Satavahana coins*. New Delhi.

Dutta, N.V. B.S. 1981. *Geology and Mineral Resources of Andhra Pradesh*. Hyderabad.

Edgar, T. & K. Raghavachari, 1987. *Castes and Tribes of South India*. 7 Volumes. New Delhi.

Edgarton, F. 1944. The Sabhaparva. *The Mahabharata*. 19 Volumes. (eds). B.S. Sukhtankar and S.K. Belvalkar. Poona. II.

Eggeling, J. (translated). 1990 (reprint). *Sacred Books of the East*, the Satapatha Brahmana. (ed). F. Maxmuller. New Delhi.

Fenwick, I.M. & B.J. Knapp. 1982. *Soils Process and Response*. London.

Filliozar, J. 1950. Intercourse of India with the Roman Empire during the Early Centuries of the Christian Era. *Journal of Indian History*. XXVIII. 23.

Fleet, J.F. 1901. Tagara, Ter. *Journal of the Royal Asiatic Society*: 548.

Foote, R.B. 1887. Notes on Some Recent Neolithic and Paleolithic Finds in south India. *Journal of the Asiatic Society of Bengal*. LVI, 2: 259-82.

Foote, R.B. 1916. *The Foote collection of Indian Prehistoric and Protohistoric Antiquities: Note on Their Ages and Distribution*. Madras.

Forbes, R.J. 1972. *Studies in Ancient Technology*. 9 Volumes. Lieden.

Francis, P.J. 1982. *Agate Beads of India*, The World of Beads Monograph Series. No 6. New Delhi.

Ghosh, P.J. 1982 a. *Glass Beads of India*, The World of Beads Monograph Series. No 7. New York.

Ghosh, A. 1953. A Remarkable Feature of South Indian Pot Making. *Man*. LIII, March.

Ghosh, A. 1973. *The City in Early Historical India*. Simla.

Ghosh, A. (ed). 1989. *An Encyclopaedia of Indian Archaeology*. 2 Volumes. New Delhi.

Ghosh, A & H. Sarkar. 1967. Beginnings of Sculptural Art in south-east Asia: A Stele from Amaravati. *Ancient India*, Bulletin of the Archaeological Survey of India. No 20 and 21 (1964 and 1965). New Delhi.

Ghosh, N.C. 1986. *Excavations at Satanikota (1977-80)*. Memoirs of the Archaeological Survey of India. No 82. New Delhi.

Gokhale, S. 1984. The Lead coin of Gautamiputra Yajna Sri Stakarni. *Journal of Numismatic Society of India*. XLVI: 47-48.

Goswami, A. 1959. *Indian Terracotta Art*. Calcutta.

Grierson, G.A. 1967 (reprint). *Linguistic Survey of India*. Delhi.

Gupta, P.L.1961. *Punch Marked Coin in the Andhra Pradesh Government Museum*. Hyderabad.

Gupta, P.L. 1972. *Gangetic Valley Terracotta Art*. Varanasi.

Gupta, P.L. 1979. Kotilingala Find of post-Mauryan Coins. *Numismatic Digest*. 3: 17-28.

Gupta, P.L. & A.K. Jha. (eds). 1987. *Numismatics and Archaeology*. Nasik.

Gurumurthy, S. 1981. *Ceramic Traditions in South India* (Down to 300 A.D.). University of Madras. Madras.

Hamilton, W. 1990 (first Indian reprint). *A Geographical Statistical and Historical Description of Hindustan and the Adjacent Countries*. 2 Volumes. Madras.9993

Hegde, K.T.M. 1981. Scientific Bias and Technology of Ancient Indian Copper and Iron Metallurgy. *Indian Journal of History of Science*. 16: 189-201.

Hultzsch, E. 1969. *Corpus Inscriptionum Indicarum. Vol I inscriptions of Ashoka*. New Edition. Varanasi.

Hunt, E.H. 1924. Hyderabad Cairn Burials and their Significance. *Journal of Royal Anthropological institute of Great Britain and Ireland*: 14.

Husain ,H.A.G. 1962. *The Economic History of India*. Calcutta. I

Imperial Gazetteer of India. 1908. Published under the Authority of His Majesty's Secretary of State for India in Council. Oxford.

Imperial Gazetteer of India. 1909. Privincial Series. Hyderabad State. Calcutta.

Indian Archaeology A Review (*IAR*). (*ed*). Director General of Archaeology in India. Archaeological Survey of India. New Delhi.

Jacobson, J. Ed. 1986. *Studies in the Archaeology of India and Pakistan*. New Delhi.

Jaggi. O.P. 1981. History of Science, *Technology and Medicine in India*, Technology in Ancient India. Delhi. I.

Jayaswal. K.P. 1916. The Empire of Bindusara. *The Journal of the Bihar and Orissa Research Society*. II, 1: 82.

Jayaswal, V.1978. *Palaeohistory of India* (A study of the Prepared core Technique). Delhi.

Jayaswal, V. 1990. Kushan caly Art of Khairadih. *Lalit Kala*. Journal of Oriental Art Chiefly India. (ed) Kari Khandelwala. Lalit Kala Academy. No 24: 61-69.

Jayaswal, V. 1990. Ethnoarchaeological study in Northern India Terracottas: A Case study. *Historical Archaeology of India*, A Dialogue between Archaeologists and Historians. (eds) Ray, A. & S. Mukherjee. New Delhi: 227-238.

Jayaswal, V. 1991. *Kushan Clay Art Ganga Plains*, A Cast study of Human forms from Khairadih. Delhi.

Jayaswal, V. & K.Krishna. 1986. *An Ethno-archaeological view of Indian Terracottas*. Delhi.

Joshi, M.C. 1975. Early Historical Uraban Growth in India : Some observation'. *Puratattva*, Bulletin of Indian Archaeological Society. No 7. (ed) B.K. Thapar. New Delhi.

Kalota, N.S. 1978. *India as described by Metatheses*. Delhi.

Kameshwara Rao, V. 1990. Some Satavahana sites in Royalseema, Andhra Pradesh. *Journal of Archaeology*. Satavahana Special. Dr. N. Rameshan Commemoration. Volume . (ed) V.V. K. Sastry. Hyderbad. III, 1: 9-12.

Kangle, R.P. 1992 (reprint). *The Kautilya Arthasastra*. first edition 1963. 3 Volumes. Delhi.

Kenoyer, J.M. 1986. The Indus Bead Industry: Contribution to Bead Technology'. *Ornament* 10, 1: 18-23.

Khan M.A.W. 1963. *A Monograph on Yeleswaram Excavations*. Andhra Pradesh Archaeological Series XIV. Government of Andhra Pradesh. Hyderbad.

Khan, M.A.W. 1969. *A Monograph on Early Buddhist Stupa at Kesanapalli*. Archaeological Series. No 27. Government of Andhra Pradesh. Hyderabad.

Knidian, K. 1987 (reprint). *Mc. Crindle's Ancient India* as described by the Commerce and Navigation of the Erythrean sea and Ancient India as described by Ktesian The Knidian. first published. 1882. 2 Volumes. Patna.

Krishna, M.S. 1982. *Geology of India and Burma*. New Delhi.

Krishnaswamy, V.D. 1984 (reprint). Stone Age India. *Ancient India*, Bulletin of the Archaeological Survey of India. No 3 (1947). New Delhi.

Krishnaswamy, V.D. 1984 (reprint) . Megalithic Types of South India. *Ancient India*, Bulletin of the Archaeological Survey of India. No 5 (1949). New Delhi.

Kuppuram, G. 1989. *Ancient Indian Mining, Metallurgy and metal Industries*. 2 Volumes. Delhi.

Larhiri, N 1992 *The Archaeology of India Trade Routes* (upto C. 200 B.C). New Delhi.

Lal. M. 1986. Origin and Development of cities in India: A Fresh Look. *Comparative Studies in the Development of Complex Societies.* The World Archaeological Xongress 1-7 September, 1986. Southampton and London. III.

Longhurst, A.H. 1990 (reprient). Excavations at Nagarjunakonda. *Annual Reprint of the Anrchaeolocal Survey of India. (1928-29).* (ed) H. Hargreaves. Delhi.

Luders, H. 1912. A List of Brahmin Inscriptions from the earliest time to about A.D. 400 with the exception of those of *Asoka' Epigraphica Indica.* Calcutta.

Mahaligama, T.V. 1957. Archaeology in south India. *Journal of Madras of University*: 141-156.

Mangalam, S.J. 1986. *Historical Geography and Toponomy of Andhra Pradesh.* New Delhi.

Mani, B.R. 1987. *The Kushan Civilization* (Studies in Urban Development and Meterial Culture). Delhi.

Margabandhu, C. 1977. Evidence of Weights and Measures During the Early Historic period. *Itihas.* IV, 1: 15-25.

Margabandhu, C. 1978. Some Etched Beads and Pendents from Kondapur. *Journal of Indian History.* LVI: 35-46.

Margabandhu, C. 1985. *Archaeology of the Satavahana-Kshatrapa Times.* Delhi.

Margabandhu, C., Ramachandran, K.S. Sagar, A.P. & D.K. Singh. (eds). 1991. *Indian Anchaeological Heritage* (SH. K.V. Soundara Rajan Felicitation Volumes). 2 Volumes. Agam Indological Series No 11. Delhi.

Marshall, J. 1955. *Texila* (An Illustrated Account of Archaeological Excavationa at Taxila between 1913-14). 3 Volumes. Cambridge.

Mate, M.S. 1969. Building in Ancient India. *World Archaeology*, Techniques of Chronogy and Excavations. I. 1: 236-246.

Michael, S.B. 1974. Prehistoric Copper Mining in North-western Zambia. *Archaeology*. October, 1974: 242-247.

Miller, J, I. 1964. *The spise Trade of the Roman Empire*. Oxford.

Mishra, K.A. 1989. *The Indian Black ware* (First Millennium B.C.). Delhi

Motichandra, S. 1950. Cosmetics and coiffeures in ancient India. *Journal of the Indian Society of Oriental Art*. VIII: 62-245.

Mukherjee, R.K. 1912. *A History of Indian Shipping and Maritime Activity from the Earliest Time*. London.

Murthi, C.S. 1965. Amaravati Sculpures in Madras Government Museum. *Bulletin of Madras Government Museum*. New Series IV.

Murthy, K.K. 1965. Some Technical Aspects of the Indian Pottery. *Orissa Historical Research Journal*. XIII, 2: 29-42.

Murthy, K.K. 1971. Pottery Making Technique in Early Indian Literature. *The Andhra Pradesh Jurnal of Archaeology*. I, 1: 73-77.

Murthy, K.K. 1982. *Mirrors of Indian Culture*. Delhi.

Murthy M.L.K. 1985. Blade-and-Burin and Late Stone Age Industries around Renigunta, Chitoor district. *Studies in Indian Archeology*. Prof. H.D. Sankalia Felicitation Volume. (eds) Deo, S.B. & M.K. Dhavalikar. Bombay: 106-128.

Muthin,S. (Editor- in Chief). 1990. *An Atlas of India*. Delhi.

Nayak, H.M. & B.R. Gopal (eds). 1990. *South Indian Studies. (*Dr. T.V. Mahaligam Commemoration Volume). Mysore.

Newbold, T.J. 1844. Notes on the Osseous breccia and Deposit in the caves of Billa Soorgumm Let $15^0 25'$ Long $78^0 15'$, South India. *Journal of the Asiatic Society of Bengal* 13, 2: 610-615.

Oates, D. 1990. Innovation in Mud brick. : Decorative and Structural Technique in Ancient Mesopotamia. *World Archaeology* (Architectural Innnovation). (ed) J. Oates. 21, 3, February 1990: 336-406.

Pal, A.C. 1991. Pottery in Archaeology. *Studies in Archaeology*. (ed) A. Datta: 149.

Paddayya, K. 1971. Radio carbon Dates and South Indian Neolithic Culture; *Antiquity*. XLV, 178 : 134-138.

Paddayya, K. & M.L.K. Murthy. 1971. Glimpses of Prehistoric Andhra Pradesh. *The Quarterly Journal of the Muthic Society.* LXII, 1, 04: 56-74.

Panikkar, K.M. 1955. *Geographical Factors in Indian History*. Bombay.

Pant, P.C. & M.Mishra. 1983. Concept of Nagar in Ancient India and its bearing on Archaeological Evidence. *Bharati,* Buletten of Department of Ancient Indian History, Culture and Archaeology. Banaras Hindu University. New Series No. 1: 100-104.

Patwardhan, N. 1984. *Hand – book for Potters*. New Delhi.

Peacock, D.P.S. (ed) 1977. *Pottery and Early Commerce*, Characterization and Trade in Roman and Later Cermics. London.

Pisipaty, S.R.K. 1997. Some observations on ceramics of the Andhra and Satavahana cultures. *Ancient Ceramics: Historical Enquiries and Scientific Approaches*. (eds) Pant, P.C. & V. Jayaswal. Delhi.

Pisipaty, S.R.K. 2006. Ceramic traditions in early Andhradesa-an appraisal. *Mahasenasiri Riches of Indian Archaeological and Cultural Studies.* A Felicitation Volume in Honour of Dr. I.K. Sarma. (ed) Chenna Reddy, P. Delhi.

Pisipaty, S.R.K. 2010. Andhra culture-an obscure phase in the early historical archaeology of Andhra Pradesh. *Recent Researches in Archaeology, History and Culture (Festschrift to Prof. K.V. Raman)*. (ed) Chenna Reddy, P. 2 Vols. Delhi. I:16

Prasad, R.C. & O. Singh. 1987. *India: A Regional Geography*. Varanasi.

Raghavachari, K. 1972-73. Dharanikota and its Western Contacts. *Quarterly Review of Historical Studies.* Calcutta. XII, 3: 1-3.

Raja Gopal, M.V. 1974. *Andhra Pradesh District Gazetteers.* Published by Government of Andhra Pradesh. Hyderabad.

Ramachandran, K.S. 1975. *Radiocarbon Dates of Archaeological Sites in India.* Archaeological Series No. 42. Government of Andhra Pradesh. Hyderabad.

Ramachandran, T.N. 1953. *Nagarjunakonda 1938.* Memories of the Archaeological Survey of India. No 71. Delhi.

Rameshan, M. (ed) 1976. *Gazetteers of India,* Andhra Pradesh. Hyderabad.

Rao, B.K.G. 1970. Development of Technology during the iron Age in south India (C. 1000 B.C. to the Beginning of the Historical Times). *Indian Journal of Historical Science.* V, 2: 253-271.

Rao, B.K.G.1970. *Megalithic Culture in south India.* Mysore.

Rao, B.S. 1948-49. The Geographical Factore in Andhra History and Archaeology. *Bulletin of the Deccan College Research Institute.* IX: 167-183.

Rao B.S. 1958. *Personality of India*; Pre and proto Historic Foundation of India and Pakistan. Baroda.

Rao, K.P. 1988. *Deccan Megaliths.* Delhi.

Rao, K.R. 1992. *Perspectives of Archaeology, Art and Culture in Early Andhradesa.* New Delhi.

Rao, M.R. 1961. *Satavahana Coins in the Andhra Pradesh Government Musume.* Andhra Pradesh Government of Archaeological Series. No 2 Hyderabad.

Rao, M.R. 1968. *Inscriptions of Andhra Pradesh.* 2 Volumes. Tirupati.

Rao. P.R.R. 1956. Asia-wide influence of Andhra Art. Buddha *Jayanti Souvenir.* (ed) P. Srinivasacharya. Hyderabad.

Rao, S.R. 1965. Shipping and Maritime Trade of the Indian People. *Expedition. 7, 3: 30-37.*

Rao, S.R. 1966. *Excavations at Amreli*: A Kshatrapa-Gupta Town. Bulletin of Baroda Museum and Picture Gallery No XVIII. Baroda.

Rapson, E. J. 1955. *The Cambridge History of India*. Delhi.

Rapson, E.J. 1975. *Catalogue of the Coin the Andhra Dynasty, the Western Kshatrapas, the Trikota Dynasty and the Bodi Dynasty*. New Delhi.

Rawson, P.S. 1953. The Surface Treatment of Early Indian Pottery. *Man* . LIII, March, 1953: 44.

Ray, A. 1983. *Life and Art of Early Andhradesa*. Delhi.

Ray Chauduri, H. 1953. *Political History of Ancient India* (From the Accession of Parikshit to the Extension of the Gupta Dynasty). University of Calcutta. Calcutta.

Ray H.P. 1986. *Monastery and Guild: Commerce under the Satavahanas*. New Delhi.

Ray, P. and S.N. Sen (eds). 1986 (second edition). *The Cultural Heritage of India , Seience and Tecnology*. 6 Volumes. first edition in 1937. The Ramakrishna Mission Institute of Culture. Calcutta.

Rea, A. 1990 (reprint). Excavations at Amaravati. *Archaeological Survey of India Annual Report 1908-09*. New Delhi.

Reddy, R.D. & S.P. Reddy . 1991. Unpublished Saravahana Coins from Kotilingala and Sangareddy. *Numismatic studies*. (ed) D. Handa. New Delhi. I.

Reddy. V.R. 1976. *The Prehistoric and Protohistoric Cultures of Palavoy, South India : with a special reference to the Ash mound problem*. Andhra Pradesh Government Archaeological Series. No 51. Hyderabad.

Reddy, V.R. 1978. *A Study of the Neolithic culture of South- western Andhra Pradesh*. Andhra Pradesh Government Archaeological Series. No 51. Hyderabad.

Reddy, V.R. 1991. *Neolithic and post-Neolithic Cultures*. New Delhi.

Rice. P. 1987. *Pottery Analysis*: A Source Book. University of Chicago Press. Chicago.

Roux, V. 1989. *The Potters, Wheel, Craft Specialization and Technical Competence*. New Delhi.

Roy, T.N. 1986. *A Study of Northern Black Polished Ware*, an Iron Age Culture of India. New Delhi.

Sahni, D.R. 1990 (reprint). The Yerragudi Rock Edicts of Asoka. *Annual Reprint of the Archaeological Survey of India. (1928-29)*. (ed) H. Hargreaves. Delhi.

Saletore, B.A. 1945. Roman Trade with Dekkan. *Proceedings of the Dekkan History Conference 1945*. Hyderabad.

Sankalia, H.D. 1957. Imported Mediterranean Amphorae from Kondapur. *Journal of the Royal Asiatic Society*: 207-208.

Sankalia, H.D.1960. Houses and Habitations through the Ages. *Bulletin of Deccan College Research Institute*. 20: 140-63.

Sankalia, H.D. 1962. From Food Collection to Unbanisation in India. *Indian Anthoropology : Essays in Memory of D.N. Majumdar*. (ed) Madan, T.N. & G. Sarana. Bombay.

Sankalia , H.D. 1963. *Pre- History and Proto-History in India and Pakistan*. Bombay.

Sankalia, H.D. 1977. *Pre-History of India*. New Delhi.

Sankalia, H.D. 1979. *Indian Archaeology* Today. Delhi.

Sankalia, H.D. & M.K. Davalikar. 1969. The Terracotta Art of India. *Marg*. XXIII, 1, December: 33-34.

Sankalia, H.D. Deo, S.B. Ansari, Z.D. & S. Ehrardt. 1960. *From History to Prehistory at Nevasa* (1954-56). Poona.

Sankaranarayan, R. 1984. Some Pages in Early Cultural History of Andhra. *Svasti Sri*. B.Ch. Chabbred Felicitation Volume. (eds) Rameshan, K.V., Prasad, A. & S.P. Tewari. Delhi: 61-65.

Saraswati, B. 1979. *Pootery Making Cultures and Indian Civilization*. New Delhi.

Saraswati, B. & N.K.Behura. 1966. Pottery Techiques in *Peasant India*. Anthropological Survey of India. Memoir No 13 (1964). Government of India. Calcutta.

Sarkar, H. 1973 (reprint). Kesarapalli-1962. *Ancient India*. Bulletin of the Archaeological Survey of India. No 22 (1966). New Delhi: 37-74.

Sarkar, H 1986 (reprint). Some Aspects of the Buddhist Monuments at Nagarjunakonda. *Ancient India*. Bulletin of the Archaeological Survey of India. No 16 (1960). New Delhi.

Sarkar, H. & B.N. Mirsa. 1987. *Nagarjunakonda*. Published by the Director General of Archaeological Survey of India. New Delhi.

Sarma, I.K. 1974. C 14 Dates, N.B.P. Ware and Early Historical Archaeology of the Penisular India'. *Journal of Indian History*. 52: 49-56.

Sarma, I.K. 1977 . *Religious in Art and History Archaeology of South India Contacts and Correlations*. Madras.

Sarma, I.K. 1978. Epigraphical Discoveries at Guntupalli. *Journal of the Epigraphical Society of India*. Mysore.

Sarma , I.K. 1980. *Coinage of Satavahana Empire*. Delhi.

Sarma, I.K. 1980 a. Important Numismatic Finds Duvuuru and Alluru distric Nellore, Andhra Pradesh. *The Journal of the Academy of Indian Numismatic and Sigillography*. 3: 12-15.

Sarma, I.K. 1982. Some Aspects of Bhattiprolu Inscriptions. *Journal of the Epigraphical Society of India*. Mysore.

Sarma, I.K. 1987. Buddhist Sites in Andhra Pradesh. *Archaeology of Andhra Pradesh, A Souvenir*. (ed) V.V. K. Sastry. Government of Andhra Pradesh. Hyderabad: 17-22.

Sarma, I.K. 1988. *Studies in Early Buddhist Monuments and Brahmi inscriptions of Andhradesa*. Nagpur.

Sarma, I.K. 1990. Historical Archaeology of Andhra in the Light of Recent Excavations at Amaravati, Nagarjunakonda and Peddavegi. *Historical Archaeology of India* (A Dialogue between Archaeologists and historians). (eds) Ray, A. & S. Mukherjee. New Delhi: 109-118.

Sarma, I.K. 1990a. Ancient Andhra Ports Religious Centers and Seafaring. *Journal of Marine Archaeology.* I. January: 19-23.

Sarma, I.K. 1990 b. Ancient port towns of south-east India, their Role in the spread of Buddhist art and Religion to China and Japan. *Researches in Indian History, Arcgaeology, Art and Religion* (Prof. Upendra Thakur Felicitation Volume). (eds) Kuppuram, G. & K. Kumudamani. 2 Volumes. Delhi. II: 551-560.

Sarma, I.K. 1992. From Peddavegi to Poompuhar (Cultural contacts and exploration on sea routes). *New trends in Indian Art and Archaeology.* (eds) Nayak, B.U. & N.C. Ghosh. New Delhi: 435-441.

Sarma, R.S. 1987. *Urban Decay in India* (*c* 300-1000) New Excavations. Nagpur.

Sastri, A.M 1982. Pre-Satavahana and Satavahana Coinage of the Deccan. *Journal of the Numismatic Society of India* (R.C. Manumdar Commemoration Volume). XLIV, I & II: 1-15.

Sastri, K.A.N. 1939. *Foreign Notices of South India.* Madras.

Sastri, K.A.N. Ed. 1957. *A Comprehnesive History of India.* The Mauryas and the Satavahans, 325 B.C.– A.D. 300. Calcutta. II.

Sastri, S.N.M. Ed. 1927. *Ancient India as Described by Ptolemy.* Calcutta.

Sastri, T.V.G. Ed. 1983. *Veddamanu Excavations and Explorations in Krishna Valley.* Birla Archaeological and Cultural Research Institute. Hyderabad.

Sastri, T.V.G., Bai, M.K. & J.V. Rao 1984. *Veerapuram* . A Type site for cultural study in the Krishna Valley. Hyderabad.

Sastri, T.V.G. 1989. Magarathi Coins and Their Chronology. *Ajaya Sr.* Recent Studies in Indology. Prof. Ajaya Mitra Sastri Felicitation Volume. 2 Volumes. (ed) D. Hansa. Delhi. I: 301-312.

Sastry, V.V. K. 1971. Terracottas from Peddabankur and Dhulikatta. *The Andhra Pradesh Journal of Archaeology*. I, 1.

Sastry, V.V. K.1983. *The Proto and Early History of Andhra Pradesh. Government of Andhra Pradesh*. Hyderabad.

Sastry, K.V.V., Subramanyam, B. & N.R.K. Rao. 1992. *Totlakonda* (A Buddhist Site in Andhra Pradesh). Andhra Pradesh Government of Archaneological Series. No 68. Hyderabad.

Sastry, P.V.P. (ed) 1972. *Epigraphia Andhsica*. Government of Andhra Pradesh. Hyderabed. III.

Sastry, P.V.P. 1978. Unknown Coins of Satavahana and their Predecessors. *Numismatic Digest*. II, 1: 10-21.

Sastry, P.V.P. 1979. Some more coins from Kotilingala. *Numismatic Digest*. III, 2: 17-28.

Sastry, P.V.P. 1989. Political System in Early Coastal Andhra. *Ajaya Sri*, Recent Studies in Indology (Prof. Ajay Mitra Shastri Felicatation Volume). (ed) D. Hande. New Delhi.

Satyanarayana, K. 1975. *A Study of the History and Culture of the Andhra* (From Stone Age to Fepression). New Delhi.

Schwartzberg, J.E. (ed) 1992. (second impression). *A Historical Atlas of south Asia*. first impression in 1978. New York.

Seenath, J. & S.H. Ahmad. 1989. *All India Anthropometrical Atlas of South Zone-Andhra Pradesh* (Analysis of Data). Archaeological Survey of India. Calcutta.

Seshadri, M. 1971. *Report on the Excavations at T. Narsipur*. Banglore.

Sewell, R. 1972 (reprint). *Lists-The Antiquarinan Remains in the Presidency of Madres*. first published in 1982. Archaeological Survey of India. New Imperial Series No VII. Varanasi.

Shah. S.L.T.D. 1938. *Ancient India*. Baroda.

Sharma, G.R. 1960. *The Excavations at Kausambi 1957-59*. Allahabad University Publication. No 1. Allahabad.

Sharma, R.S. 1983. *Material Culture and Social formation in Ancient India*. New Delhi.

Singh, A.K. 1988. *Indo-Roman* Trade. New Delhi.

Singh, B.P. 1973. A Technological Study of Terracotta Figurines in India Before the Emergence of the Mould. *Journal of the Oriental Institute*. XXII, 3: 378-393.

Singh, B.P. 1985. *Life in Ancient Varanasi*, An Account Based on Archaeological Evidence. Delhi.

Sigh, R.L. (ed) 1971. *India: A Regional Geography*. National Geophysical Society of India. Varanasi

Singh, R.N. 1988. Ancient South Indian Metallurgy: A Reappriasal. *Studies in Ancient Indian History* (D.C. Sircar Commemoration Volume). (eds) Gupta, D.K.K., Bhattacharya, P.K. & R.D. Choudhury. Delhi.

Singh, T.R.R. 1979. Prehistoric and Early historic Sites in Karimnagar Region, *Andhra Pradesh*. Andhra Pradesh Journal of Archaeology. II: 1-10.

Singa, B.P. (ed) 1969. *Potteries in Ancient India*. Patna.

Sircar, D.C. 1991 (reprint). *Select Inscriptions*, Bearing on Indian History and civilization. 2. Volumes. first edition in 1942. Delhi.

Sitapati, P. & V.V. K. Sastri 1980. *New Satavahana Sculptures from Andhra Amaravati*. Archaeological Series. No 54 Government of Andhra Pradesh. Hyderabad.

Soundara Rajan, K.V. 1958. Studies in the Stone Age of the Nagarjunakonda and its neighborhood. *Ancient India*. Bulletin of the Archaeological Survey of India. No 14. New Delhi: 49-113.

Sundara Rajan, K.V. 1985 (reprint). Stone Age Industries Near Giddalur, district Kurnool. *Ancient India*. Bulletin of the Archaeolocal Survey of India. No 8 (1952). New Delhi: 64-92.

Spate, O.H.K. & A.T.A. Learmonth. 1984 (third edition). *India and Pakistan, A General and Regional Geography*. New Delhi.

Srinivasachary P. (ed) 1956. Buddha Jayanti Souvenir. Hyderabad.

Srinivasan, K.R. & N.R. Banerjee. 1953. Survey of South Indian Megaliths. *Ancient India*. Bulletin of the Archaeolocal Survey of India. No 9. New Delhi: 103-118.

Srinivasan, P.R. 1963. Bronzes of South India.. *Bulletin of the Madras Government Museum*. Madras. VIII.

Stein, B. 1976. *Essay on South India*. New Delhi.

Subrahamanyam, B.R. 1964. Apperarance and Spread of Iron in India, An Appraisal of Archaeological Data. *Journal of the Oriental Institute*. Baroda.

Subrahamanyam, B.R. 1966. Iron Age in India-its beginnings. *Journal of the Maharaja Sayaji Rao University*. Baroda.

Subrahamanyam, K.R. 1989. *Buddhist Remains in Andhra and the History of Andhra* (Between 225 and 610 A.D.). New Delhi.

Subrahamanyam, R. 1964. *Salihundam – A Buddhist site in Andhra Pradesh. Andhra Pradesh* Government Archaeological Series. No 17. Hyderabad.

Subrahmanyam, R. 1968. *The Guntupalli Brahmi Inscriptions of Kharavela. Epigraphical* Series. No 3. Government of Andhra Pradesh. Hyderbad.

Subrahamanyam, R. 1974. *Asokuni Erragudi Silasasanamulu* (in Telugu). Hyderabad.

Subrahamanyam, R. Banerjee, K.D., Khare, M.D., Rao, B.V., Sarkar, H., Singh, R. Joshi, R.V. Lal, S.B.., Rao, V.V. Srinivasan, K.R. & K. Totadri. 1975. *Nagarjunakonda (1954-60)*. Memoris of the Archaeological Survey of India. No 75. New Delhi. I.

Thapar, B.K. 1985 (reprint). Maski, 1954: A Chalcolithic Site of the Southern Deccan. *Ancient India*. Bulletin of the Archaeolocal Survey of India. No 13 (1957). New Delhi: 4-142.

Thapar, B.K. 1967. Prakash 1955: A Chalcolithic Site in the Tapti Vally. *Ancient India*. Bulletin of the Archaeolocal Survey of India. No 20 & 21 (1964 & 1965). New Delhi: 5-167.

Tripathi, V. 1986. From Copper to Iron-A Transition. *Puratattva.* Bulletin of the Indian Archaeolocal Society. No 15. New Delhi: 75-79.

Ushakantha, S. 1982. Megalithic Monuments of Andhra Pradesh. *The Eastern Anthropologist.* 35, 1: 25-36.

Varma, K. M 1970. *The Indian Technique of clay Modeling.* Calcutta.

Venkatachalam, K. 1948-49. The Origin of the Andhras. *Journal of Andhra Historical Research Society.* Prof. R. Subba Rao Shashtipurti Volume. XIX, April: 154.

Venkataramanaian, N. 1971-72. Prehistoric Remains in Andhra Pradesh. *Journal of Andhra Historical Research Society.* I-I: 20-25.

Venkataramanaian. N. & P.V.P. Sastri (eds). 1972. *Epigraphic Andhrica.* Government of Andhra Pradesh. Hyderabad. II.

Vincent, A.S. 1972. *Coins of Ancient India* (Catalogue of the Coins in the Indian Museum). Calcutta.

Wacher, J. Ed. 1990. *The Ron an World.* 2 Volumes. London.

Wadia, D.N. 1970 (reprint). *Geology of India.* London.

Warmington, E.H. 1974 (second edition). *The Commerce Between the Roman Empire and India.* London.

Wheeler, R.E.M. 1955 . *Roman beyond the Imperial Frontiers.* Harmondsworth.

Wheeler, R.E.M. 1984 (reprint). Brahmagiri and Chandravalli, 1947: Megalithic and other Cultures in the Chitaldurg district, Mysore. *Ancient India.* Bulletin of the Archaeological Survey of India. No 4 (1947-48). New Delhi: 181-310.

Wheeler, R.E.M., Ghosh, A. & Krishna Deva. 1983 (reprint). Arikamedu: An Indo-Roman Trading station on the East coast of India. *Ancient India.* Bulletin of the Archaeolocal Survey of India. No 2 (1946). New Delhi: 17-124.

Yazdani, G. 1941. Excavation at Kondapur: An Andhra twon (200 B.C.-200 A.D.). *Annals of the Bhandarkar Oriental Research Institute.* XXII: 171-185.

Yazdani, 1960. *The Early History of the Deccan.* London.

Yusuf. S. 1936-37. Paithan Excavation. *Annual Report of the Archaeological Department of His Exalted Highness the Nizam's Dominions.* Hyderabad.

INDEX

G

H

I

J

K

R

S

V

W

Y

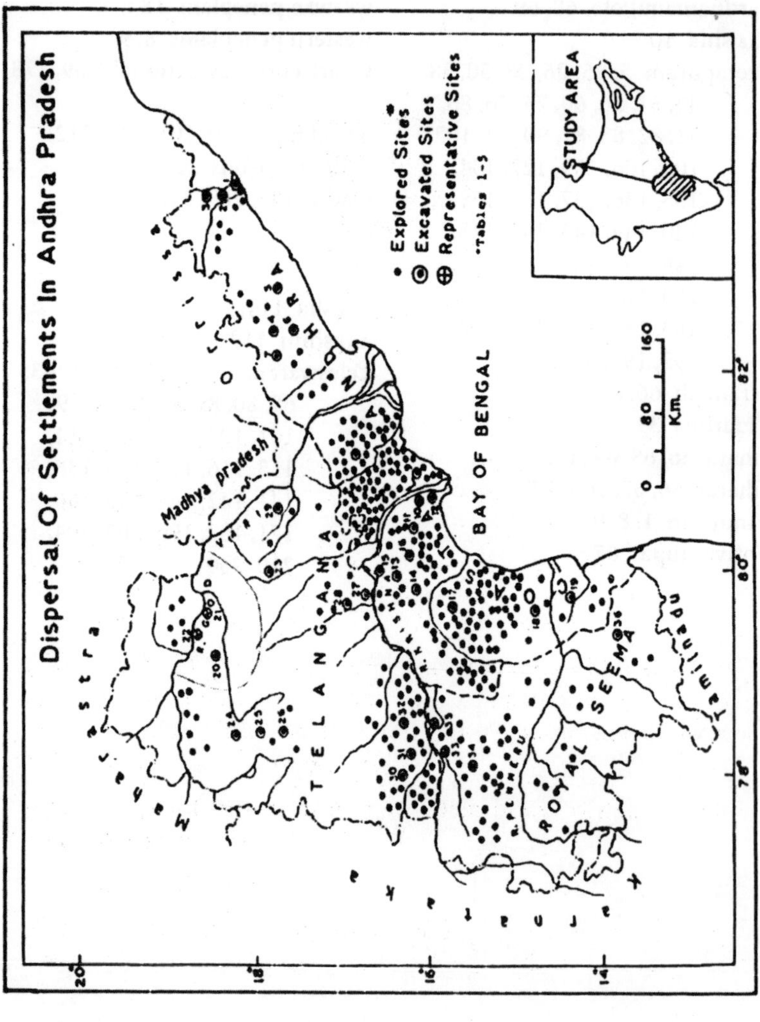
Dispersal Of Settlements In Andhra Pradesh
Explored Sites*
Excavated Sites
Representative Sites
*Tables 1-5
STUDY AREA
BAY OF BENGAL
Madhya pradesh
TELANGANA
0 80 160
Km.

Map–I

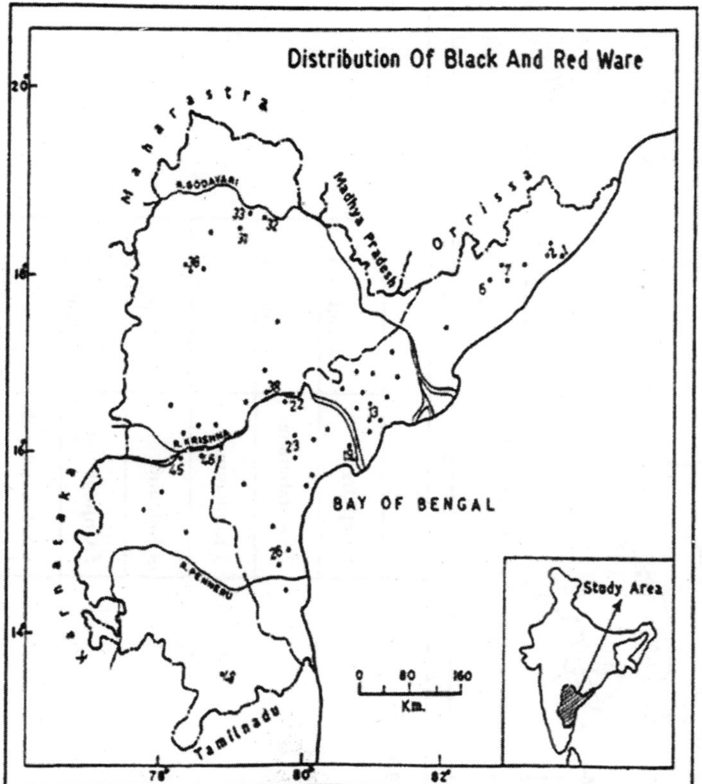

Map–II

1.Calingapatnam	2.Mukhalingam
3.Salihundam	4.Lingarajupalem
5.Guntupalli	6.Kantamanenivarigudem
7.Peddavegi	8.Agiripalli
9.Allur	10.Annangi
11.Bobbellapadu	12.Chintalapadu
13.Gantasala	14.Kandrapadu
15.Kesarapalli	16.Kommavarapupadu
17.Raghavapuram	18.Vijayawada
19.Amaravati	20.Chebrolu
21Mallipadu	22.Nagarjunakonda
23.Vaddamanu	24.Vaikuntapuram
25.Vipparala	26.Chandravaram
27.Inalapadu	28.Jonnavada
29.Kotesvaralayam	30.Budigepally
31.Dhulikatta	32.Kotilingala
33.Peddabankur	34.Ismaikhanpet
35.Kandi	36.Kondapur
37.Kakanur	38.Yeleswaram
39.Polakonda	40.Chagatur
41.Chellipad	42.Chinnamarrur
43.Utnur	44.Yapaladevipadu
45.Satanikota	46.Vamulapadu
47.Veerapuram	48.Guddimallam

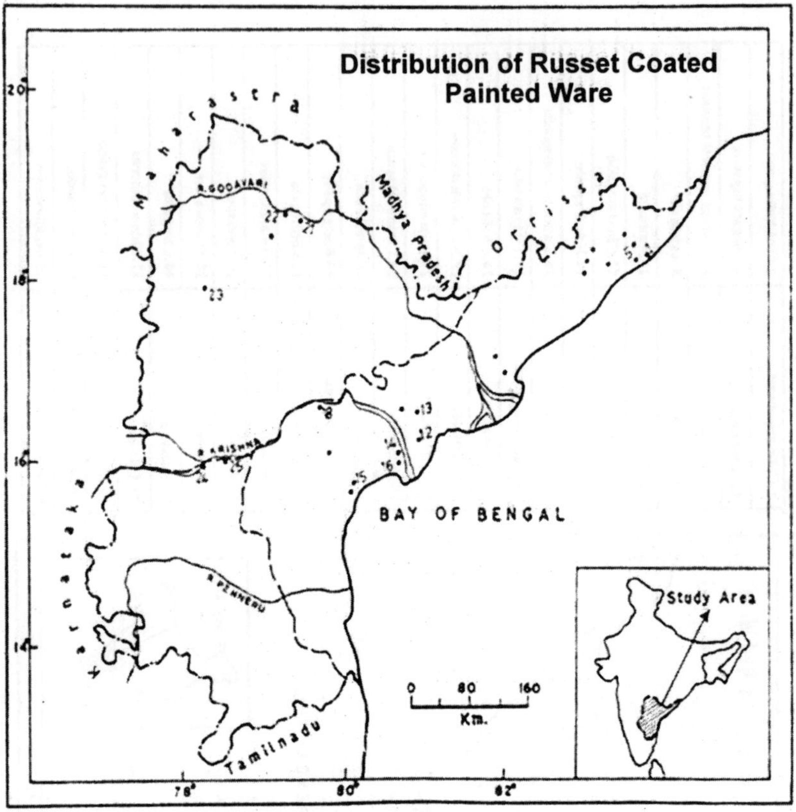

Map–III

1.Kotilingala	8.Tolkatta
2.Peddabankur	9.Gurjala
3.Kondapur	10.Manjra
4.Kakanur	11.Jangoan
5.Gujulabanda	12.Rekulapadu
6.Nelakondapalli	13Satanikota
7.Panigiri	14Veerapuram

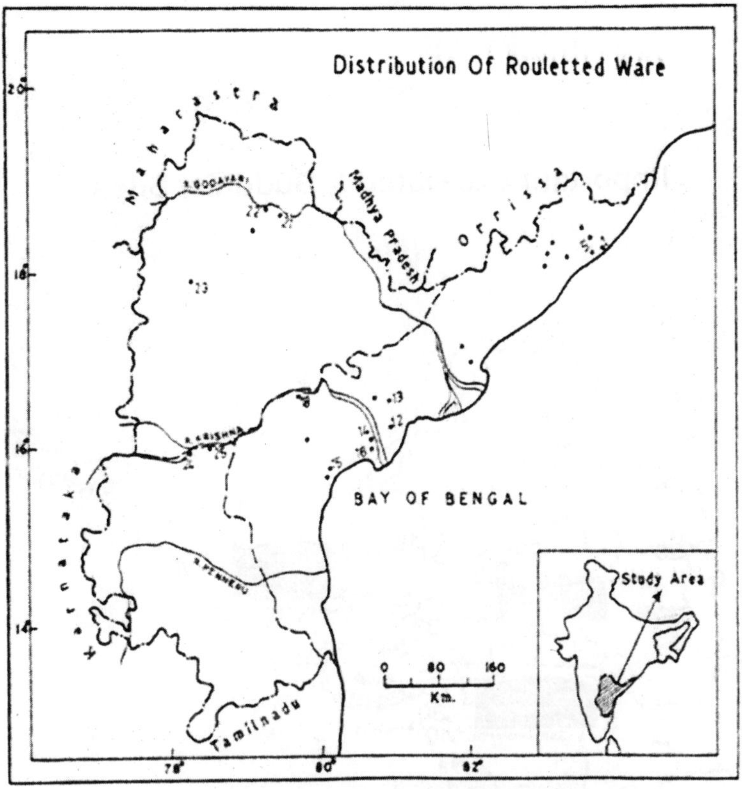

1.Calingapatnam	2.Chintamandi Dibba
3.Mukhalingam	4.Neredubandagudu
5.Salihundam	6.Simhapura
7.Bhavikonda	8.Pithapuram
9.Nagarlapet	10.Paritala
11.Annanesi	12.Gantasala
13.Kesarapalli	14.Amaravati
15.Chebrolu	16.Dharanikota
17.Mallipadu	18.Nagarjunakonda
19.Vaikuntapuram	20.Dhulikatta
21.Kotilingala	22.Peddabankur
23.Kondapur	24.Satanikota
25.Veerapuram	

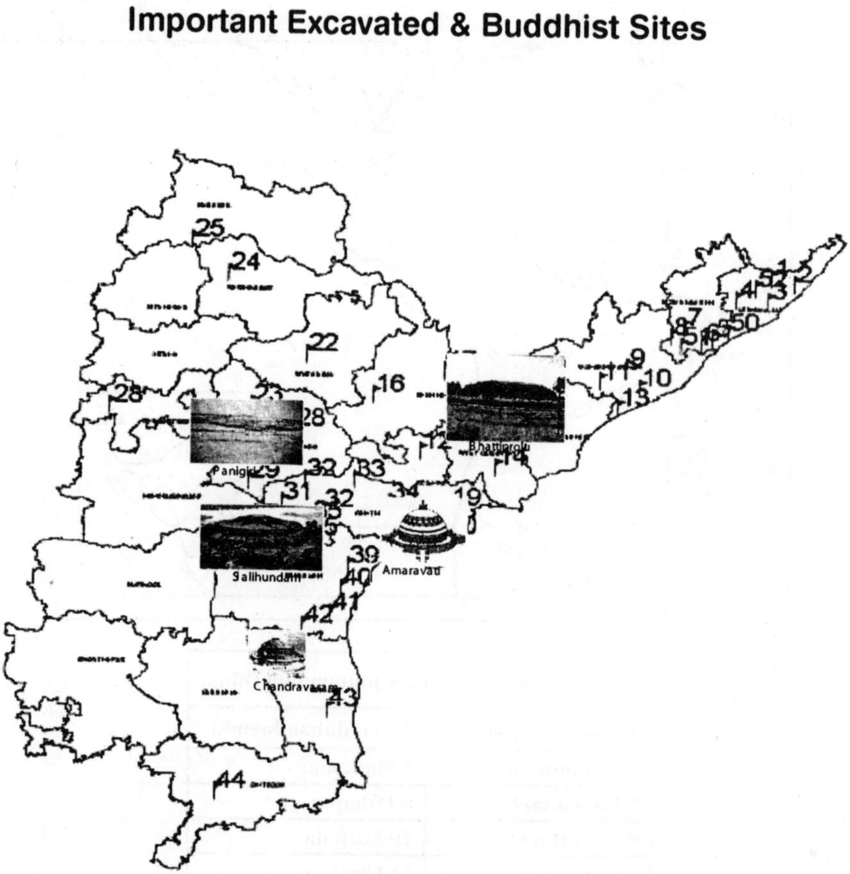
Important Excavated & Buddhist Sites
Panigiri
Salihundam
Bhattiprolu
Amaravati
Chandravaram

Map–V

S No	Name of Site	District	Region	Significance
1.	Calingapatnam	Srikakulam	Coastal Andhra	Port
2.	Mukhalingam	"	"	Religious
3.	Salihundam	"	"	"
4.	**Dantapuram**	"	"	"
5.	Bhavikonda	Vishakapatnam	"	"
6.	Gopalapatnam	"	"	"
7.	Pavuralabedu	"	"	"
8.	Thotlakonda	"	"	"
9.	Peddavegi	West Godavari	"	Early Historical
10.	Gantantasala	Krishna	"	Religious
11.	Agiripalle	"	"	"
12.	Amaravati	Guntur	"	"
13.	Bhattiprolu	"	"	"
14.	Dharanikota	"	"	Fortified town
15.	Kesanapalli	"	"	Religious
16.	Mallipadu	"	"	Early Historical
17.	Nagarjunakonda	"	"	Religious
18.	Vaddamanu	"	"	"
19.	Chandravaram	Prakasham	"	"
20.	Dupadu	"	"	"
21.	Nandalur	"	"	"
22.	Duvvuru	Nellore	"	Early Historical
23.	Kotamitta	"	"	"
24.	Dhulikatta	Karimnagar	Telangana	Fortified town
25.	Kotilingala	"	"	Political centre
26.	Peddabankur	"	"	Early Historical
27.	Polakonda	Wàrangal	"	"
28.	Kandi	Medal	"	"
29.	Kondapur	"	"	Craft centre
30.	Rekulapadu	"	"	Early Historical
31.	Yeleshwaram	Nelgonda	"	Religious
32.	Vardamankota	"	"	Early Historical
33.	Panigiri	"	"	Religious
34.	Gajulabanda	"	"	"
35.	Arlagaddagudem	"	"	"
36.	Tirumalagiri	"	"	"
37.	Byragulagutta	Khammam	"	"
38.	Chagatur	Mehboobnagar	"	"
39.	Peddamarrur	"	"	"
40.	Yapaladevipadu	"	"	"
41.	Satanikota	Kurnool	Royalseema	Fortified town
42.	Siddarajalingapuram	"	"	Early Historical
43.	Veerapuram	"	"	Rural centre
44.	Gudimallam	Chittor	"	Religious

Detail of Map-V

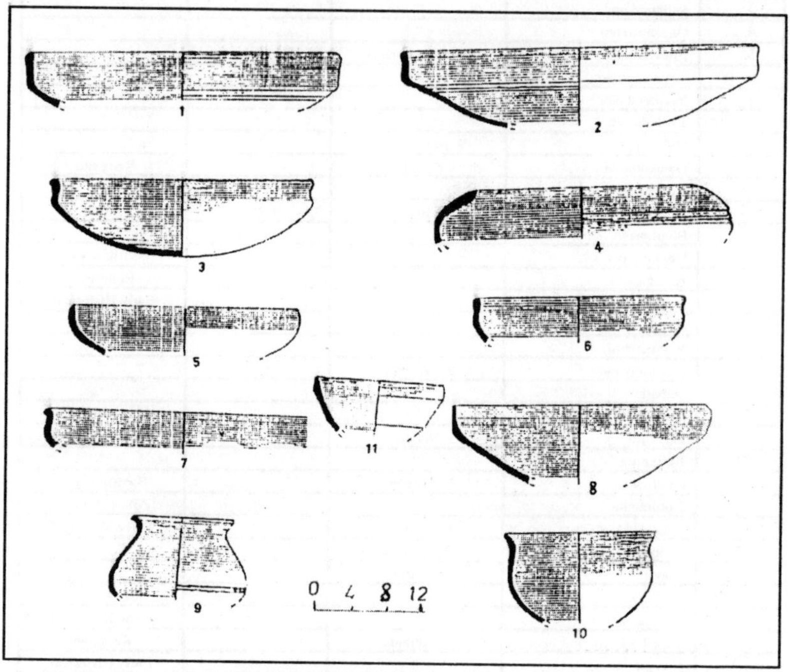

Fig. 1
Black and Red ware
1, 2, 3, 8 – carinated bowls, Kotilingala
4, 5 – convex side dishes, Peddabankur
6, 7, 8 – bowls, Kotilingala
9 – globular vase, Kotilingala
10 – round based bowl, Peddabankur

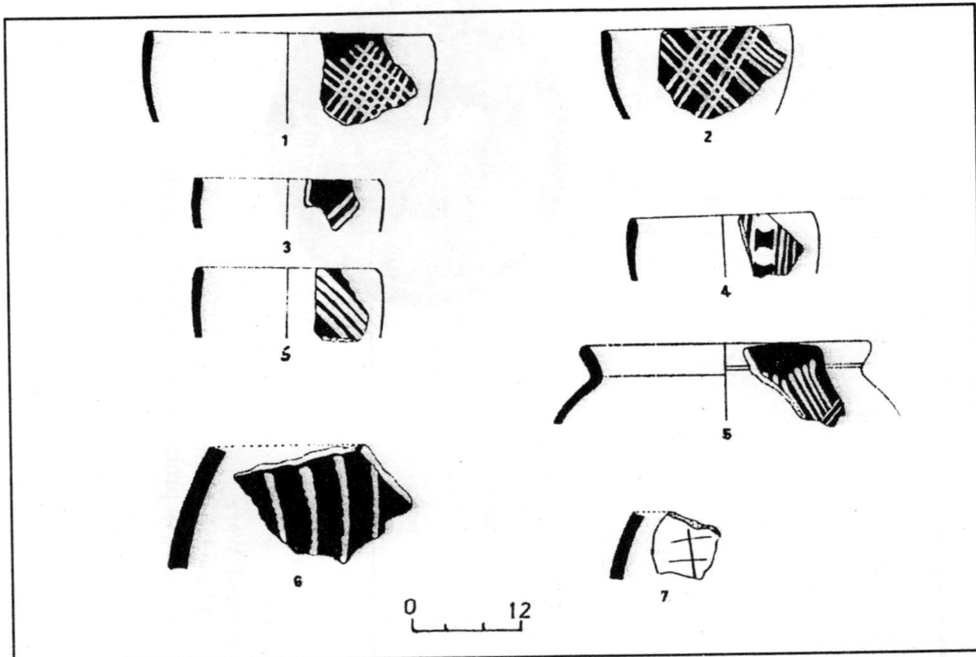

Fig. 2
Russet Coated Painted Ware
1-4 Bowls of Black and Red ware with a group of radiating lines Intersect each other making criss-cross (1 & 2), Veerapuram
5 vase of Red ware, painted with a group of radiating lines, Kotilingala
6-7 sherds of Red ware, Kotilingala

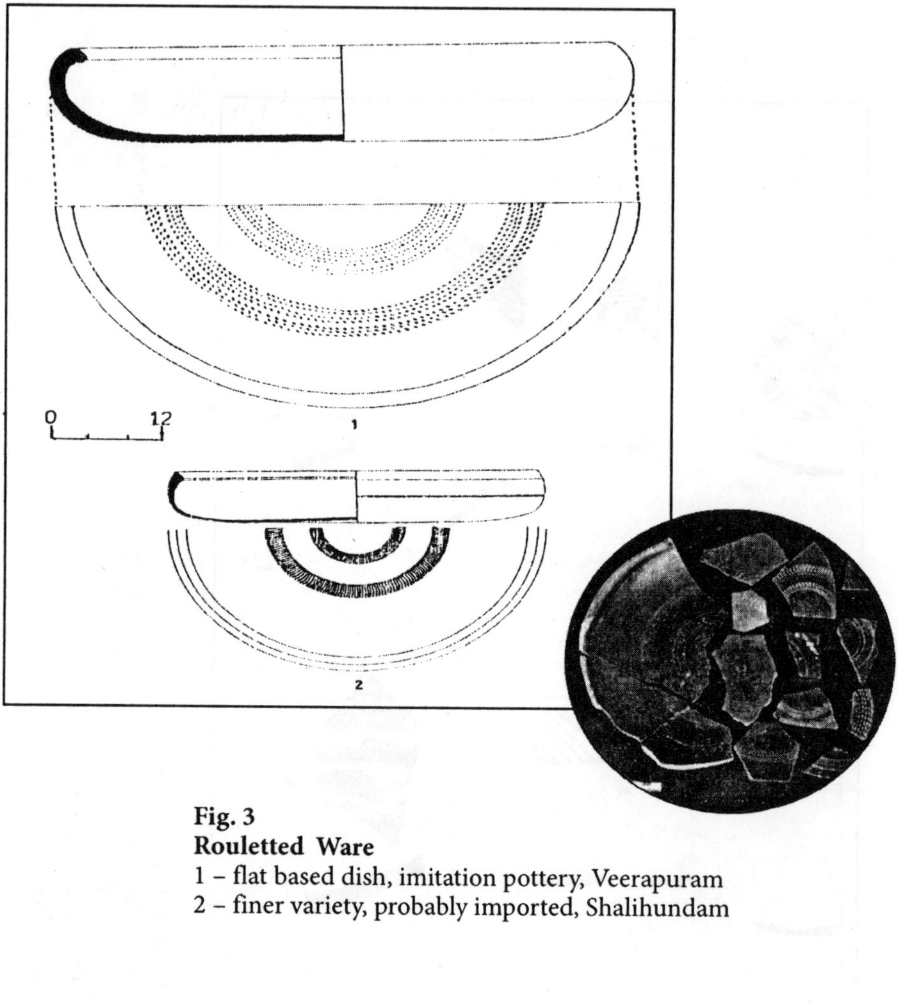

Fig. 3
Rouletted Ware
1 – flat based dish, imitation pottery, Veerapuram
2 – finer variety, probably imported, Shalihundam

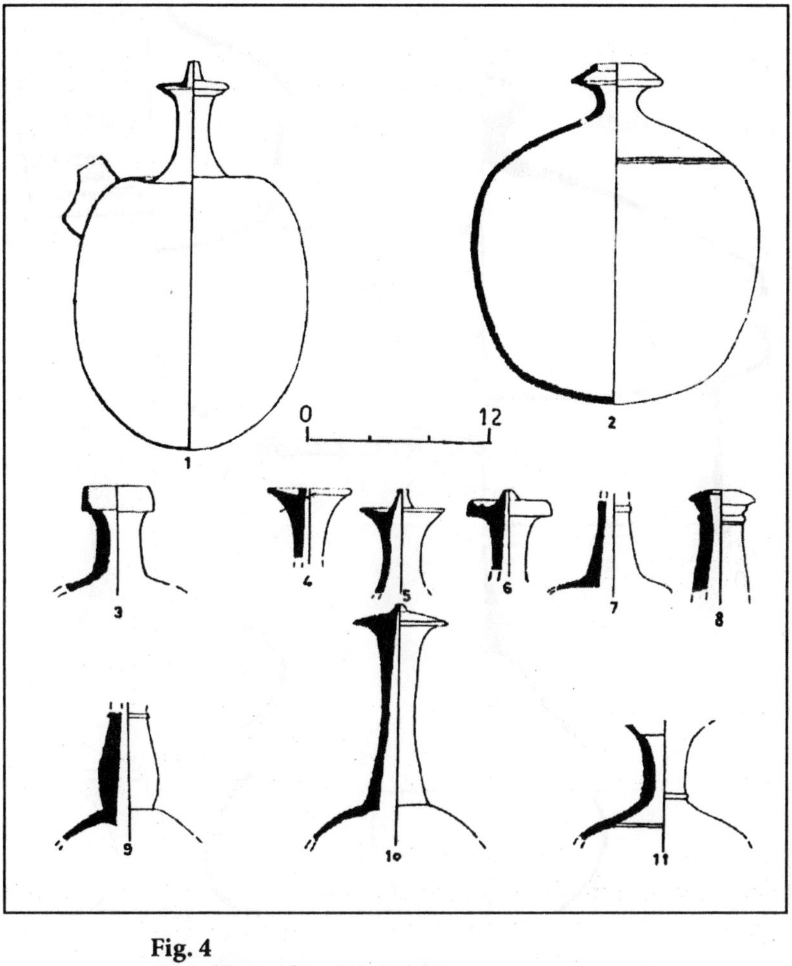

Fig. 4
Sprinklers of Red Polish Ware
1 – deluxe Red ware with a highly burnished surface having straightened narrow neck, Yeleshwaram
2 – Red ware jar with a perforation in the form of a hole on the shoulder, Yeleswaram
3-11 sprinklers of Red Polish ware

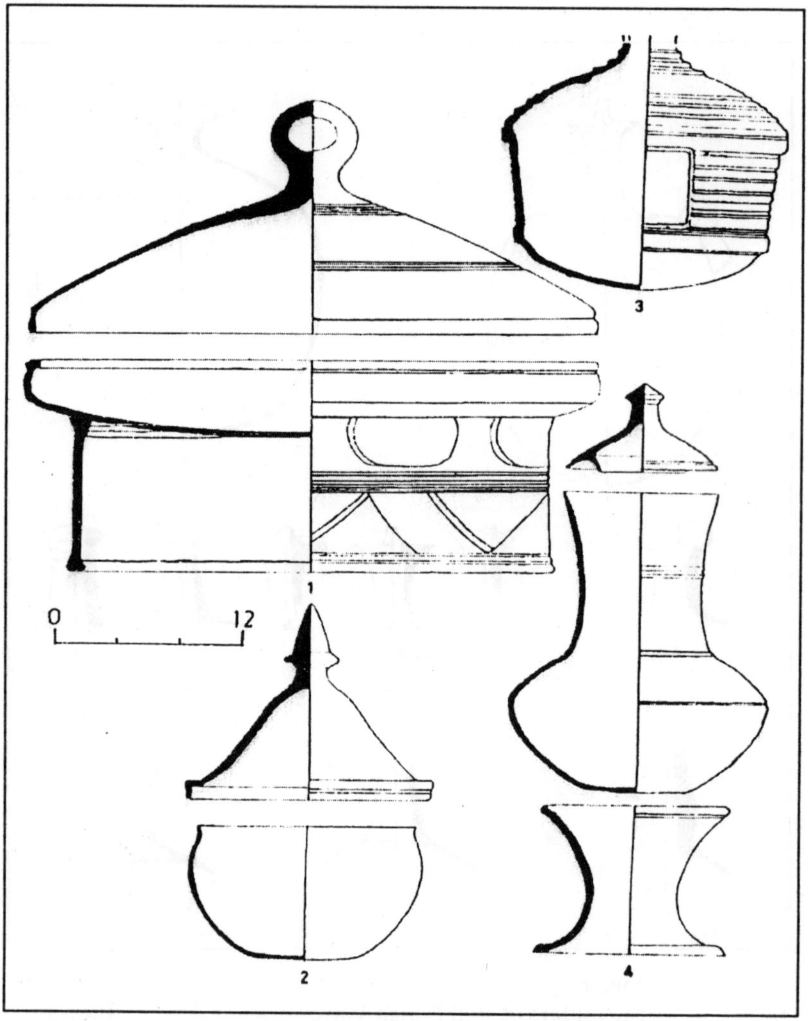

Fig. 5
Rare pots from Yeleswaram
Brazier or a hot case , Black ware
Tulip-shaped vase with funnel shaped lid, Black and Red ware
Lantern with a shutter or door, Red ware
Hour glass stand, Black ware large neck vessel with knobbed lid, Black Polished ware (curtsy from Yeleshwarm pavilion)

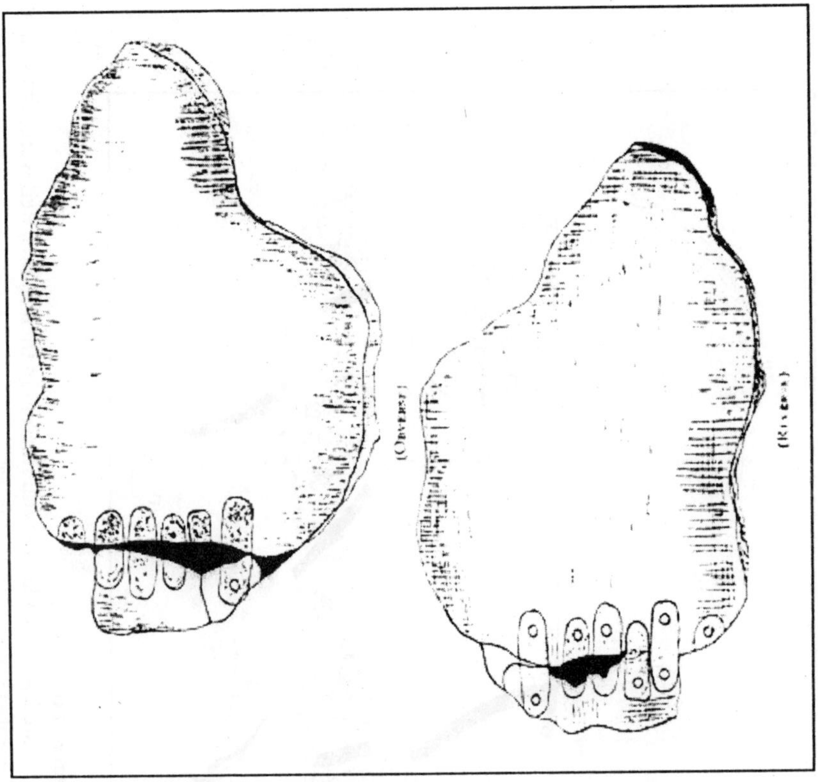

Fig. 6
Fragments of Red ware pottery
Storage Jar with iron joints & rivets, Kondapur
(curtsy form Kondapur museum)

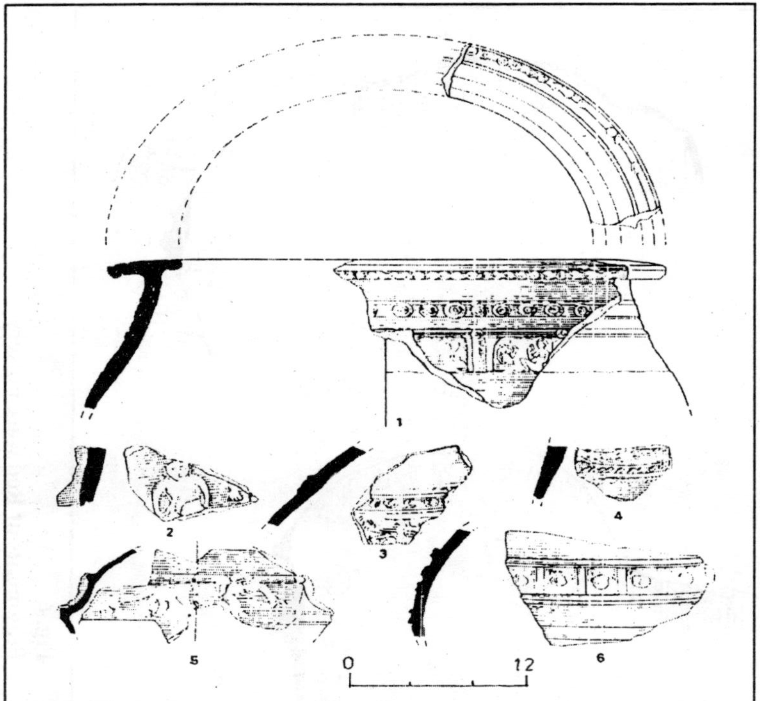

Fig. 7
Decorated Pottery
1 – decorated with two ladies with mirrors in their hands, Red ware, Yeleswaram
2-6 decorated pot sherds, Red ware

Plate I: Terracotta Female figurines in different hairdo Kondapur

Plate II A: Terracotta spout Dhulikatta

Plate II V: Ivory seal Dhulikatta

Plate III: Cup shaped Terracotta objects Showing divinity at top Peddabankur

Plate IV A: Iron objects Kotilingala

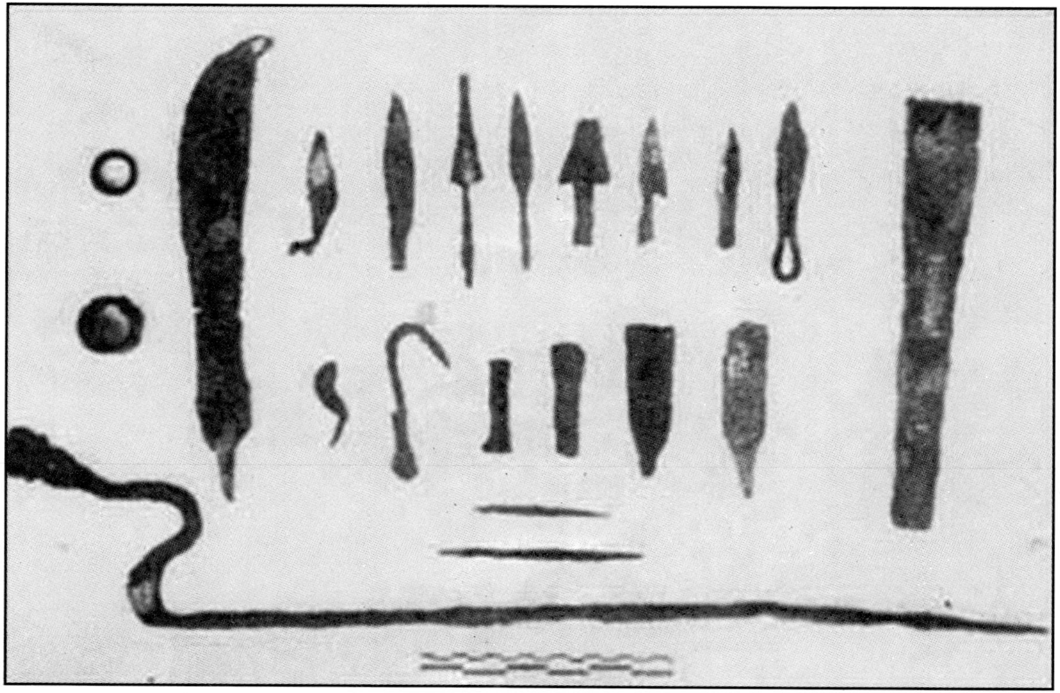

Plate IV B: Iron objects Peddabankur

Plate V: Bronze Ankadhatri Dhulikatta

Plate VI: Palace complex, Dhulikatta (curtsy from State Archaeology, A.P.)

Plate VII: Castel like enclosures, Peddabankur (curtsy from State Archaeology, A.P.)